The Fitful Republic:
Economy, Society,
and Politics in Argentina

The Fitful Republic: Economy, Society, and Politics in Argentina

Juan E. Corradi

Westview Press / Boulder and London

Latin American Perspectives Series, Number 2

Copyright © 1985 by Westview Press, Inc.

Published in 1985 in the United States of America by Westview Press, Inc., 5500 Central Avenue, Boulder, Colorado 80301; Frederick A. Praeger, Publisher

Library of Congress Cataloging in Publication Data
Corradi, Juan E., 1943–
  The fitful republic.
  (Latin American perspectives series; no. 2)
  Bibliography: p.
  Includes index.
  1. Argentina—Economic conditions. 2. Argentina—
Social conditions. 3. Argentina—Politics and government.
I. Title. II. Series.
HC175.C668 1985   330.982'064   84-25794
ISBN 0-8133-0110-6
ISBN 0-8133-0111-4 (pbk.)

Printed and bound in the United States of America

10   9   8   7   6   5   4   3   2   1

For Lela and Chelo

Contents

Foreword

In this book Juan E. Corradi presents a detailed, insightful, and interpretative analysis of political, economic, and social life in Argentina. He places his discussion in historical context by reviewing developments since the colonial period, but he concentrates on events from 1930 to the present, a period in which military intervention and control have been predominant. He is concerned primarily with questions of development and lack of development and directs attention to the impact of capitalism on dependent societies. He despairs that the problematic of dependency and the use of dependency as a critical perspective have progressively become cast as theory in an abstract and useless context. He prefers instead to locate his theory in concrete facts and actual events; interwoven through the historical discussion is a class analysis of life in Argentina, written in strong personal and interpretative terms. His book portrays the rise and fall of Perón after the Second World War; the attempt to escape the legacy of Peronism through a period of reform under Frondizi; the return to dictatorship; the reemergence of Perón; the disintegration of Argentine society in the wake of his death; and the recent "democratic" opening prompted by the military defeat of the Malvinas (Falklands) war with Great Britain and the subsequent electoral period.

Dr. Corradi, who teaches sociology at New York University, writes as expatriate, sympathizer, and skeptical intellectual. The present acccount is an updated and expanded version of his lengthy chapter in *Latin America* (Ronald H. Chilcote and Joel Edelstein, editors), a volume of essays published in 1974 and reprinted many times but now out of print. The book was used widely in university classrooms, and we have encouraged the authors to substantially revise and update their chapters for publication in the Latin American Perspectives Series published by Westview Press.

Corradi's original piece was in great demand and, given the dearth of serious studies on Argentina, it is particularly appropriate that it appear in its present form. Readers will find this account interesting, clearly presented, and useful, for Corradi has successfully combined historical narrative with profound analysis of the Argentine political economy.

Ronald H. Chilcote
for the Collective of Coordinating Editors,
Latin American Perspectives

Preface

Understanding the complexities of modern Argentina requires a theoretical effort and an attention to detail that surpass by far the country's importance in the concert of nations. The task is bound to tax the patience of non-Argentines who are curious and well disposed but unwilling to become specialists. I have designed this book with that problem in mind—also for readers who may not be experts but who nonetheless request, and deserve, some basic elements of judgment.

The following pages began as a chapter written for a massive volume on Latin America published in 1974. Subsequent work has changed my intellectual interests and some of my views. Argentina, which has not been my home for many years, is no longer my country, by choice; and yet I cannot be indifferent to it. It is at once too close and too far. I had to overcome a resistance to return to it in the pages of this book. But the gravity of developments in recent years and the attention they have drawn made me take a closer look. Much of this book is a product of those reflections.

The book endeavors to present the varied roles played by social groups in the modernization of Argentina. It seeks to account for the attainment of a high level of modernity in a country whose economy has manifested a notorious incapacity for self-sustaining growth. More specifically, it attempts to illuminate the political predicament of a modernized but marginal society; the persistent swing between tyranny and tumult.

There are several general considerations behind my undertaking. I have long been disappointed by the quality of theoretical reflection that has accompanied research on issues of development. I have been skeptical of the thesis that considers socioeconomic development as a road to carbon copies of Western democracy. The observation that political democracy is frequent among the rich nations of our time and a rare occurrence among the poor and weaker countries cannot be extrapolated and used to gauge a general trend. Yet not long ago, much within political sociology consisted of attempts to relate levels of wealth to types of political regime. The unique experience of some of the wealthiest lands was elevated to the status of a yardstick allowing researchers to formulate theoretical expectations about the less-developed countries. Processes of social change in the latter were reduced to the recapitulation of familiar sequences. If they did not conform to the expectations, the society that displayed them was treated as a deviant case. In this way the sociology of development was turned into a plethora of studies on "obstacles" and "exceptions" to a prefigured march of history. A correlational perspective in comparative sociology was extrapolated in the service of a progressive and optimistic interpretation of history. In essence, it was the old Whig interpretation in a new scientific guise.

I have never found convincing tales of history in which present enlightenment is contrasted with the benighted conditions of one's own past or with the backwardness of contemporaries, in which history is regarded as marching, with occasional setbacks, toward a better world, and in which moral and political issues appear unambiguous. Nor has a radical version of this kind of sentimentalism been more acceptable to me than the liberal variety that has always been more fashionable in academic circles. This book displays an alternative view. If it is true that, whatever else it may be, social science is also an essay in persuasion, then I argue to discourage historical progressivism, whether lineal or dialectical. Even Engels once spoke of "the enlightened prejudice that since the dark Middle Ages a steady progress to better things *must* surely have taken place." This prejudice prevents us from seeing that progress, if any, comes from tension, that it gives rise to as much suffering as happiness, and that it is no more sure, or convincing, than regress. The Whiggish interpretation of history that was smuggled into the studies of development implied that the causal processes active in less-developed countries were essentially the same as those once operative in the now advanced West. This assumption was highly questionable with regard to the experience of the less-developed countries and was actually also untenable in the light of the comparative history of modernization.

Later, the field of Latin American studies underwent a thorough overhaul in the categories of analysis. Subsequent work sought to integrate social and economic facts in a polemical framework of theory that ran counter—not without exaggeration—to the "working truths" of earlier development studies. The main thrust of that new effort has been to examine how Latin American development has been related to the principal aspects of world development in each of its stages. Focusing on the role of investment and finance in Latin America, many studies sought to determine the structural features of a system of international stratification and their repercussions on the organization of local societies. The force of their argument resided in the rejection of hitherto widely accepted theses about the stages of economic growth, their evolutionary assumptions, and the typologies based on them. They offered instead a conception of development and underdevelopment that treated these conditions as the poles of a single world process. The goal was to unravel the structural tensions that beset Latin America. Together, these studies formed a constellation that was baptized with the name of "dependency theory."

Unfortunately, the new approaches succumbed time and again to the temptation to explain historical processes as the abstract unfolding of forms. They subsumed the struggles through which some groups dominate others under rigid systemic principles that made the outcome of conflict seem preordained. They did not consider modular movements, the alliances that maintain institutions while opening the possibility of their transformation. History's trick on those pretensions is, of course, to make social scientists dupes of their own grids, victims of the unexpected. In this context, the displacement of the sociology of development that flourished in the fifties and sixties by a spate of neo-Marxian theories in the seventies did not at all dispel the dangers of a variety of academicism that may be called "systemic abuse." Among ontogenetic theories, the tendency has been to reduce politics and ideology to mechanical schemes of class conflict. Among "world-system" theories, the tendency has been to deduce politics and ideology from a global logic. In Latin American studies, that is precisely what happened to the problematic of dependency, as Fernando Henrique Cardoso pointed out. What had been originally a critical perspective, a fluid attempt to analyze the establishment and disestablishment of alliances between historical actors, was turned progressively into a "theory" of the international system from which changes in local social structures were derived. Proponents of such premature "theory" even went as far as to operationalize the original insight. They specified a series of variables, tested hypotheses, and measured "degrees" of dependency. Critics of the theory responded in kind, in what would soon become a little Byzantine debate.

After more than a decade of studies undertaken under the banner of dependency theory, one thing has become clear: The more systemic the approach has been, the more impoverished the resulting diagnosis. The time had come to descend from the heights of "dependency" to the concrete examination of "dependent societies," that is, to the inspection of historical modes of development, of the specific manner in which societies act upon themselves and are acted upon by other, more powerful societies. It is a more modest but more fruitful undertaking.

From the perspective of traditional paradigms, Argentina is a paradox in that it fails to display the features of "political maturity" that are expected from its level of development. Part of the explanation may lie in the structures of dependency. But only part. It is legitimate to ask of Argentina questions such as these: Could it be that the development of dependent capitalism and the achievement of a high level of modernization, when joined, lead away from a political system of the type of liberal democracies? Could they lead, instead, toward protracted political crises verging on bloody chaos? But we must beware of the *post hoc, ergo propter hoc* fallacy. Things, as Max Weber would have reminded us, could have been different. Like Weber, we should focus our attention on historic turning points.

protracted
political
crises

In pursuit of all these issues, I have examined a broad array of information, ranging from aggregate data to qualitative analyses, and even the insights of novelists. Above all I have applied myself to reexamining a large number of studies on Argentina that stake out the gamut of social science specialties, some of which are truly fine. The richness of social research is that, beyond its originally conceived products, it continues to lend itself to second and third gleanings and yields new fruits. I have subjected the studies thus perused to three interrelated sets of questions: (1) What have been the determinants of economic growth in Argentina? In what sense does its development differ from that of other societies? (2) What processes have led to a high level of modernization in a context of peripheral development? What is the modernization profile of Argentina? (3) What is the political predicament of a highly modernized society that is subjected to the strains of peripheral growth? My general conclusion is that such a society follows a path to crisis that is flanked by authoritarianism and chaos. Beyond this, there are reasons to consider Argentine society, if not the exemplar of a type, at least a wayward pioneer in a journey that is fraught with some distinct but somber political prospects.

How are the citizens of the still prosperous and free societies of the West to evaluate Argentina? They can engage, as some have done, in self-righteous condemnation of the excesses to which Argentines have recently abandoned themselves; or they may patronizingly dismiss the case as typical of exotic and hopeless mores. This book carries a different message. It suggests that what has occurred in Argentina could happen elsewhere. Even to the U.S. reader it whispers that perhaps *de se fabula narratur.*

Juan E. Corradi

Acknowledgments

During the time in which I have been occupied with the issues discussed in this book, I have enjoyed the help and encouragement of a great many persons.

Professor Ronald Chilcote first provided me with the opportunity to put my thoughts on paper. Gino Germani, José Luis Romero, and Kalman Silvert were interlocutors whose wisdom I miss. Many others have helped me greatly with their expertise and remarks in seminars and conversations. Among them I wish to thank the participants in the seminar on Argentina that I cochaired at the Center for Inter-American Relations in 1976, in particular Natalio Botana, Adolfo Canitrot, Tulio Halperín Donghi, Noé Jitrik, Manuel Mora y Araujo, Guillermo O'Donnell, and Juan Carlos Portantiero. As friend and colleague, Juan Carlos Torre has been an infallible source of good sense. Some ideas in this book have been inspired by him. I am indebted to my friend John Saxe-Fernández for the opportunity to present some of my ideas in his institute in Mexico City. Some of my best friends took particular trouble to encourage me at different stages of the project: Pedro Cuperman, Uri Eisenzweig, Volker Meja, Charles and Laura Nathanson, Paul Piccone, Luisa Valenzuela, and Victor Zaslavsky. To them my thanks and recognition.

The responsibility for the outcome is, of course, solely mine.

J.E.C.

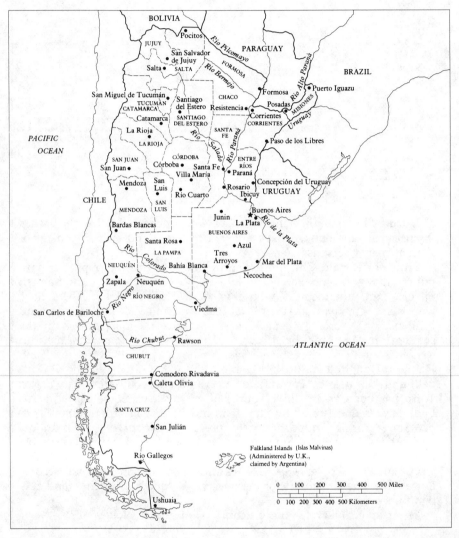

Argentina

Introduction

Argentines have always prided themselves on being different from their Latin American brethren. They are for the most part white, European, urbanized, well fed. The Spanish philosopher Ortega y Gasset thought he had perceived in them an imperial vocation, though he warned that Argentine grandeur rested more on promise than on accomplishment. He should have known: Centuries before, Spanish grandeur had come to naught.

For decades Argentines believed they were a chosen people. *"Dios es argentino,"* they boasted. Chosen they were, but not by deities. British imperialism had elected the *pampas*—those wide open spaces, or so they must have seemed from London—to supply the British Empire with foodstuffs. Argentina became a pampered informal colony. Cattle multiplied, wheat ripened under the sun, immigrants arrived on the shores of the River Plate to gather the harvests, railways and ports gave up loads of produce to the world. Thus it seemed natural for Argentines to be exempted from the fate of their subcontinent—poverty. They did not know the laws of their well-being. Heedless of the artificiality of good fortune, they became complacent and presumptuous, and even tried to show others the light.

But circumstances changed in the world and Argentina was left behind. Argentines found to their amazement that they had little or no control over the forces that had once made them prosperous—that is, they found that they were dependent. Before, they had thought the pie would get forever larger and everybody would have his or her share. Now, the pie had shrunk. They suffered dictatorship and exclusion. Finally, grudgingly, they began supplying themselves with what the world had given them till then—the products of industry. National enterprise began replacing imports from the industrial metropolises. And

1

so industrialists and workers appeared on the scene. The old Argentina refused to concede its own eclipse. It clung to privilege with force, corruption, and fraud. Where one form of economic existence had prevailed, two modes of accumulation now struggled for supremacy: the agrarian and the industrial. They struck a bargain, and from that dubious marriage came something misshapen: a society in which an incomplete industrial system drew funds from an inefficient rural structure. The creature could not grow without constant protection from the state. As different members of this body—classes, interest groups, and so on— were precarious, the state began to maneuver and compensate for their weakness. So the slender body gave rise to Caesar's head—a cumbersome authoritarian state, which paid off now one sector, now another. Just as the old agrarian Argentina had paid off a sizable middle class during the apogee of exports, the new Argentina paid off the working class when international prosperity shone briefly during World War II. Caesarism turned into populism—a revolution on the cheap. Peronism added much but resolved little: It was accretion, not creation. The cumbersome system collapsed when exceptional international circumstances charged and funds to underwrite the payoffs ran out.

Thereafter Argentines tried to dismantle what they had built and found they could not. They tried to set the clock back and it would not run. They tried social and political cannibalism, but every major group was too strong to be wiped out. These once-arrogant people came to see failure as their central historical experience: failure to develop by themselves, failure to have confidence in each other, failure to understand the sources of their misery. A country of immense material promise, human diversity, and a spectacular past found that after all it was not that different from the rest of the continent. Its more industrialized economy had fallen prey to stagnation or mere fitful growth; its resources ended up in foreign hands; its elites engaged in a type of politics that Argentines had scorned as suitable only for tropical republics. Dependency, stagnation, political decay, and violence have been bitter staples for these erstwhile exceptionalists.

In some, the counsel of despair produced a preoccupation with explaining their experience as a failure unique to their circumstances. To others there is nothing unique about Argentina; they view its failures *sub specie aeternitatis*, as containing lessons for all humanity, including the advanced nations of the West. It is, however, *sub specie temporis* and *sub specie regionis* that Argentine phenomena require explanation. Argentina is one of the most industrialized of the major countries of the Third World, but it belongs to that world. A higher proportion of its population is urban than in many European countries. The working class is highly organized and comprises two-thirds of the work force. This singular configuration has created forms of behavior and institutions not commonly found in the underdeveloped regions of the planet, but

Argentina remains a peripheral capitalist society, a nonmetropolitan country, a Latin American nation, a fitful republic. In their own ways Argentines will have to struggle against the same evils that have beset sister nations in order to do better and to find a path to rational development.

PART 1
Land of Promise

In a rock-stratum are embedded crystals of a mineral. Clefts and cracks occur, water filters in, and the crystals are gradually washed out so that in due course only their hollow mould remains. Then come volcanic outbursts which explode the mountain; molten masses pour in, stiffen, and crystallize out in their turn. But these are not free to do so in their own special forms. They must fill up the spaces that they find available. Thus there arise distorted forms, crystals whose inner structure contradicts their external shape, stones of one kind presenting the appearance of stones of another kind. The mineralogists call this phenomenon *Pseudomorphosis.*

By the term "historical pseudomorphosis" I propose to designate those cases in which an older alien Culture lies so massively over the land that a young Culture, born in this land, cannot get its breath and fails not only to achieve pure and specific expression-forms, but even to develop fully its own self-consciousness. All that wells up from the depths of the young soul is cast in the old moulds, young feelings stiffen in senile works, and instead of rearing itself up in its own creative power, it can only hate the distant power with a hate that grows to be monstrous.

—Oswald Spengler, *The Decline of the West*

1

The Colonial Legacy

The Uneven Development of Metropolises: Spain

Argentine underdevelopment and international dependency have their roots in the colonial period, in the specific manner in which Spanish mercantilism affected the River Plate region. Spain's search for precious metals led to the colonization of Latin America. Different regions developed at different rates according to their ability to service the requirements of the mother country for natural resources and labor. During the fifteenth century, the displacement of international commerce from the Eastern Mediterranean to the Atlantic fostered the supremacy of the maritime powers on the ocean and the North Sea. The discovery of the American continent—both a result and a catalyst of the world's commercial revolution—faced those powers with the challenge of directly organizing production by articulating capital and labor. The colonial territories were transformed into appendixes of a system designed to pump wealth into royal treasuries. There were different means of funneling the colonial surplus into metropolitan centers: royal enterprises managed by functionaries; indirect methods, such as taxation; and the participation of royal capital in private enterprises. The system rested on mercantilism and monopoly.

An important consequence of the agrarian and limited level of development of metropolitan economies was the restriction of exchange with the colonies to exotic comestibles, precious metals, and a few raw materials. Precarious means of transportation limited trade to products of high value and small volume.

The availability of natural resources and the accessibility to maritime routes of trade patterned settlement and colonization. The existence of exploitable labor was an essential consideration, and its supply was rendered more flexible by a large slave trade. The rigid pattern of centralization that characterized the metropolitan society was extended to the colonies. It prevented the formation of any class with strong local roots that would be tied more to local markets than to metropolitan interests. The situation in Latin America was the opposite of what existed in the New England colonies. Whereas in the latter, production was organized by autonomous settlers in small and medium-sized enterprises geared to dynamic local markets and the division of labor became fairly complex, in most of Latin America, large-scale monolithic enterprises utilizing slave or servile labor and under the management of merchants and landowners with links to the royal bureaucracy yielded a very different social and political order, characterized by rigid social stratification and external dependency. Under this system, economic growth increased the wealth of the metropolitan treasury and the colonial elites, but did not diversify the productive structure and did not develop the colonial economy.

Despite the creation of a vast overseas empire in the sixteenth century and its control of those areas until 1824, Spain itself was an economic dependency of Europe. From 1500 to 1700, Spain and Portugal expanded overseas, creating in turn dependent areas without much positive feedback. In the course of that process they failed to modernize their internal social and economic structures (Stein and Stein, 1970, Part 1).

That failure was not, however, an historical accident. Nor was it the product of a peculiar system of values. At the onset of its colonial experience, Spain was an imperfectly organized nation, an economy oriented to the export of a few primary products, a society lacking a dynamic bourgeoisie. Centuries of territorial expansion, the Reconquest, and the struggle against Muslim culture had strengthened the role of a militant aristocracy and the church. The exploitation of the colonies made the restructuring of the Spanish semifeudal, land-based, aristocratic economy and society unnecessary. The mercantilist expansion overseas in fact contributed to the development and entrenchment of the Spanish aristocracy, the bureaucracy, the service sector, and the church. As the economy—under the impact of capitalism—came to rest on foreign and colonial commerce, Spanish domestic manufacture contracted and raw materials were exported and returned as manufactured goods for domestic consumption and reexport to the colonies, while colonial gold and silver flowed to England to compensate for the deficit in the balance of trade. The acquisition of empire resulted in the proliferation of the patrimonial political structure. The military establishment was impressive, but Spain did not consolidate the economic and political bases of its might. Trade with the colonies was a monopoly benefiting the Crown and supporting large numbers of parasitic merchants. In fact Spain was the first "Latin American" nation in terms of most economic and social indicators. So acute was its dependency on other capitalist powers that by 1700 Spanish guild members were often front men for foreign merchants.

The aversion to manual labor, the importance of family connections, and the aristocratic life-style in general that so characterized Spanish culture cannot be tautologically derived from an alleged value system or national character. Nor can Spanish "feudalism" be explained solely in terms of its own social and political structure. These features of society are better understood in terms of the uneven development of capitalism, that is in terms of worldwide networks of dependency, conceived as a complex chain of metropolis-satellite relations in which each satellite "serves as an instrument to suck capital or economic surplus out of its own satellites and to channel part of this surplus to the world metropolis of which all are satellites" (Frank, 1969, 6). The colonial expansion not only laid the foundation of Latin American underdevelopment, it simultaneously reinforced the subordination of Spain and Portugal to the dominant capitalist economies of England, Holland, and France. Thus Western European, Iberian, and Ibero-American economies were interlocked by 1700. England became the dominant center of world capitalism—a process greatly accelerated by the industrial revolution. Spain, like Portugal, became an appendage of its colonies in America. The latter began to move toward the British orbit.

The Uneven Development of Colonies: Argentina

From 1500 to 1700, Spain developed a colonial mining sector to maintain its economy and international position. Mexico and Peru became the main poles of colonial development in the sixteenth century. This development took place through private entrepreneurship in which miners, merchants, and the state collaborated and shared the profits. Miners and merchants in America, merchants in Seville, and ultimately the bourgeoisie of Western Europe reaped the benefits accruing from the extraction of gold and silver and from the exploitation of Indian labor. Those benefits also paid for the administrative costs of empire and went to ecclesiastical and secular officials. The export orientation of Latin American economies was shaped during this period. Large estates with a relatively immobile labor force, devoted to agriculture and ranching, were the principal subsectors of the mining nuclei. On the ruins of preconquest agrarian societies, the Spaniards built a mining export sector and a supportive *hacienda* system with catastrophic consequences for the native populations. Disease, overwork, and culture shock were the price paid by those people for the remolding of communal societies along profit-oriented lines.

The colonial world was characterized by a striking contrast between the main export and production centers and the backward peripheral regions. In the former, the growth of services and the concentration of labor, the royal bureaucracies and their personnel produced a civilization of administrative cities, military garrisons, and busy export trade. In the peripheral regions, far away from established trade routes and deprived of the natural resources coveted at the time, scattered and poor populations barely made a living on subsistence crops and subsidiary production for the more dynamic regions. The territory of Argentina belonged during most of the colonial period to these imperial backwaters. The predominance of the Pacific port of Lima-Callao in the export of Peruvian gold and silver impeded the emergence of Buenos Aires as a commerical center until nearly two centuries after it was founded (1536–1580).

The provinces—later the vice royalty—of the Río de la Plata were among the less adapted of all Spanish colonies in America to the commercial and economic policies of the Spanish imperium. They counted among the last territories to be added to the colonial empire. They were removed from the already established highways of transatlantic commerce, poor in readily exploitable mineral wealth, and thinly populated by nomadic societies. During most of the colonial period, the pulse of economic life in Argentina was faint indeed. The great *pampa* region was given over mainly to the hunting of wild cattle, an activity that could not be properly called stock raising, since no systematic effort was made to improve the breeds or to commercialize the produce. In the colonial *estancias* cattle were hunted and slaughtered mostly for their hides, the only good that could be shipped to export markets. Tallow was also exported, and a certain amount of salted beef was sent to the West Indies and Brazil. Eventually, sheep raising developed and some wool was exported. Here and there corn and wheat were raised, but flour had to be imported to feed the population of this *finisterre*. Despite the increase in the military and strategic importance of Buenos Aires, which in the eighteenth century led to the creation of a viceroyalty on the River Plate, the economy of Argentina remained rustic and picturesque, yet hardly productive. In point of fact, the socioeconomic configuration of Argentina was, throughout the colonial period and well into the nineteenth century, the opposite of what it looks today. As one traveled from the eastern seaboard toward the northwest, approaching the silver mines of Potosí, one met with increasing activity and prosperity. Raising mules and producing foodstuffs for the mines of Upper Peru gave impulse to the local economies. But this stimulus barely reached the grasslands of the littoral. There self-sufficiency and economic stagnation prevailed. The large landed estate—the *latifundium*—was the dominant form of property. The fiscal and political needs of the Crown in this region of scarce resources resulted in large land grants to individuals.

Though land ownership was concentrated early in a few hands, land values remained very low until the nineteenth century, when cattle breeding and grain culture in the *pampas* came to meet the needs of European industrial capitalism.

From the beginning, the basic interests of the River Plate territory were sacrificed to the interests of the Lima merchants and to those of the royal treasury. Mercantilist policies imposed the total prohibition of commerce. An open port on the shores of the River Plate would have made the whole territory east of the Andes commercially a tributary to Buenos Aires. Hence, if those markets were to be preserved for the commerce of Lima, it was essential that Buenos Aires be prevented from developing into a transit point for imports from Europe. Moreover, from the standpoint of royal fiscal policy, the concession of trading privileges to Buenos Aires had to result in the loss of revenue through contraband and a negative balance of trade. Thus Buenos Aires was closed to all overseas traffic until well past the middle of the eighteenth century. It was also isolated from internal markets by tariff walls, that is, internal, or so-called "dry" customs, and restrictions on the flow of specie. The Argentine economy was all but strangled. In order to survive, the colony waged a surreptitious struggle against those policies, mostly through contraband. As the population and wealth of the colony grew those restrictions were challenged more often and more openly.

The administrative and commercial reforms undertaken by the Bourbons in the eighteenth century liberalized or altogether abolished many of the restrictive measures and opened the gates to the economic development of the Río de la Plata, and especially of Buenos Aires. The territories were at last in a position to utilize the advantages of the more direct route to markets through the port of Buenos Aires. Import prices fell and export prices rose. The province and the city of Buenos Aires were visibly at the head of the economic expansion of the eighteenth century. The province of Buenos Aires, and generally the *pampa*, was the most important producer of exportable commodities. The city now became the only port of a vast territory, the terminus and transit point of a large interprovincial and overseas commerce.

Yet Spain could not meet the challenge opened by the economic development of its colonies. It simply lacked the economic capacity to absorb all of the colony's produce and to satisfy the latter's growing demand for manufactures at a reasonable price. Spain functioned as an onerous intermediary between the River Plate and other countries, particularly England, which rapidly became the largest consumer of the colony's produce as well as the main supplier of commodities. The Spanish liberal reforms of the eighteenth century were bound to remain an empty gesture so long as Spain's economic advance continued to lag behind that of the rest of Western Europe and North America. Even the economic development of the colonies had outgrown the halfhearted liberalism of the Bourbons. Argentina, and Spanish America in general, were ready for a new pattern of dependency—a neocolonial pact with the new industrial powers.

Technically, the solution was opening the port of Buenos Aires to all commerce. However, such a liberalization of trade was hard to achieve without breaking the unity of the empire. Opening the port was a direct threat to the merchant-monopolists, who, together with the crown officials formed the upper crust of colonial society. Conversely, "free trade" would directly benefit the nonmonopolist merchants and the landowning cattle breeders. The latter became an interest group standing for free trade and its preservation through political independence. Their opponents included not only the *peninsulares* and the monopolists of Buenos Aires, but also the producers of the interior provinces who had been protected by the isolation of Buenos Aires from internal and external markets.

2
The Making of a Nation

Independence and Neocolonialism

By the end of the eighteenth century, when the viceroyalty of the Río de la Plata—comprising what is now Argentina, Uruguay, Paraguay, and Bolivia—achieved economic importance, the Spanish Empire was subservient to British capitalism. Spain had regressed from first- to third-rate power status. English vessels not only carried goods to Spain for domestic sale and reexport to the colonies, but began to penetrate the Spanish dominions directly. France—a less dynamic power—was also competing for control of the trade with the Iberian world. Interested in preventing the collapse of Spain, in 1700 France succeeded in placing a Bourbon king on the Spanish throne. This event inaugurated a period of bureaucratic reform designed to prop the tottering imperium. These reforms, far from constituting a "bourgeois revolution," represented a variety of defensive modernization, which failed nonetheless to protect the empire from the massive encroachment of British capitalism. Those efforts most likely belong in the same historical category as the flurry of reforms under the dowager empress in early twentieth-century China. They came to naught as the end of eighteenth century approached. Spain entered a severe crisis, not just economic but political and military as well, which culminated with the collapse of central authority before the Napoleonic armies in 1808.

Britain's industrialization demanded raw materials for production and a direct access to Latin American markets. The growing economic potential of the River Plate region had already prompted British interest, and in 1806 and 1807 the Buenos Aires *estancieros* and merchants repelled two British invasions, without aid from Spain. When Napoleon occupied Spain and placed his brother on the throne, Argentines seized the opportunity to force upon the kingless viceroy a document granting them free trade with England. This act amounted to a declaration of economic independence, or rather a shift toward a new type of dependency. It was soon followed by political independence. In 1810 the Buenos Aires liberals set up an autonomous governing junta. Six years later the de facto independence was ratified by a national congress. Representative government and independence were the ideological rallying cries of the *porteño* coalition of merchants and landowners.

A question that has troubled Argentines since at least the nineteenth century is this: Why did two once-colonial areas, the United States and Argentina, develop so differently after independence? The question has often received fantastic answers.

By 1870 the United States had emerged as perhaps the second industrial nation of the world, while Argentina became a major producer of staples and foodstuffs for Europe. The comparative question is especially poignant since the environment in which the English settled was similar in important ways to that of the first Iberian colonists in the Río de la Plata. In both cases settlers hoped to discover mines of precious metals. Yet no mines were found. Even if they had been found, labor to operate them was not readily available, for West Europeans in the River Plate region as well as in North America did not have to confront or incorporate substantial Indian cultures. They pushed aside the nomadic Amerindian inhabitants, killed most of them, and isolated the survivors on unproductive lands. True, Indians and the offspring of unions between Spaniards and Indians formed a substantial sector of the early colonial population of Argentina. Since then, however, successive waves of immigration absorbed most of the *mestizos* and drove the Indians into remote parts of the national territory. The Indian of Argentina ultimately remained as unincorporated and forgotten as the Indian of the United States. At present, the combined Indian and *mestizo* population constitutes less than 3 percent of the national total. Agriculture was unknown among the Indians of Argentina except in the northwestern part of the territory, where some rudimentary cultivation was practiced. Almost all of the indigenous groups were nomadic and depended on hunting and gathering as their primary means of subsistence. The population remained scattered in small groups.

The indigenous cultures were almost immediately changed by contact with the Spaniards who arrived in the sixteenth century. The most important factor in the change was the acquisition of horses that had escaped from Spanish settlements. The introduction of the horse created greater mobility and ease in hunting, which led to the formation of larger bands of as many as one hundred to five hundred people. They frequently raided European settlements well into the nineteenth century. Contact between Indians and Spaniards was primarily hostile. Sustained exposure to Western culture and techniques resulted in the defeat of the native populations and in the loss of their cultural identity. Those who were not killed in the final decades of the nineteenth century were driven into remote parts of the frontier provinces, and their former lands were converted into farms and estates.

In the 1830s, Juan Manual de Rosas, a *caudillo* who achieved control of Argentina for near a quarter of a century and paved the way for national unity, opened vast territories for settlement at the expense of the Indian population. Pushing the Indians out of the *pampas* was the historical equivalent of enclosures in Argentina. (Centuries before, the transformation of fields into grasslands for grazing sheep, as a result of the development of the wool industry, had thrown thousands of English peasants off their lands and condemned them to starvation.) And in 1879, General Roca, another Argentine strongman, finally "pacified" the Indians with the help of the railroad, the telegraph, and the Remington rifle. Genocide was carried out in several one-sided campaigns.

In seeking a basis for comparing U.S. and Argentine development, analysts are frequently led back to the European culture complexes from which English and Iberian colonists migrated and from which they borrowed their images of social organization. A "social heredity" thesis has been developed along these lines suggesting that, in contrast to Spain, English settlers in North America came from a modernizing England that generally treated literacy, tolerance, individual rights, entrepreneurial initiative, and capital accumulation as inseparable elements of the process of growth. There is some truth to these assertions, but they fail to provide an adequate explanation of different patterns of colonial development. For instance, they fail to account for the structural differences between the northern and southern settlements in the United States.

A more satisfying account stresses the so-called external factors in development differentials. Thus, due to limited agricultural possibilities on the eastern seaboard, the northern English colonies developed shipbuilding and mercantile occupations, while the southern colonies created an export-oriented agriculture based upon slave labor—a structure not dissimilar to the Brazilian sugar estates of the seventeenth century, which became the prototype of plantation economies in the Americas. In other regions of Ibero-America, production was organized on the basis of servile Indian labor in the mines. But throughout the Americas, North and South, settlement was guided by essentially the same capitalist goals. The difference lies rather in the outcome of the same capitalist input upon different natural and social environments, and in the feedback of colonial developments on metropolitan societies.

Of great significance for the development of the United States was the growth of trade with the ex-metropolis. By contrast, the Spanish colonies found neither trade nor financial assistance in their metropolis, itself economically weak and dependent. The growth and diversification of the colonial economies in Latin America were not accompanied by a parallel development of the mother country. The forces making for underdevelopment were at work on both sides of the Atlantic; on the one side the decline of the mother country; on the other, the distortion of the colonial economy—with capitalist dependency at both ends.

We can now reformulate the comparative question: Why did Argentina develop in such a way that its postcolonial relations with the capitalist world became subordinate rather than complementary? Why did the River Plate region fail to play the historic role that the North played in U.S. development—a financial center for other agricultural regions and a supplier of manufactures?

Indeed, the similarities between the northern colonies and the River Plate were many. Both regions were modern colonies as defined by Marx (Marx, *Capital*, I, 25). Both were characterized by a lack of mineral wealth and exploitable native labor. Capitalism was established in both regions. Population grew at a rapid rate in both. Both areas initiated an independence movement. There was, however, one crucial difference. The New England colonies had little fertile land—only forests providing timber for shipbuilding and a sea that was far more hospitable to economic enterprise than the land. To the west lay vast territories suitable for appropriation by a landowning class that could have been capable of living off agrarian rent. But by the time the western frontier was opened, a society of small capitalists had firmly entrenched itself on the coast. This prevented the early concentration of landownership and the establishment of an agrarian aristocracy. Land in North America would eventually become accessible to ownership by independent settlers and immigrants.

The vast natural prairies of the River Plate, on the other hand, were initially accessible to Spanish colonists, who proceeded to appropriate enormous tracts of land and then simply sat back while the natural multiplication of cattle increased their value. This class of landowners became the nucleus of an export-oriented agrarian bourgeoisie. Land rent became the historical substitute for primitive accumulation on the *pampas:* It was capitalist accumulation on the cheap. The landed bourgeoisie thus established a civilization of hides and beef based much less on productive human labor than on the lavishness of nature and the demand of foreign markets.

Dependency and misdevelopment were the prices that Argentina paid for the effortless enrichment of its ruling class. Cattle ranching, which was to become the backbone of the Argentine economy, was a productive activity that required little human intervention. At the beginning of the nineteenth century, one foreman and ten peons could look after ten thousand head of cattle on the grasslands. Cattle multiplied at a fabulous rate in the mild climate. It is therefore wrong to charge Spain with the responsibility for feudal colonization in explaining Argentine underdevelopment. The hackneyed reference to feudalism is sadly overworked and leaves a good deal unsaid. It is misleading, indeed, both in principle and in fact. On the one hand, it implies a comparison of stages of development, as though the experience of Latin America, instead of differing in kind from the European or North American, were merely less mature. On the other hand, it ignores the sharp contrasts between them, not only in spirit and quality, but in circumstance and detail. The fact was that the natural wealth of the *pampas* stimulated the growth of a certain neocolonial capitalism with few labor and capital needs, oriented to the outside world and oblivious of the internal market. There was not an ounce of feudalism in this, but many tons of beef.

Capitalism and Class Conflict in the Nineteenth Century

The growing disparity in the rate of economic development between the various parts of the Spanish Empire was accompanied by a weakening of the bonds that held them together. The political and social unity of the metropolis and the colonies, on the one hand, and of the several colonial administrative areas, on the other, became increasingly tenuous on account of that uneven development. These processes led to the independence of the Latin American colonies. In the River Plate, the groups that benefited most from the Revolution of 1810 were those connected to the grazing industry, overseas commerce, and the portion of intercolonial trade that emanated from or passed through Buenos Aires.

Political independence opened the country to foreign trade, broadening the market for hides and other cattle products. Land appreciated in value, and cattle owners flourished. Commerce followed in the wake of grazing. The volume of trade increased and its terms became more advantageous than ever before. The benefits were reaped by the merchant class of Buenos Aires.

The interior provinces, however, suffered from free trade. They had achieved economic integration and self-sufficiency behind the protective shield of Spain's commercial and administrative policies. They had attained a crude industrial development catering to the internal market. After emancipation they could not withstand foreign competition. The Revolution of 1810 accelerated the economic deterioration of the interior. The provinces could only survive economically under conditions of fairly broad political autonomy as a defense against the economic encroachment of European manufactures pushed by Buenos Aires. Economic self-defense stood behind the federalist conception of state organization sponsored by the interior provinces.

The economic problem became a political contest in which *federales* fought *unitarios*, pitting states rights against Buenos Aires centralization. The program of centralization expressed the interests of those concerned with the expansion of overseas and domestic commerce: the merchants of the city port. They wanted to make internal markets accessible to foreign goods.

The cattle breeders of the province of Buenos Aires, on the other hand, relegated commerce to a subordinate position. They were interested primarily in the expansion of their industry. They wanted to monopolize for the province the economic gains of the revolution and viewed with suspicion any attempt to nationalize the port of Buenos Aires and its revenues. These cattle interests sponsored a federalism that was not—as with the interior provinces—the expression of economic self-defense. Their federalism represented rather the particularistic supremacy of the most privileged province in the union.

These deep economic cleavages made effective national organization nearly impossible for decades after the formal proclamation of Independence in 1816. Factionalism and political confusion were rampant. It was impossible to determine a new pattern of social and economic relationships and to anticipate a unified political structure. Moreover, the mobilization of the lower strata of the population, now demanding a share of the new order, upset the calculations of the commercial and intellectual elites.

At the beginning of the struggle for independence, the creole elite as a group preferred monarchical institutions, provided economic policy was modified. It finally chose a republican structure. Internal conflict was not resolved, however, by agreement on a republic. There still remained crucial issues: What kind of a republic: federal (decentralized) or unitary (centralized), presidential or parliamentary, popular or elitist, democratic or aristocratic, liberal or conservative? The conflict over political organization mirrored sharp differences over the existing and future structure of society, over access to and distribution of power, and over the course of economic change. At stake was the issue of who would inherit the revolution.

Not only was the elite divided along economic lines of cleavage: For the first time the rural population, the *gauchos* and the farmers, as well as the middle and lower classes in the cities had entered the political arena. The nation plunged into a series of civil wars. At the root of these wars stood the central trend in the economic development of independent Argentina: the shift of the economic center of gravity from the interior towards the seacoast brought about by the rapid expansion of the latter and the simultaneous retrogression of the former.

The uneven character of the economic development resulted in a self-perpetuating inequality. The country became divided into poor and rich provinces. The interior provinces were forced to relinquish ever-larger portions of the national income to Buenos Aires and other provinces of the East, which were quick to utilize their geographical advantage and superior capital means. In short, as Argentina became caught in the web of neocolonial relations after independence, the flow of wealth was redirected towards the seacoast in what amounted to a process of internal colonialism. The satellization of the interior took place by a rather circuitous route: Argentina successively fell under the sway of premature centralization (unitarism) that overestimated the potentialities of the national economy, went through a period of civil wars and provincial autonomy, came under the hegemony of Buenos Aires, and

was finally unified as a nation under the supremacy of the *pampa* and
the city-port.

The half-century after independence featured a triadic conflict between
Buenos Aires, the western provinces, and the riparian provinces of the
East. The substance of conflict was bare. The revolution had linked the
economy of the country to overseas markets at the same time that it
separated the interior from areas it had formed an integral part of during
the colonial era. So the economy of the interior was not only exposed
to the devastating competition of overseas industries in the eastern
markets, but was also deprived of those markets in which European
competition was least effective, namely those of Bolivia and Peru, which
after independence remained outside Argentina. In order to offset the
injurious commercial liberalism of Buenos Aires and prevent irreparable
loss, the western provinces sought political autonomy and interprovincial
trade by means of regional treaties. They thus fought for a type of loose
political organization that would guarantee their autonomy and at the
same time stabilize interprovincial relations. Such was the programmatic
core of Argentine federalism: a movement that sought the redistribution
of national income in favor of the interior and a better balanced national
economy (Burgin, 1946, Ch. 5).

The provinces of the littoral, especially Santa Fe and Entre Ríos,
resembled Buenos Aires in that they produced hides, meats, and other
by-products of the cattle-breeding industry. Like Buenos Aires, these
provinces depended upon foreign markets for a considerable part of
their income. Thus, whereas the Revolution of 1810 went too far for the
western provinces, it did not go far enough for the littoral. Economic
reform had not gone beyond the opening of Buenos Aires to foreign
commerce. These provinces rebelled against the stifling supremacy of
Buenos Aires, which had monopolized the economic gains of the revolution. They wanted direct contact with foreign markets—a practicable
program, since the rivers of the littoral were accessible to oceangoing
vessels. This bitter rivalry added much to civil strife in the decades
following independence. The conflict took place not only between
unitarios and *federales*, but also among the latter.

The unitary party represented the interests of a small and articulate
class of wealthy merchants and intellectuals sponsoring free trade and
liberalism. The *federales*, on the other hand, were concerned primarily
with local interests, which varied from region to region. Therefore, they
basically agreed on the desirability of home rule and on curtailing the
powers of the central government, but seriously disagreed on a number
of other issues. For instance, Buenos Aires federalists resisted the nationalization of customs revenues and their distribution *pro rata* among
the provinces. They equally opposed opening the rivers of the littoral
to foreign navigation. The country was finally pacified under the dictatorship of Rosas, who became governor of Buenos Aires in 1829.

Rosas would, in contemporary terminology, be termed a despotic but
also modernizing "nation-builder." He prepared the ground for economic

and political reorganization of the country. He was a strong representative of the cattle-breeding industry of the province of Buenos Aires—a Buenos Aires federalist. He presided over the federal reorganization of the country, which gave regional hegemony to the stronger provinces, such as Santa Fe in the littoral and Córdoba in the interior, and made Buenos Aires, as the strongest province, the arbiter of Argentine development.

Rosas' governorship represented not the unitary program of the merchant and intellectual elites of the city, but the power of the Buenos Aires cattle industry. The *unitarios* had been in power until then. They had hoped that with the help of foreign capital and European political institutions the country could be rapidly modernized. Their policies were rather premature and hardly corresponded to the social and economic realities of the time. They provoked the resentment of the interior and the suspicion of the cattle breeders of Buenos Aires. The latter instead proclaimed the principle of economic and political autonomy of the provinces, but insisted upon complete freedom in shaping the economy of Buenos Aires. This became Rosas' program.

For most interior provinces Rosas' government represented the continuation of the economic status quo. Buenos Aires continued to exercise control over the country's economy; it kept internal ports closed to overseas trade and appropriated the nation's customs revenues. Thus, Rosas' federalism expressed the hegemonic interest of the most powerful province. Provincial federalism, on the other hand, expressed the desire of the interior to bring Buenos Aires under the federal control of the provinces.

The economy of Buenos Aires rested solidly upon large-scale cattle breeding and foreign commerce. Abundance of cheap land and free access to foreign markets were essential to the economic development of the province. The federalist party of Buenos Aires, represented by Rosas, rose to its position of leadership on a program of defense of the economic and financial interests of the province. It was basically opposed to the nationalization of customs revenues, the opening of the river ports to overseas traffic, and the protection of domestic industries in the interior. Hence the tensions between Buenos Aires and the rest of the country continued under Rosas.

Buenos Aires federalism under Rosas was preferable to the rule of the *unitarios*, as far as the interior provinces were concerned. But it was still a selfish and domineering regime. Unlike the *unitarios*, Rosas formally recognized the principle of autonomy for the provinces. Moreover, his administration was extremely popular in Buenos Aires.

Rosas established a dictatorial regime by 1835, which, unhampered by parliamentary procedure, proceeded to take swift action restoring the economy of the province of Buenos Aires, shattered by wars, revolutions, and drought. His regime was very popular not only among the landowners and the *gauchos* in the countryside, but also among the meat producers, the artisans, and the small merchants in the city. But it was essentially a program of isolation from, and political domination over, the rest of the country, injurious to the most vital interests of other regions of Argentina. In order to realize such a program, Rosas needed the undivided support of his whole province, and lacking that, unlimited authority and power to use and dispose of the province's political and financial resources. His methods were contrary to the liberal tradition of the pro-independence elite, but they were in accord with the practices of the times. Postindependence political structures in Latin America shared by that time the same basic elements: strong executives and wide discretionary power. It was the period of unifying autocracies, which are usually associated with the early phases of political modernization.

The Landed Bourgeoisie

Rosas seldom went beyond the confines of the immediate interests of the province and the class he represented. This was the class that would shape Argentine dependent development. Buenos Aires pursued an independent economic course. It disposed of the produce of its pastoral industries in foreign markets, and in those markets it satisfied its demand for manufactures and foodstuffs. Ever since the opening of Buenos Aires to foreign trade the province had been drawn into the orbit of the European and North American economy. The province of Buenos Aires, home of the Argentine landed elite, found its place in the world market and was determined to keep it at all costs. It was a dependency of Europe and it satellized—when it did not altogether ignore—the rest of the nation.

Rosas was above all concerned with the prosperity of the pastoral industries. The central problem was the growing scarcity of free land. Twenty years after the opening of Buenos Aires to foreign trade, grazing was rapidly approaching the limits of profitable expansion. Cattle breeders were pushing southward into Indian territory in search for cheap land. Territorial expansion through military conquest of Indian land became the basic policy of Rosas and the ranchers. Within one year alone, Rosas brought under military control vast territories until then inhabited by Indian bands. He pushed the Indians south of the Río Colorado in the La Pampa and Neuquén provinces, opening up a territory that extended to the west as far as the Andes, and as far as Cape Horn to the south. Some six thousand Indians were killed during the campaign.

Once control over Indian territory was secured, the government proceeded to transfer large tracts to private owners. Many Argentine *belles familles* can trace their origins to the land grabbers of that time (Oddone, 1967, V, VI). Why did Argentina not become a nation of farmers instead of producing this capitalist "aristocracy" of cattle barons? Here again, a glance at comparative economic opportunities yields some answers that do not hinge on the metaphysics of value systems and Spanish heritage.

In the days following independence, enterprising elites laid plans to populate the *pampa*, to expand the area under grain cultivation, and to make the provinces and the country agriculturally self-sustaining. Successive national administrations subsidized immigration, relying on private initiative and fertile soil. These considerations were deemed sufficient to insure prosperity to agriculture just as they insured the continued expansion of cattle breeding. But it soon became clear that domestic agriculture had none of the economic advantages that grazing enjoyed. Agriculture called for proportionately larger investments of labor, which was notoriously scarce and expensive. Second, methods of cultivation were primitive, and the yield was low in spite of the excellent quality of the soil. Machinery and agricultural implements were required. Third, the high cost of transportation forced the farmer to move closer to cities where land prices were higher. Finally, unlike the cattle breeder, the farmer had to contend with an often ruinous foreign competition. The domestic market was small, and because foreign wheat and flour were usually of superior quality, domestic farmers had small chance to survive. Agriculture therefore continued to occupy a minor position in the expanding economy of the *pampas*. It only became important much later, when a landed cattle aristocracy was already well entrenched. Agriculture then developed on the basis of tenancy and sharecropping arrangements. The early and natural flow of capital into ranching produced something approaching a land monopoly and a powerful landed stratum. One must be careful not to assume that either of these traits was proof of institutionalized feudalism. A scholar not suspect of Marxist leanings puts it bluntly: "Argentine agro-pecuarian enterprise is free capitalist enterprise and always has been since the revolution and even earlier" (Ferns, 1969, 124).

Public land was not only sold at low prices and in enormous tracts: It was also simply given away by the government in the form of land grants to friends and hangers-on. By 1840, Rosas had "liberated" public lands, assuring the pastoral industry a plentiful supply at reasonable prices, and had extended the southern frontiers of the province. Argentina became a paradise for *estancieros* and *saladeristas:* Cattle breeders and meat and hide producers were the groups that derived the greatest benefits from this regime.

Cattle breeding and meat production were export-oriented activities. A policy of economic laissez-faire suited these interests best. Their markets were abroad, and from abroad came goods against which the artisans, farmers, and wine producers of the interior could not compete. Thus large-scale merchants, cattle breeders, and meat producers were free traders, whereas producers who did not depend upon foreign trade fought unsuccessfully for protectionism. Industrial protection and economic nationalism were time and again sacrificed. Domestic manufacture seldom received an adequate stimulus. It never gained a foothold in postcolonial Argentina. Ranching was by far the most attractive investment, geared to a foreign rather than a domestic market. The economic greatness of Buenos Aires and with it the strength of the nation for many years to come derived from the soil. Buenos Aires did not raise the standard of economic revolt against Spain in the name of industrialization on the European pattern. Economic revolution and Argentine capitalism germinated on the pastures of the *pampa*, among cattle breeders. They were the class that ultimately propelled the economic growth of Argentina, and subordinated the rest of the country to its interests. Their role would change in the course of the nineteenth century from that of a particularistic pressure group in one province to that of a national ruling class—*la oligarquía.*

The Rosas regime consolidated the power of this class and prepared the ground for national unification. Rosas fell when his policies had outlived their usefulness and their historic role. The mounting resentment of other provinces and the mounting costs of his heavy-handed rule brought about his demise in 1852.

The Imperialism of Free Trade

After the fall of Rosas, a liberal aristocratic Argentina was born, which was in the heyday of its glory on the eve of World War I, collapsed in 1930, and has been in agony since then.

Rosas was overthrown by a coalition of cattle interests of the littoral and liberal bourgeois intellectuals, eager to work out a constitution and to establish a policy of modernization. The single most divisive issue was the place of the city and the province of Buenos Aires with respect to the rest of the country. The issue was finally settled in 1880 when the city of Buenos Aires was separated administratively and politically from its province, converted into a national capital, and so became the hub of Argentine society as a whole.

Underlying that issue was the relative position and power of the mercantile and financial interests with respect to the landed interest. It has been speculatively suggested (Ferns, 1969, 314) that if Buenos Aires had succeeded in keeping its political independence, it would have been possible for its class of financiers and entrepreneurs to undertake their own independent capital accumulation and become, in other words, the nucleus of a national and industrial bourgeoisie. The province of Buenos Aires probably had enough resources and people and the use of the harbor of Buenos Aires was intensive enough to warrant the supposition that private and public internal capital accumulation and reinvestment could have taken place.

As it was, the landed interest under the leadership of provincial politicians prevailed. These were not national financial and industrial entrepreneurs but a class of modernizing landlord-liberals devoted to rapid economic growth of the market opportunities for ranching, sheep breeding, and grain farming; to the import of capital to develop the infrastructure of railways, docks, and commercial facilities; to the increased supply of labor through immigration and to the further expansion of the frontier by building railways and applying the "final solution" to the Indian problem. They came to be known as the "generation of 1880," the first truly national ruling class.

The capital requirements of their project of modernization were so large that both the landowners and their governments became debtors of international finance capital: the governments to build railways and ports; the landlords to fence their land, dig wells, install Australian tanks and windmills, buy farm machinery, and acquire high-grade breeding stock. From the beginning, British capitalists were the largest foreign investment interest. British diplomacy during this foothold period unerringly supported the more daring projects of national political integration, such as the integration of Buenos Aires in the republic, and equally supported the more grandiose projects of economic expansion they knew were well beyond the capacities of Argentine capital.

In the end, saddled with a vast foreign investment, Argentina was obliged to export or go bankrupt, and this meant concentration upon a limited range of exportable staple products with all the social, political, moral, and intellectual consequences of acute dependency. An American rural sociologist put it this way:

> A society depending almost altogether on an extensive production of cheap raw products is a slave of export markets, on the one hand, and the exploitation of its lower classes, on the other hand. It is, therefore, socially unhealthy, both domestically and internationally. (Taylor, 1948, 207)

The generation of 1880—a debtor ruling class—had the political power to assert its interests and to ensure its well-being. As opposed to other Latin American "enclave" economies, in Argentina the upper class secured control over the principal means of production, even though the financing and commercialization of the produce were largely in foreign hands (Cardoso and Faletto, 1969, 42–47). There was a certain degree of political autonomy amidst economic dependence. The dominant Argentine interests and their creditors often compromised with each other, shifting the burden of the compromises to wage workers, the middle strata, and the unpropertied classes generally. Dependency was continuously negotiated.

And so modernization took rapid hold on the *pampas*. Within a generation, the social life of the country was altered. A striking feature of this change was the expansion of grain production, which led to the emergence of Argentina as a major supplier of grain for industrial markets. Lands formerly idle or used for wild pasturage were converted to the tillage of wheat, corn, alfalfa, and flax. Crop acreage and production went up. Livestock products became a basic pillar of Argentine specialization in foodstuff production. Here again, technological innovations led to a marked increase in productivity. Successful experiments with refrigerated shipping led to the establishment of freezing plants to prepare meat for overseas markets. Because the demand for better grades of meat could hardly be provided by the wild or semiwild cattle of the *estancias*, a true stock-raising industry was developed. Improved breeds were imported from Europe, and care and vigilance of these refined breeds led to the consolidation and rationalization of property rights. The application of new business techniques was eminently compatible with the existing system of *latifundia* and with the social order it had produced. In fact, the new wave of capitalism—now in its imperialist stage—on the *pampas* came to reinforce the pattern of land tenure and consolidate the power of the landed bourgeoisie. The developing livestock industry led to fencing cattle in ranches rather than letting them graze on the open range. Further enclosures were made necessary by the intermingling of crop lands and cattle ranches.

Much of the cultivation of crop lands on the ranches was carried out by tenants. Tenancy had been largely unknown in Argentina before, but the growing world demand, the new dependency, the rationalization of production, and the inflow of external migrants rapidly changed the situation (Jefferson, 1926). Immigrants and their descendants became the nucleus of a class of tenant farmers, as sharecropping and other rental arrangements were worked out in order to develop agriculture in a context of superconcentration of property and rising land values.

Perhaps the most revealing feature of the whole process was the development of the railroad system, initiated around 1885. By 1914 most of the trunk lines across the *pampas* had been completed and a network of feeder and branch lines had been created. The radial pattern of the railroad lines expressed their true economic function: All of the major lines spread out from the capital city like spokes from the hub of a great wheel. There was little cross-linkage between internal points, since the vast majority of the goods carried by rail were destined for the capital city for shipment overseas. The peculiarity of the rail network helped Buenos Aires maintain economic and political hegemony over the nation, for the sake of export goods (Scalabrini Ortiz, 1964).

In this way the new Argentine economy was the product of technical advances in manufacturing and transportation that originated in the capitalist metropolises, and of an international system characterized by freedom of trade, movements of capital to the "open spaces," and large labor migrations. The modernization of Argentina, and perhaps even the creation of the nation itself, came about as the result of foreign needs and was implemented by railroads, steamships, and refrigerated shipping.

Until the closing days of the nineteenth century, the Argentine economy operated under a system of paper currency. Price inflation was a constant feature. None of the unpropertied classes had any political power in this society, so they had scant means of resisting the effects of prices rising faster than incomes. There were, however, countervailing factors:

Labor—especially skilled labor—was scarce, and this factor pushed wages upward. If the upper classes used the hammer of inflation too harshly, then immigrants would simply cease to come en masse to Argentina. Thus compromises had to be devised with the lower classes as well as with the imperialist interests. The upshot for several decades was a moderately open, modernizing society. Variety, in people and opinion, was progressively tolerated. Social mobility was high. The world conjunction was favorable, and Argentina enjoyed natural advantages.

Historians discern four stages in the development of what is sometimes called, apologetically, "the free, open society of the landlord-liberals" (Ferns, 1969, 98): (1) an initial stage of integration into the international capitalist division of labor, completed in the 1860s; (2) a critical stage connected with the financial crisis of 1890–1896; (3) a "golden age" of high prosperity from the Boer War to World War I; and (4) a stage of maturity that ended with the international crisis of 1929. In brief, the first stage involved national political unification and the choice of dependent development through foreign investment over autonomous accumulation. This period set the foundations of national indebtedness as development of export agriculture and stock raising was financed from abroad. Argentine wealth was land. Investment in railways, or generally in joint-stock enterprise, was foreign, and heavily British.

The flow of foreign capital began as a sustained process in the 1860s and continued almost uninterruptedly until 1890. The intensity of this flow was such that in 1888 to 1889 almost half of the new issues in the London capital market were made on behalf of enterprises in Argentina and nearly a quarter of a million immigrants from Europe entered the country. During all this time more goods were flowing into Argentina than were being exported. In 1890 a crisis developed; the important London banking firm of Baring Brothers was threatened with bankruptcy on account of its Argentine accounts. The Argentine economy was simply not producing enough to satisfy all the demands on it. Such crises were familiar in the capitalist world before the First World War. In the Middle and Far East, as well as in other countries of Latin America, those crises led to gunboat diplomacy, that is, to a direct political and military intervention by the imperialist powers in order to administer the community so that foreign capitalists could be paid. The United States frequently behaved in such fashion vis-à-vis its southern neighbors.

In 1890, Argentine dependency on Britain had reached such intensity that the repudiation of debts was considered unacceptable to the landed bourgeoisie, tied as it was to the international market for commodities and capital. Having ruled out autarky, this class turned to the United States as an alternate potential moneylender. The result was disappointing: The Americans wanted to expand their share of Argentine markets but were unwilling to open up their own to Argentine produce. Moreover, they demanded special legislation to protect their interests, and they even wanted a naval base. This type of big stick imperialism, from which other Latin American republics suffered so much, was far less attractive to the Argentine beef aristocracy than the subtler and more intelligent manipulations of Lord Rothschild. The British banking establishment offered better terms. Argentine agro-pecuarian production promised a growth of such magnitude that the country's mortgage of its future did not alarm the avant-garde of the London banking community. And indeed Argentine production of wheat, linseed, wool, mutton, and beef did expand enormously. The price of Argentine exports began to rise, the country resumed interest and debt service payments, and foreign investment was resumed in the late 1890s.

The crisis was overcome before the outbreak of the Spanish-American and the Boer Wars. The golden age of Argentina then dawned. Argentina entered the twentieth century enraptured in a dream of unlimited prosperity. To cite Victor Hugo: "situated in the moon, kingdom of dream, province of illusion, capital Soap-Bubble" (*Les Misérables, Saint Denis*, VIII, Ch. 3). Such was the mood of the times. Exports multiplied at a fantastic pace. The landed bourgeoisie and its commercial allies grew enormously rich and adopted a veneer of French culture and English manners.

Liberalism and Prosperity

Internationally, Argentine dependent modernization hinged on a world market for foodstuffs unrestrained by tariffs, quotas, and controls. Between 1896 and 1914, the price of foodstuffs improved markedly, while the prices of industrial products tended to fall. Argentina bought certain competitive advantages in the international conjuncture but was to pay dearly for them in the long run. That favorable conjuncture began to change after World War I, was never restored to a state so favorable to Argentina as it had been before, and turned against the country after 1930.

Internally, two main factors made economic growth possible: a large supply of good land, and the availability of a large immigrant labor force.

We have already seen how, from revolutionary times onward, land in Argentina was distributed in large blocks to a small number of families. These possessed estates often as large as entire English counties. In 1914, 78.34 percent of all land was in farms of more than 1,000 hectares (2,470 acres). According to the census of that year there were 2,958 properties of 5,000 to 10,000 hectares (12,350 to 24,700 acres); 1,474 from 10,000 to 25,000 hectares (24,700 to 61,750 acres); and 485 with more than 100,000 hectares (247,000 acres) (Taylor, 1948, 185; Oddone, 1967, 182–186). In the more remote National Territories, fewer than 2,000 persons owned as much land as Italy, Belgium, the Netherlands, and Denmark combined (Oddone, 1967, 273)!

To briefly sketch the social history of the Argentine *latifundia:* Some of them came into existence by free land gifts in a long period when land had little value, and the competition for landownership and use was slight; some of them came into existence much later—some as late as a few generations ago. Profitable cattle production made that land valuable, and so rich cattlemen became the nucleus of the upper class. Later they were joined by rich sheepmen, sugar-plantation owners, and some rich owners of cereal farms.

The history of tenancy, on the other hand, is the story of hundreds of thousands of European immigrants pouring into the country seeking land that had become so valuable that owners would seldom release title to it for colonization purposes. They instead colonized it with tenants, or employed wage labor.

The relationship between the agrarian classes changed with economic development. During the initial period of paper currency and loose credit policies (before the Baring crisis), inflation benefited landowners and working farmers and oppressed wage earners as prices rose faster than wages. After the crisis, tighter credit and deflationary policies alienated renting farmers from landowners. The system of land rental and sharecropping worked smoothly as long as land was freely available and the international prices of produce rose faster than the prices of goods consumed by farmers and ranchers. When the external market situation changed and land became less available, tensions erupted between the landowning class and the tenant farmers. The latter swung towards the opposition parties after 1912 (Cortés Conde and Gallo, 1967, III).

Argentina became one of the principal absorbers of European immigration before the First World War. Yet neither the expulsion from Europe nor the attraction of the New World reveals the whole story. Given the prevailing ownership structure, the immigrants could hardly be expected to "take root" in the soil. Had it not been for the initial concentration of rural property, immigration could well have yielded a more egalitarian social system, based on family medium and small holdings as an offshoot of European societies. Historically, such systems have developed either by way of land reform or revolution, or through the colonization of farmlands carried out under governments in which landlords did not have a prevailing interest. One could speculate that such agrarian structure could have made agricultural diversification much easier when the impact of external demand ceased and when industries began to require a regular supply for the city markets. As it was, Argentina developed a feeble system of tenancy. It is worth mentioning that nearly half of the immigrants who arrived in Argentina in the period of massive intercontinental migrants returned to their lands of origin.

And yet the people of no nation—with the possible exception of the United States—are more thoroughly the offspring of European immigrants than the Argentines. The magnitude and impact of European immigration after 1853 have been so great as literally to remake the ethnic composition of the country. Between 1890 and 1914 over 4 million foreigners poured into the country. Many returned home after a brief stay, but immigration left a residue of about 2.4 million to settle permanently. By the eve of World War I, close to a third of the population had been born abroad, which gave Argentina the distinction of a higher proportion of immigrants to total population than any other major country (Germani, 1962, 197; Solberg, 1965, 35–37).

The movement of immigrants and emigrants into and out of Argentina was uneven over the years of recorded data, which began to be collected in 1857. The broad outline of the economic and political forces that attracted and repelled them is fairly well known. There were three crests and three troughs of immigration, matched to some extent by trends in emigration. The increase in the flow of immigrants was modest and consistent until about 1880. Then it began to grow by leaps and bounds. The number of immigrants increased from 26,000 in 1880 to almost 219,00 in 1889 (Taylor, 1948, 91). Immigration declined and emigration rose during the years of crisis and political instability, 1890–1895. Then the upward trend recovered, and from 1904 until the outbreak of World War I hundreds of thousands of immigrants poured into the country each year, reaching high points in 1910 and 1912. It was during this period that seasonal workers moved back and forth between the harvests of southern Europe and Argentina. They were called *golondrinas*, or swallows, because they migrated annually. In that way, Italian and Spanish laborers met a peak requirement at times of harvest without putting a strain on the system of Argentine *latifundia*. Gradually the mechanization of wheat harvesting diminished the migration of these "swallows." But out of the flux there were thousands who after a season or two chose to stay in Argentina. The First World War provoked a sharp decline in immigration. The third and last high tide began in 1920, and lasted until the debacle of 1930. With the Great Depression the process came to an end. External immigration, which shaped Argentine society in the era of agrarian prosperity, gave way to internal migration from the provinces to Buenos Aires as an essential component of industrial development.

Italians first, and then Spaniards, composed more than three-fourths of the immigrant contingents. French, Poles, Russians, Ottomans, Germans, and Austro-Hungarians trailed behind. Reflecting the trend toward the near-monopoly of landownership by the native bourgeoisie, agriculturists constituted a steadily diminishing proportion of all immigrants. Day laborers, merchants, and mechanics constituted steadily increasing percentages and concentrated in the cities (Beyhaut et al., 1965, 85–123). This explains a unique and probably most significant fact about population development in Argentina: The center of population moved toward the coast rather than toward the interior. The majority of the people in a predominantly agricultural country came to live in cities: overurbanization in an agrarian society. Ecological disequilibrium resulted in a fan-shaped distribution of natural resources and population, with the hub of the fan located approximately at the city of Buenos Aires— an icon of outward growth and dependency.

Immigration provided a mass of laborers, some qualified personnel, and a small number of entrepreneurs. However, the characteristics of Argentine economic expansion, under British international control and under circumstances that left the basic agro-export structure unchanged, tended to channel entrepreneurial initiative away from industrial activity and into commercial and speculative ventures while increasing urbanization very quickly. The upshot was a distorted social structure. Under the continued dominance of the landed bourgeoisie the social mobility of the newcomers ended up inflating a disproportionately large tertiary sector, characterized by a large number of unproductive activities. Immigration, therefore, furthered modernization but left intact the productive structure of society.

Several decades of prosperity seemed to support the development schemes of the "generation of 1880." Facts and figures seemed to justify the euphoria of the ruling class: Population grew at a rate of 3.2 percent a year between 1869 and 1929; productivity rose at an average of nearly 5 percent; total capital increased at a similar yearly rate; income per capita jumped from 2,308 pesos (at constant 1950 prices) in 1900–1904 to 3,207 pesos in 1925–1929 (Ferns, 1969, 121). The national censuses of 1869, 1895, and 1914 reveal impressive changes: The 1.9 million residents of 1869 were joined as of 1914 by 5.9 million immigrants, of whom 3.2 million became permanent residents. The land under cultivation increased from 1.5 million hectares in 1872 to 25 million hectares in 1914. The railroad network was 35,800 km long in 1914. British investment in Argentina increased from 5 million pounds in 1865 to 365 million in 1913. The city of Buenos Aires grew by 786 percent between 1869 and 1914. White-collar workers represented 6 percent of the working population in 1869; by 1914 they were 21 percent—some 595,000 middle-class individuals, concentrated mostly in Buenos Aires, in a nation with no significant industrial base (Merkx, 1968, 79–93)! As wealth increased, politics were liberalized.

Argentina could even afford to misrepresent itself before other Latin American republics as a champion of the weak against Yankee imperialism. In 1890, the first Pan-American conference was held in Washington. On the agenda was a project for the creation of a Pan-American customs union, promoted by the United States on the maxim "America for the Americans." Argentina strongly opposed the project with the maxim "America for humanity." In those days U.S. imperialism had already begun to parade under the banner of Pan-Americanism. Argentina's universalism, on the other hand, expressed the confident defense of its dependency on England. The ideological conflict persisted until after World War II (Whitaker, 1954, Ch. 5).

As the century came to a close, political parties of the middle class—notably the Unión Cívica Radical, or Radical Civic Union—emerged, trade unions developed, and the groundwork was laid for universal male suffrage. This period has been widely interpreted as one of development toward democratic gradualism. Such an interpretation is made superficially reasonable by the fact that economic growth was followed by a decade and a half of domestic rule. *Post hoc, ergo propter hoc* arguments are treacherous: There are deeper reasons to suspect that the boundary conditions of Argentine democratization were narrow.

The first point to be made is that the process of change in Argentine society during the early part of the twentieth century can in no way be seriously described as "the passing of traditional society." Argentine underdevelopment is a concrete historical process through which societies that have already achieved a high level of development have not necessarily passed.

"Traditionalism" and "modernity" are terms that fail to describe Argentine social change. Argentina had been a dynamic capitalist society for at least half a century. The landowning class had long made the transition to commercial agriculture in the nineteenth century. Landowners had been quick to exploit expanding export markets for their crops and to link Argentina to world capitalism. The landed bourgeoisie had called for, and received, capital and labor from abroad. Massive immigration, concomitant rapid urbanization, and even some subsidiary industrialization indeed changed Argentine society. But it was a different type of change from that which is typically construed by social scientists when they write about "transitional" societies in which "traditional" patterns are weakened. These metaphors are rooted in the specific historical experience of the European transition from feudalism to capitalism. They tend to hypostatize the internal change of past societies. There industrialization involved the transformation of peasants into industrial workers. The increasing hegemony of the bourgeoisie reflected the mobility of indigenous classes and the growth among them of role distribution based on achievement. Not so in peripheral capitalist societies like Argentina. Here modernization was not an internal transformation. It was rather a change induced by the development of a worldwide capitalist division of labor that pushed certain countries into the role of agro-pecuarian exporters. It then grafted onto the agribusiness nucleus an urban, semi-industrial, service-oriented society, literally from the outside, by means of external financing and foreign immigration.

Society thus came to be organized around a dependent export sector. After massive immigration and rapid urbanization, the productive structure of society remained basically the same. Modernization was superstructural, pseudomorphic.

An analogous situation existed in politics. New political parties—notably the Unión Cívica Radical—representing the growing urban middle sectors and some marginal agrarian groups entered politics, as it were, from the outside. These parties embodied the demands of outsiders who had not been integrated into the land-based authority structure. Their strength was neither a consequence of the weakened power of the dominant class nor the manifestation of a superior mode of production. Their participation in politics depended instead on the prosperity and self-confidence of the class of landlord-liberals. After 1930, when that prosperity and self-confidence were undermined by events beyond anybody's control in Argentina, the landed bourgeoisie did not hesitate to close the political system on the tacit rule of privilege: "last hired, first fired."

The Middle Class in Power

As export development reached sufficient magnitude, a middle class emerged that did not challenge the existing economic order, but demanded political participation and equality, i.e., the extension of citizenship.

The word "pseudomorphic" describes the processes of modernization associated with export development, because Argentina became a bourgeois society before becoming an industrial nation. Historically, middle-class societies have been associated with the industrial revolution. In Argentina, however, the structure and the fabric of bourgeois-democratic society was superimposed on agro-pecuarian foundations. The growth of an urban middle class resulted here from the international division of labor, which permitted Argentina to import modern superstructures and join them to a dependent, nonindustrial mode of production.

At the time of these developments, the Argentine government was still the preserve of the landed elite. It was an oligarchy: "A government resting on a valuation of property, in which the rich have power and the poor man is deprived of it" (Plato, *The Republic*, Book 8, 550-C). With the growth of the new middle class came demands for opening the system through popular suffrage. Moreover, in times of crisis, such as the Baring crisis of 1890, members of the oligarchy were not above recruiting allies from the middle class. It was such a coalition that founded the Unión Cívica in 1890. Shortly thereafter middle-class members seceded and formed the Unión Cívica Radical—Argentina's first modern political party.

The Unión Cívica Radical never represented a united, coherent class, but was rather an aggregation of disparate groups and individuals. Initially, it was more representative of the old middle class, which was largely creole and in which independent farmers were heavily represented. It eventually came to encompass the new middle class, which was drawn mainly from the descendants of Spanish and Italian immigrants—the growing white-collar strata of clerks and bureaucrats, and the petit bourgeoisie of shopkeepers. The leadership of the party was dominated by landed interests not closely tied to world markets. Hipólito Yrigoyen, the party leader who became president of Argentina in 1916 and again in 1928, was himself a marginal landowner.

The party's heterogeneous class composition and the general prosperity of the nation prevented it from articulating a serious challenge to the established economic order. The basic demand of the radicals was popular suffrage. The rest was mostly a lofty-sounding and vague ideology.

Under Yrigoyen's leadership the radicals abstained from electoral participation at the time—electoral politics was rigged and merely a facade for oligarchic control—and twice launched revolts. Radicals frequently conspired with the military in the hope of inducing officers to attempt a coup. The oligarchy became increasingly concerned about such tactics and the more enlightened elements of the elite finally granted universal male suffrage in 1912. The radicals returned to electoral politics. In 1916 Yrigoyen was elected to the presidency.

Once in power, *radicalismo* operated well within the limits of the status quo in a manner acceptable to the dominant landed interests. *Radicalismo* generally eschewed serious reference to economic problems, in part to avoid cleavages among its heterogeneous constituency. Radical economic policies supported the establishment. The radical program sought the extension of political participation and the redistribution of the benefits of export development. In brief, it sought to extend both geographically and socially the institutional structure of agrarian Argentina.

The same programmatic and ideological ambivalence was characteristic of other middle-class parties such as La Liga del Sur, which later became the Partido Demócrata Progresista, a party based in the province of Santa Fe. Moral indignation and the concern over formal democracy consumed a large amount of the political energy available to the middle-class parties. The political trajectory of these parties, their programs and ideologies, were determined by the process of economic expansion. They called for more participation, for the end of economic abuses and political corruption. But they expressed a fundamental consensus about the content and direction of economic growth. Middle-class insurgency erupted during the periodic crises to which the economic system was subject. Those crises produced spontaneous "explosions" of middle-class anger, prompted some reforms, and then subsided. A closer scrutiny of the main middle-class subgroups shows their incapacity to formulate alternatives in the field of economic policy.

The industrial sector was too weak to formulate alternative economic policies. Moreover, the middle-class parties did not really represent this sector and did not incorporate its demands in their programs. The commercial sector was in a similar position: Commercial capital was largely concentrated in import-export trade that depended on the agropecuarian sector. The rest was scattered among small merchants and shopkeepers—most of them Spanish and Italian immigrants. These groups were nonpolitical: Their main motive for migration had been to improve their economic lot by acquiring money or property—something they could try without applying for Argentine citizenship. The rural middle class fought for better grain prices and lower rents, but never challenged the tenure system. In brief, the middle sectors had economic interests in many ways parallel to the interests they opposed, namely, the big landlords, meat packers, and ranchers.

That basic economic consensus extended even below the strata of farmers, shopkeepers, and white-collar workers. For instance, after the stabilization of the currency around the turn of the century, a certain coincidence of interest developed among wage-workers and the big exporters. Labor leaders and working-class parties, especially the socialists, became strong advocates of price stability, which they associated with free trade. They thus opposed any policy that aimed at industrial protection. Strikes and agitation, which were frequent after 1900, were aimed at obtaining better working conditions and higher wages in the industrial plants but they in no way represented a challenge to the export establishment.

This is not to minimize the radicalism and militancy of the working-class movement. Two political currents provided leadership to the proletariat during the export period. One was anarcho-syndicalism, which was very influential in the strikes before 1916. The other was the Socialist Party, founded in 1896, which espoused reformist policies.

As a consequence of immigration, European ideas about trade unions, socialism, and anarchism flourished among the railway employees; the workers in the processing and milling enterprises, in the building industry, and in the ports; and among the numerous groups of waiters and servants who supplied the services demanded by the wealthy. Strikes and anarchist violence were common events, especially around 1905. In 1909 there was a general strike in which a clash between demonstrators and troops resulted in four dead and forty-five wounded. Later that year the chief of police of Buenos Aires, Colonel Falcón, was blown to bits by a bomb. Anarchism flourished when larger industrial concentrations began to replace artisan shops, drawing more and more handicraftsmen into the ranks of the proletariat. Anarchism thus expressed the radicalization of a vanishing stratum of the working class. The evolution of the working-class organizations reflected that trend. The first workers' societies were established along immigrant-ethnic lines. By 1891, the movement had a short-lived central federation, the Federación de Trabajadores de la Región Argentina. The next organization, the Federación Obrera Argentina (FOA), founded in 1904, was crushed, but reorganized itself as the Federación Obrera Regional Argentina (FORA). This new central union was controlled by anarchists and syndicalists.

The socialists, who had created the Unión Central de Trabajadores (UCT), eventually came to dominate the working-class movement, superseding the anarcho-syndicalist period. However, as the economy expanded the social mobility increased, their own constituency became more "middle class." Their position as a working-class party began to deteriorate, and they suffered several defections. The most significant of these, in 1918, led to the formation of the International Socialist Party, which joined the Third International and was a forerunner of the Argentine Communist Party.

The organization of labor was part of the continuing capitalist consolidation of the economy. So was its systematic repression. Anarchist militancy was met by the ruling class with the Law of Residence, passed in 1902, and the Law of Social Defense, passed in 1910, which empowered the government to deal directly with immigrant leaders by deportation. Troops were frequently used against demonstrations. In this, the middle-class government of the *radicales* fared no better than its conservative opponents. In 1919, a metalworkers' strike in Buenos Aires became the nucleus of a series of solidarity strikes in the rest of Argentina. Soldiers were called out, and for a whole week the strikes were forcibly put down. This came to be known as the "Tragic Week" of January 1919. In 1920 to 1921, some two thousand workers were massacred in Patagonia by the military.

Radicalismo and the Consolidation of the Export Economy

The growth of exports stimulated the development of subsidiary industries, many of them concentrated in foreign hands. The meat-packing industry was the nucleus of subsidiary industrialization. U.S. investments prevailed in this sector, followed by British and local capital. In 1927, the United States controlled over half of meat exports, Britain over a third, and Argentine interests the rest. In the commerical sector, firms like Bunge & Born—founded by Belgian financiers with worldwide connections—controlled flour mills, chemical and industrial firms, and loan associations. They virtually monopolized the export of grain, and, being middlemen for other products, they also came to control the available foreign exchange.

Banking, however, was under national control, which allowed the landed bourgeoisie to finance production independently. In other words, the landed bourgeoisie controlled production and local financing, while European and U.S. interests controlled the packing and commercialization of the export produce.

The Argentine economy continued to specialize in the export of meats and cereals. The area under cultivation in grains and forage increased fourfold between 1900 and 1929, always under elite control. Cereal exports grew even faster than meat exports. In 1925, the Argentine contribution to total world export was: maize, 66 percent; flax, 72 percent; oats, 32 percent; wheat, 20 percent; and meat, 50 percent (Daniels, 1970, II, 2).

As long as the economy continued to expand, *radicalismo* did not pose a threat to the dominant classes. The system could sustain substantial reforms and extended political participation. Oligarchic control was loosened. Before 1912, the oligarchy had retained control of the essential offices of the state through the management of the electoral machinery and the political use of the police and the armed forces to get their own people to the polls and to count the ballots in their favor. In 1912 the Saenz-Peña Law, forced through a reluctant congress by an enlightened president, provided for a compulsory, secret ballot to be conducted by the armed forces. The latter would act as a neutral agency in the preparation of the voters list from the registry of all male citizens obliged to enroll under the law of compulsory military service. They were charged with the duty of seeing that all voted secretly and only once, and that the votes were counted impartially. Genuine elections were at last possible as a means of selecting the members of the formal power structure. These political reforms brought radical and socialist representatives to Congress, and in 1916 they brought Yrigoyen to the presidency.

The radicals came to power in the middle of World War I. To their credit, they stuck to a policy of strict neutrality. They also nationalized the petroleum industry. But the war created other opportunities as well: High prices for Argentine products were offset by the reduction of capital flows and by a rise in the price of imports. Scarcity and high prices gave an advantage to national industries. Yrigoyen's administration did not seize the opportunity to consolidate the advantages by tariff protection and other similar measures. Surpluses were used to reduce foreign indebtedness rather than to increase domestic capital.

If economically the radical regime was unimaginative, socially it was sometimes repressive. When peace came to Europe with its wake of revolutionary unrest, Yrigoyen struck at the working class in what was one of the worst periods of repression and official violence in Argentine labor history before 1955. Yrigoyen left the Argentine economy almost exactly as he found it: dependent on the big export industries and foreign markets. His shortcomings were not, however, accidental. Rather, they expressed the "middle-mass" consciousness of store owners, clerks, and employees of public utilities, for whom "*radicalismo* is a sentiment, not a program," as the saying went.

The hegemony of the landed bourgeoisie was never questioned. Not only did the landed elite ultimately determine economic policy; the landed oligarchs held a majority in the senate, and were often appointed to cabinet posts. Marcelo T. de Alvear, the second top leader of the *radicales* who succeeded Yrigoyen in 1922, was himself a member of the old "aristocracy." Again, he did nothing to change laissez-faire economic policies.

The undisputed economic hegemony of the landed elite throughout this period of middle-class government is even more clearly revealed by the vicissitudes of the Argentine socialist movement. That movement was born in the 1880s when inflation devoured the incomes of the incipient working class. With the subsequent expansion of Argentine exports, the favorable terms of trade stabilized the currency. Thus, the success of the elite's economic program won for them the support of the socialists, who from then on sought reform and not revolution. Social mobility also contributed to the bourgeois tendencies of the socialists. Eventually they became junior partners of the establishment. These are the historical roots of a spectacle that would puzzle some observers in 1945, when socialists and communists demonstrated against Perón in the company of reactionary landlords.

Yrigoyen was reelected in 1928. One year later the Great Depression engulfed the capitalist world. As prices of grain and meat fell, Argentina's gold stocks flowed abroad to pay for imports into the country. In order to protect gold holdings, the government suspended the free conversion of paper pesos into gold. The price of imported manufactured goods did not fall as did that of Argentine exports on account of the sudden contraction of industrial production in the metropolitan countries. This diminished the goods and services available to the mass of the people. Customs revenues fell and the state, devoid of other tax resources, could not meet its payments to the innumerable beneficiaries of the political patronage system that the *radicales* had carefully cultivated. Everybody was more or less worse off.

The economic malaise interacted with a social and political crisis. The international crisis awakened authoritarian and reactionary trends among the landed upper class that found its economic basis threatened and therefore turned to political levers to preserve its rule. Its members called on the military to overthrow the government.

On September 6, 1930, General José Felix Uriburu deposed the president and proclaimed martial law, striking down a decade and a half of democratic rule and, more generally, a liberal system that had endured for sixty-eight years. Uriburu was an officer with landed, conservative family connections. He was inspired by European fascism, which he misunderstood as an aristocratic movement. He was backed in this venture not only by the landed elite, but also by anti-Yrigoyen radicals and by the right-wing Independent Socialist Party. But his dictatorship was ineffective and short-lived. It was soon replaced by a "limited democracy" type of government based on the restriction of popular participation, under General Justo.

The year 1930 marked the return of the landed upper class to political power, within a context of international crisis and under the imperative to industrialize. The Prussian training of the army cadres, the increasing impact of fascism on the European continent, and the frictions between Yrigoyen and the armed forces over military appropriations were all considerations that facilitated the army coup. Moreover, the Argentine army had always been "political": Compulsory military service, established in 1901, was designed with political socialization in mind. The army was charged with overseeing elections. In Argentina the draft card and the voter registration card are one and the same document for males over eighteen years of age. In brief, the Argentine armed forces have always been oriented to "civic action" programs. Internally, politicization was also traditionally intense: Officers' lodges, or secret pressure groups, have always been a feature of army life (Orona, 1965; Potash, 1969, 11–18, 37–38).

Social scientists have long known that the Argentine armed forces are not the preserve of the landed elite. The traditional upper class has comparatively little family and class connection with the armed forces with the exception of some elite branches of the service. This was true in 1930, even though General Uriburu had family connections with the landed upper class. The fact remains that the Argentine armed forces are fairly meritocratic in organization, with relatively open recruitment from different social classes. They are a ladder for upward mobility. But this overwhelmingly middle-class composition of the armed forces does not prevent them from pursuing policies which are pro–status quo and anti-popular. They often engage in such policies precisely as representatives of an ambivalent and contradictory middle class (Nun, 1969).

3

The End of an Era

The Structural Crisis

Although of unprecedented severity, the Great Depression of the 1930s was not sudden or cataclysmic, turning buoyant prosperity into ruin. In fact the economic position of Argentina—as of most primary producing nations—was very weak and insecure during the 1920s. Both prices and demand for primary commodities had been falling, and the disparity between these prices and those of manufactured goods in world trade was growing wider. Given the insecurity and dependency of its position, Argentina belonged to one of the sectors of the world economy least able to resist the effects of a severe trade depression. Even without the Depression it is difficult to see how in the long run the position of a dependent economy such as Argentina's could have been less critical.

The onset of the Depression accentuated all the weakness of the situation and revealed the shaky basis of the liberal period. Its most obvious manifestation was the fall in the volume and value of international trade. But the main problem in the 1930s was the failure of primary-product prices to recover, and the closely related deterioration in Argentina's terms of trade. The severe reduction in export earnings sharply lowered the purchasing power of the country for imported goods and particularly for manufactured commodities. The share of imports in the total supply of goods fell from 52.9 percent in 1929 to 34.9 percent in 1938 (United Nations, *Economic Survey of Latin America 1949*). The gap left by this reduction of imports began to be filled by home-produced goods. Argentine production, at constant prices, increased by 9 percent between 1929 and 1938 while exports fell by 37 percent. The necessity to produce commodities that could no longer be imported reoriented economic activity toward the home market.

Argentina negotiated unfavorable trade treaties in the 1930s, as the Depression weakened its position more than that of the exporters of manufactured goods. Manufacturing countries helped their own balance of payments by protecting domestic agricultural production and this further limited the exports of the primary producers. Britain gave preferential treatment to its primary-producing dominions—Canada, Australia, and New Zealand—in the Ottawa agreements of 1932. In order to regain access to British markets Argentina signed, in 1933, the Roca-Runciman Agreement, which granted the British government import licenses for 85 percent of Argentine beef exports, while Argentina retained only 15 percent. These arrangements tended to divide the Argentine landowning interests. Grains gave way to meats as the most important export product. The stockmen themselves were split into two factions: breeders and fatteners. Fatteners purchased the bred cattle and, owning land closer to the seaports, sold their livestock directly to the meat packers. A stabilized world demand for chilled beef gave them a monopoly control over sales to the export market. This monopoly, reinforced by their control over the Argentine Rural Society, sustained the privileged position of the fatteners among the stockmen and made them the dominant sector of the landed class. Put briefly, the Roca-Runciman Agreement guaranteed Argentina a fixed but reduced share in the British market for meat and bound the British to limit their encouragement of British agricultural producers by subsidies. In return Argentina agreed to stabilize its tariffs on industrial products, to reduce tariffs on some manufactures, and to preserve free entry for fuel. Argentina also reformed its exchange controls so as to facilitate the remission of interest and profits on British-owned investments. It undertook also to defend British-owned transport enterprises (street cars) against competition from automotive transport.

The principal feature of these agreements was the entrenchment of the past and of one class by tightening the bonds of dependency and consolidating the position of the dominant sector of the landowning class. In other words, privilege was further concentrated at the top and losses were distributed among the rest of the community. It was the beginning of the economic and technical sclerosis that cost the Argentine landed bourgeois first place as competitors in the world market for food and raw materials like wool and linseed. Their policies narrowly followed their immediate class interests. To the lights of these frightened conservatives, their short-sighted efforts were a success, but they proved to be a disaster in the long run. They did little to find new markets by attracting new capital and reducing production costs through technological improvement. Argentina today is still paying for the trusteeship of its economy to this class in the 1930s.

During the decade following 1935, Argentina became an industrial nation. But it changed without becoming different in several important respects. During this period, Argentina drifted in search of an alternative model of growth and modernization to that of outward export expansion. The different attempts proceeded from guesswork and social mending to more conscious planning.

The military-conservative group in power faced an economy seriously affected by the world crisis. Exports declined drastically; the prices of produce fell rapidly; unemployment increased; the budget was imbalanced; the state operated with diminished sources of revenue; and the peso had to be devalued. The government had to engage in a policy of regulating the economy and of financing as well as transferring to the popular strata the heavy losses of the agro-pecuarian producers. The currency was depreciated, and the government fixed minimum prices for grain, assumed control of all operations in foreign exchange, and established a system of import licensing. The conversion of external and internal debts reduced the state deficit considerably. The transformation of blocked foreign funds into "loans" to the government also contributed to stabilizing the situation. Public works—such as the construction of roads—reduced the impact of unemployment. Financial mechanisms were strengthened and concentrated with the creation of a central bank.

The aims of the conservative coalition in power during the thirties did not go beyond preserving the status quo, yet such a task involved establishing economic controls, and under the umbrella of a controlled economy industry began to grow. Thus the decline of the import capacity of the economy acted as a strong incentive to national industrialization. The process of import substitution led to what has been called an unintegrated industrial economy (Ferrer, 1963, IV)—unintegrated insofar as the process was mostly concentrated on light industry, thus postponing, rather than solving, the problem of economic dependence. Nonetheless, the number of industrial workers began to grow considerably and very rapidly, as did the size and the importance of unions. The landed elite that had indirectly unleashed this process was soon confronted with the demands of an expanding proletariat and with the kernel of what could be labeled a "national industrial bourgeoisie."

Until 1930 industry was subsidiary to the main export sector. After 1930 it began substituting imports and established an important foothold in the economy. Between 1900 and 1930 the proportion of manpower employed in industry remained fairly constant (around 25 percent) compared with 36 percent engaged in primary activities. Major industrial enterprises such as the meat-packing industries depended on the export economy. They were not the nucleus of autonomous industrialization. Thus, one should not construe the tensions between ranchers and meat packers over prices and terms of sale as a class struggle between farmers and industrialists as in, for example, the conflict between the western agricultural provinces of Canada and the protectionist industrial interests in Ontario and Quebec. The large service and commercial sectors of the Argentine economy used more manpower than agriculture and ranching. This large tertiary sector contained few elements of autonomous growth, for in the main the commercial and service apparatus of society was geared to serving the needs of the dominant agricultural and ranching industry and its beneficiaries. There was a high degree of articulation between these three sectors of the economy until the thirties, with the primary export sector dynamizing the other two. Social conflict took place then less along sectorial lines than along class lines within sectors. In the absence of a clear-cut division between an agrarian and an industrial interest, conflict erupted within sectors, between workers and employers. Thus labor was organized first in the railways, which were big employers of skilled labor and part of the agricultural economy. Conflict was institutionalized in this sector before World War I. Not so in the meat-packing industry, which pursued a policy of paternalism and brutal opposition to the formation of unions. In the commercial sector there was a similar opposition to working-class organizations on the part of employers. For the working class this was a period of anarchist and syndicalist intransigence.

Industrialization

This social and economic constellation changed after 1930. As a response to depression and war, Argentina became an industrial society. By 1944 industrial production constituted a larger proportion of total production than ranching, the production of cereals, and agricultural raw materials. And yet then, as today, these traditional export activities still played as strategic a part in the economy as they had before World War I. Argentina today is still heavily dependent on foreign suppliers for industrial goods and fuel and is still paying for them almost exclusively with exports produced in the rural sector. This peculiar situation indicates that industrialization has not been autonomous, that external dependency has changed but not disappeared, and that the transition from an agrarian to an industrial economy has taken place without anything resembling a social revolution.

Industrialization has taken place on the basis of import substitution. Since the 1930s the proportion of consumer goods in Argentine imports has steadily fallen. But the proportion of capital equipment, steel, and metals has risen to four-fifths of all imports. These facts again suggest a profound structural weakness. The flaw of the Argentine industrialization pattern has been known to economists for some time. They have pointed to the fact that Argentine industry is predominantly a consumer goods, "light" industry, which has grown up without making the country less dependent on foreign suppliers. It sustains its growth by relying on the basic industries of the dominant industrial countries. It is a high-cost industry incapable of meeting international competition, and hence is unable to support its own demand for fuel, raw materials, and capital equipment. On account of these developments, it is incapable of improving the agro-commercial industries by inducing a reduction in the cost of export farming and ranching on which it depends for foreign exchange for its supplies. Thus, the vicious circle of stagnation is closed.

The stalemated system that is Argentina today stems from an industrialization program tailored to suit the interests of the dominant sector of the landed bourgeoisie. In fact, the original industrial program of the thirties was not opposed by any powerful social group. Industrialization was part of the defensive strategy of the agrarians who sought to decrease imports to the level of exports. Industry thus came into being as a by-product of their adaptation to less favorable conditions in the world market. The new economic order was born warped and its subsequent growth locked in a set of self-reinforcing weaknesses.

Argentine industry was dependent on the export sector for surplus capital and therefore subject both to the low efficiency of that rural sector and to fluctuations in world markets. It was also dependent on the basic industries of the imperialist countries. It was concentrated in the littoral and especially around Buenos Aires, thus reinforcing the dominance of this region over the rest of the nation. The main consequence of industrialization was to redefine the nature of Argentine dependency and to produce a regrouping of social forces, that is, new conflicts and alliances of social classes.

Industrialization spurred the growth of a large urban proletariat. The increased demand for labor in the import substitution industries and soaring unemployment in the countryside (the world crisis and the emergence of the United States and Canada as exporters of wheat had severely damaged Argentine agriculture) combined to produce a mass exodus to the urban centers. That is why, despite the cessation of immigration, industrial employment figures showed a steady rise during the years of world depression, and later during the war. Agrarian conditions provided a large reservoir of potential workers, and the new industry attracted them like a magnet. Not only the agrarian crisis led to internal migrations. Technological development had accentuated an age-old phenomenon: the crowding out of the small farmer by giant enterprises technically better equipped. This trend was later accelerated by the wartime rise of meat prices, which led many *estancieros* or ranchers to use land for grazing instead of leasing it for agricultural purposes. The shift to grazing before and during the Second World War added to the surplus of labor in the countryside, since ranching requires fewer hands. During the 1935 to 1946 period, half a million persons entered the industrial labor force, an increase of over 100 percent. Large amounts of surplus value were extracted from these workers for investment in industry and services. By increasing the cost of foodstuffs, high agricultural prices in the internal market further reduced the available income of workers and funneled industrial surplus value to the agrarian elite. This latter aspect brought the interests of the new industrial bourgeoisie into a conflict of somewhat classic proportions with the agrarians. It was a conflict over consumer markets on the surface, and a conflict over the appropriation of surplus value underneath.

At least initially, the protagonists of this conflict were distinct social groups. Despite the *estancieros'* marked preference for urban living, few entered the new economic sectors opened up by import-substituting industrialization, though many functioned as urban professionals. Sociologist Gino Germani commented: "Industrialization was produced outside this group [the landed bourgeoisie]; already during the first phase of industrialization . . . virtually all the *non*-agricultural activity was in the hands of immigrants" (Germani, 1965, 172).

The conflict was aggravated by the Law of Exchange Control introduced by the central bank, which made available to the industrial sector foreign exchange generated by the agrarian export sector. On the other hand, the wage freezes forced upon workers by the conservative governments of the period produced wide discontent among the masses, making them available for political mobilization.

PART 2
Uneasy Under One Roof

True, indeed, behind this fantastic
farce, enacted on the visible stage
of society, solid things and stupendous
labors are to be discover'd, existing
crudely and going on in the background,
to advance and tell themselves in time.

. . . but the fear of conflicting and
irreconcilable interiors, and the lack
of a common skeleton, knitting all close,
continually haunts me.

—Walt Whitman, *Democratic Vistas*

4

The Old Order
and the New

Patterns of Industrialization

We have seen how until the 1920s the Argentine economy was organized in terms of the international division of labor structured by British imperialism. The cattle ranchers were the staunchest defenders of this arrangement within the country. The agro-pecuarian export system did allow, however, the growth of a food industry in order to supply world markets. This was the extent to which the system tolerated industrialization. It was external demand that stimulated the growth of those industries. The combination of abundant raw materials, low costs, and a growing external demand fostered the growth of this subsidiary industrial sector and its fast concentration, and lured foreign capital—British and U.S.—to invest in it. Socially, the economic system was supported by the ranching faction of the landed upper class, British capitalists, and import-export merchants. Politically, the consensus about the system extended to all significant parties, conservative, radical, and socialist alike. Conservatives and radicals defended the agro-pecuarian producers and their markets. Socialists defended consumers and the purchasing power of wage earners and thus were drawn into the prevailing consensus.

This anti-industrial constellation of interests was slowly but steadily subverted by marginal national capitalists emerging from the ranks of the urban middle sectors and immigrants and by the mounting pressure of international industrial monopolies eager to establish a productive foothold in the country. Capital from these different sources began to flow into new branches of industrial activity.

The national capitalists had the hardest time. The First World War provided some "natural" protection for their incipient industrial establishments. These managed to survive, despite hardships and the open

47

hostility of the dominant class. The industrialists gathered around two organizations: the Argentine Industrial Union (Unión Industrial Argentina) and the Argentine Confederation of Commerce, Industry, and Production (Confederación Argentina del Comercio, la Industria y la Producción).

On the other hand, U.S. and Continental European capital began to dispute the primacy of British investments in Argentina. U.S. capital in particular increased its influence considerably after the First World War. At the end of that war, the United States ranked first among suppliers of Argentine imports. Moreover, in order to secure their position in the Argentine market, U.S. corporations began to make direct, "tariff-hopping" investments. U.S. capital arrived in Argentina to find traditional areas of investment, such as railroads and public utilities, preempted by British capital. Meanwhile, the United States was itself a large producer of foods and raw materials, which meant that its markets were closed to Argentine produce. The U.S. economy was, in this respect, competitive vis-à-vis the Argentine economy. U.S. investment flowed mostly into light industry, especially into the production of consumer durables. By the 1920s several subsidiaries of the most important U.S. industrial corporations had already established a foothold in Argentina. The Argentine trade balance with the United States yielded then, as always, consistent deficits.

The Argentine agrarian establishment regarded this industrial nucleus with alarm and attempted to thwart it by manipulating fiscal and credit policies. But despite official disfavor, industries managed to survive and even to increase production in the twenties. In brief, the twenties witnessed a modest spreading of industrialization outside the traditional export sector and its related industries. During those years some significant U.S. investments took place as well as some displacement of British and European goods by U.S. manufacturers in the import market. Those trends ran against the best interests of the British and of the Argentine agrarians. The state—operating then with limited autonomy— tried to mediate between these diverse interests. But neither the incipient industrial national bourgeoisie, nor the incoming U.S. corporations, nor the state—controlled at the time by middle-class politicians—challenged the hegemony of the dominant British interests and their landed Argentine allies.

But, as we have already seen, the crisis of 1930 brought about a drastic reduction in the value of Argentine exports on account of import controls instituted in Great Britain. With this came a correlative weakening of the capacity to import manufactures. In short, the neat division of labor and the free trade policies to which Argentina was accustomed went to pieces. Argentina simply could not obtain the amount of manufactured goods that it had previously imported. To maintain imports would have meant an intolerable trade deficit. To reduce them to the new level of exports meant an equally intolerable retrenchment of consumption. After three long years of waiting for the world capitalist economy to recover, the Argentine ruling class, now firmly entrenched in power by force, decided to launch a program of import substitution through "contained" national industrialization. In the eyes of this class these were temporary measures in order to weather the crisis, effective only until international trade resumed and with it, Argentina's role as leading agricultural and cattle exporter. This expectation limited industrialization to certain branches of industry and placed it under the auspices of an alliance of classes in which the agrarians remained dominant and the industrial bourgeoisie assumed the role of a junior partner. It was an alliance between sectors of classes rather than between whole classes.

Both the agrarian and the industrial bourgeoisie were internally differentiated on the eve of the crisis. The ranchers were divided, as we have seen, into breeders and fatteners, the former depending on the latter. The industrialists were divided into those investing in so-called "natural" branches (that is, those industries closely tied to the export sector) and "artificial" branches, such as metallurgic industries. During the first years of the Depression, intraclass conflicts erupted, as each of these sectors tried to maintain its position and pass on the brunt of the crisis to other groups. In the end, it was the lower classes that suffered most. Nevertheless, some sectors of the dominant classes, notably the breeders among the agrarians, lost power.

After three years of crisis and sectorial strife, an alliance was formed in 1933 between the cattle fatteners, represented by the Argentine Rural Society, and the industrialists, grouped in the Argentine Industrial Union. The economic ministry was put in the hands of a team of ex-Independent Socialists, headed by Federico Pinedo. The class alliance and the ministerial team in power stimulated the diversification of industries and allowed the growth of new branches—especially textiles—in order to replace imports. But this was throughout a controlled process, under the undisputed hegemony of the oligarchy. Room was made for a new class of industrial entrepreneurs, side by side with the landed interests and the older industrial establishments linked to the export economy.

The new industrial bourgeoisie accepted the agrarian definition of the situation and tried to prosper within that framework. Interestingly, this group failed to generate an ideology of its own and to put forth a different program of economic development. In spite of this apparent lack of consciousness and daring, the new bourgeoisie had a definite social identity. Despite inadequate data and conflicting interpretations, the evidence seems to indicate that agrarian wealth played neither a direct nor a decisive role in industrial development and that neither foreign nor domestic monopolies managed to take over the industrialization process of the thirties and forties. Available data show that concentration in industry remained fairly low during this period (Jorge, 1971). In brief, industrialization represented the emergence of a new and distinct social stratum that neither overlapped with the landed bourgeoisie nor was ancillary to foreign monopolies. Import-substituting industrialization took place through the mobilization of urban savings. Entrepreneurial leadership emerged from middle and immigrant sectors. The landed elite had only invested capital in some food and beverage industries in an earlier period but did not participate in the new industrial ventures of the thirties and forties. Foreign capital did develop certain industrial branches but in fact lagged behind the more dynamic national sector and failed to satellize it during those decades. But the new industrial bourgeoisie failed to articulate its own economic designs for the nation. After 1943 it joined a new alliance of classes that culminated with Peronism, but it did not dominate that populist coalition either. Finally, after the fall of President Perón in 1955, as we shall see, it rapidly lost power and was ultimately satellized by foreign corporations, especially by the U.S. multinationals that gained a decisive foothold in the economy after 1958.

These vicissitudes raise the issue of the undeveloped or "false" consciousness of the industrial class. Without attempting to provide an exhaustive answer, it would seem that the political impotence and the ideological timidity of the industrial bourgeoisie initially had to do with its overwhelming foreign origins. The industrial census of 1935 indicates that 60 percent of all industrial entrepreneurs in Argentina were foreign born. They were mostly concentrated in the new branches of industry—those developed for import substitution. In other words, it was an industrial, but hardly a "national" bourgeoisie. To this fact should be added that traditionally a very low percentage of immigrants to Argentina became naturalized citizens. They thus tended to remain alienated from politics. This feature may help to explain the fact that during the period of industrialization Argentina knew no "party of industry." In this as in other aspects of Argentine social change the resilience of the original agro-pecuarian structure proved to be a decisive limiting factor with long-term political consequences. As new, relatively modern groups—including an industrial bourgeoisie—developed, they were grafted into the agrarian structure but remained socially, politically, and culturally separate. Only gradually did they become interwoven into a closer framework of mutual interdependence. The landed elite—retaining control of the state during a crucial phase of industrialization—impeded the full development and integration of these groups into new institutional frameworks. Furthermore, the earlier political integration of native non-industrial middle sectors during the heyday of agrarian prosperity increased the isolation of the new industrial bourgeoisie from the existing political structures. The so-called middle-class parties, like the Unión Cívica Radical, were simply not receptive to the new industrial interests.

The textile industries, favored by the local abundance of raw materials, were the fastest growing sector of manufacturing during the thirties. Other industries followed: Machinery, electrical appliances, and rubber tires were developed by foreign capital. The latter's participation in the industrialization process was significant but did not overshadow the mobilization of domestic savings for industrial development. Between 1935 and 1946 the number of industrial establishments grew from 40,000 to 86,000. National capital flowed into small and medium-sized establishments, while foreign capital established larger enterprises. The growth of small and medium-sized national industries was indeed so massive that throughout this period, industrial concentration remained low on the average (Jorge, 1971, V).

Industrial growth was accompanied by an impressive growth of the working class. The number of workers doubled between 1935 and 1946. Workers thus became the principal occupational category in the forties. These two related processes—the increasing importance of industry and the development of the proletariat—clearly overflowed the expectations and prospects of the conservative coalition in power. Official disfavor could not prevent the development of metallurgic industries, which were more threatening to the export sector than the textile establishments. A new industrial bourgeoisie with no more than very tenuous links to the landed bourgeoisie, a working class whose ranks were continuously expanding by the incorporation of new workers from the rural areas, and other less strategic groups such as the disaffected rural middle class, the rural proletariat, and even some displaced sectors of the landed classes formed the ingredients of a new coalition of social forces. This coalition began to take shape during the Second World War and finally found political expression in the populist movement led by Juan D. Perón in the forties. Peronism is incomprehensible without a survey of the patterns of industrialization that developed in the thirties and especially without a study of labor developments during this same period.

Toward a New Coalition of Classes

A strong labor movement existed in Argentina already in 1930 when the oligarchy-inspired military coup overthrew the radical government of Yrigoyen. Thereafter, the industrialization process described above brought thousands of new workers—mostly internal migrants—into the industrial centers of Buenos Aires and the littoral. The number of unions and their membership went up. The presence of labor organizations established during the years of external immigration, with their tradition and experience in labor struggles, provided a base for the mobilization of the new mass of workers and for the articulation of their interests. But there were strains. The labor movement was divided and subjected to continuous repression at the hands of the conservative regimes from 1930 until 1943. Communists, socialists, and syndicalists competed for control over the labor movement and over the leadership of the newly founded trade union congress, the Confederación General del Trabajo

(CGT). Communists were strong among the metal, textile, and construction workers. Transport workers were organized in more moderate unions. By 1942 the CGT had split into two rival groups. Government controls kept salaries consistently depressed and official repression demoralized the movement.

During the forties, Peronism would unify the working-class movement by mobilizing the more recent sectors of the proletariat but also making strong inroads among the older and more established organizations. The "old" and "new" working classes were more united in the expression of their interests and in their support of Peronism than has been customarily acknowledged by social and political analysts. In fact many of the demands of the working-class organizations in the 1930s found continued expression in the labor policies and in the ideology of Peronism.

What took place from 1935 to 1946 was a process of national capitalist accumulation based on the compression of wages and under the political control of a class coalition dominated by landed elements. Peronism represented the vindication of the mass of repressed workers who had born the brunt of a rather "classic" form of accumulation based on the existence of a reserve army of laborers, compressed wages, and political repression (Murmis and Portantiero, 1971, Part 2). Productive expansion eventually reduced unemployment, but wages were not allowed to rise and workers' demands went unheeded until 1943, when Perón became secretary of labor of a new military regime that seized power from the conservatives and closed the decade of reaction known as *la década infame* or the "infamous decade." In short, the growth of industry resulted in the eventual takeover of government by a populist leader who combined appeals to a long-suppressed but growing working class, promising to bridge the gap between accumulation and distribution in the name of social justice, with appeals to industrial entrepreneurs in the name of national economic development.

It is fruitful to contrast the Argentine experience with that of other countries—notably Brazil—in which populist regimes outwardly similar to Peronism also attained power. Brazilian populism under Vargas had seized power before the advent of Perón in Argentina. Once in power, the Brazilian populist coalition launched a program of industrialization *with* distribution of income to the workers. The workers were thus firmly tied to the state apparatus. In Argentina, on the other hand, populism gained power after a period of accumulation without redistribution, during which workers, bereft of state protection, created their own organizations. The populist regime had to negotiate labor support first and only after obtaining it did it progressively attempt to control the movement by linking workers' organizations to the state. Nevertheless, the labor movement in Argentina never became an absolute creature of the government, which explains the endurance of Peronist unions after Perón and under strongly antilabor regimes.

The Argentine working-class organizations proved stronger and more autonomous than their counterparts in other Latin American nations.

This continued strength of trade unions indicates that what occurred under Perón—as we shall see shortly—was more than just government manipulation of working masses from above. It meant the strengthening of organizations encompassing the majority of the industrial working class—organizations capable of defending the interests of this class after the fall of the populist government. Ultimately it meant that economic development could not take place in Argentina disregarding the proletariat: This class had the power to veto any attempt to maximize industrialization while minimizing social change—a favorite strategy of multinational corporations in other countries of the region. The strength of the working class is the other side of capitalist stagnation in Argentina in the latter part of the twentieth century.

The process of industrialization from the mid-thirties until the advent of the Peronist government in 1946 involved the establishment and disestablishment of alliances between different classes and sectors of classes. Six features were of particular import in these developments. First was an initial industrializing alliance in the thirties consisting of the largest cattle interests and industrialists. Second was the agrarian split into a dominant faction composed of cattle fatteners and a subordinate group of cattle breeders. The displaced landowners became the element most strongly opposed to any project of industrialization. Their opposition found political expression in those political parties now excluded from participation (Unión Cívica Radical and Partido Demócrata Progresista). Third, the growth of a large industrial labor force with new recruits from the rural interior, bereft of political protection, and under classic conditions of labor exploitation produced a union movement independent from the state. The fourth feature was the development, during the Second World War, of a new set of industries, under the automatic protection afforded by the conflict between the industrial nations. This "new wave" of import substitution under the exceptional conditions of the war gave prominence to new entrepreneurs who had little organization among themselves and who were not represented by the traditional parties. They turned toward the state in search for more institutionalized protection for their industries as the war came to an end. Fifth, a transformation occurred in the economic role of the state, which increasingly intervened in economic matters and acted as an arbiter between different social classes. The state apparatus gained increasing autonomy during this period. Sixth was a new intervention by the armed forces, this time in favor of a coalition of workers and new industrialists. Thus, a new class coalition was structured after 1943. Three years later, Peronism attained power and maintained it for nearly a decade.

Peronism forged an unstable alliance between those sectors of the industrial bourgeoisie in greater need of state protection and the urban proletariat, through the medium of the state and military bureaucracies and under the banner of a national developmentalist ideology. Its most significant feature was the incorporation of the working-class movement and its mobilization from above. The military, which captured the state by means of a coup in 1943, allied itself with recent industrialists in need of protection and vindicated the pent-up demands of the working class through welfare measures and redistributive policies. State protection and the enlargement of the consumer market were conditions *sine qua non* of the continued development of national capitalism. On the other hand, the populist mobilization of working people was a political expedient designed to buttress the legitimacy of a military regime that had repeatedly failed to win the allegiance of other social groups, notably the middle sectors. These circumstances lend a unique historical identity to Peronism and disallow any facile assimilation of this Argentine phenomenon to other social movements of the twentieth century, especially European fascism.

The Origins of Peronism

At this point it may be helpful to return to the historical narrative from 1930 onward to assess the series of episodes that were a prelude to Peronism. The revolution of 1930, after having attempted to establish a corporatist system of fascist inspiration, opted for a less extreme solution: the formal restoration of the constitutional regime with the systematic use of electoral fraud. Short of all-out dictatorship, this was the only way the landed upper class could keep the middle-class *radicales* out of power. Thanks to this device, a coalition of conservatives, anti-Yrigoyen radicals, and ex-socialists elevated General Justo to the presidency with the support of the army. Justo managed to institute a political restoration with remarkable skill. Under his conservative administration a group of politicians who had once been socialists undertook to revamp the battered agrarian economy through state controls and intervention. One of the indirect consequences of those measures was, as we have seen, the growth of industry. The set of reforms undertaken by the conservative regime amounted to a sort of Argentine New Deal, whose purpose was to buttress the export establishment and, secondarily, to allow the growth of import-substituting industries as a way to balance the system. The repeated recourse to electoral fraud behind a constitutional facade was hardly a way to legitimate the power of the landed elite. However, they maintained themselves in power for a decade, largely because the center and left parties did not offer massive opposition. Had the latter done so, the conservative group in power would undoubtedly have resorted to direct dictatorship, particularly under international circumstances that favored authoritarian solutions throughout the world. Behind the political impotence of the center and left parties stood the inability of the social groups they represented to formulate an alternative economic project for the nation. The *radicales* had become seriously compromised in the political corruption of the conservative regime. The left parties were fearful of provoking a fascist backlash by their actions. The government, on the other hand, attempted to enlarge the basis of its power by stimulating a Catholic renaissance that derived its inspiration from Spanish fascism during the years of the civil war in Spain.

When Britain turned against the fascist powers, the ideological tension in Argentina abated somewhat. The conservative coalition placed a new man in power. This was Dr. Ortiz, who ascended to the presidency thanks to an unprecedented use of violence and fraud in the elections of 1937. Ortiz tried to reincorporate the *radicales* into the political system and gave them the governorship of the province of Buenos Aires through the simple political expedient of allowing honest elections in that province. Thus 1940 seemed to be the year of a return to cleaner democratic politics in Argentina. But democratization was opposed by ultraconservatives who wanted a more authoritarian system. The latter's interests were favored by the illness of the president, who delegated power in the hands of his archconservative vice-president Dr. Castillo, and died. Castillo soon returned to the political practices of the early thirties. Internationally, he fostered a brand of neutrality that catered to the profascist sentiment of a significant sector of the Argentine ruling circles without, however, alienating British support.

This feature of Argentine international relations deserves an explanation. British benevolence towards Argentine profascist neutrality during the war was based on pure self-interest. It is not difficult to reconstruct the constellation of interests prevailing at the time. Engulfed by the war, Britain's hold over the Argentine economy weakened precisely at a time when its foodstuff needs were critical to sustain the war effort. British interests feared that if Argentina were to join the Allies, Germany would impede the flow of goods from Argentina to Britain. Germany, on the other hand, increased its investments in Argentina as a way of establishing an imperialist foothold in Latin America. A policy of neutrality thus favored the flow of German capital to the country and the flow of Argentine exports to Britain. As a consequence, the ruling sector of the Argentine landed bourgeoisie found itself in collusion with both the British and the Axis interests and in conflict with the United States. U.S. attempts to include Argentina in mutual defense agreements and bring the country into its own economic orbit failed repeatedly. British and Argentine commercial interests resisted the pressure. War documents recently declassified by the U.S. National Archives—especially the Churchill-Roosevelt correspondence from 1939 to 1945—reveal that Churchill's reluctance to abide by an economic embargo against the pro-Axis Argentine government was one of the more acrimonious disagreements between the British and U.S. governments during the war.

As a result of Argentine neutrality, the United States favored Brazil with economic and military aid. The resulting economic and military rivalry between these two South American countries was a leading cause of the Argentine military coup of 1943. As pressures from the United States increased, as the rivalry with Brazil—now favored by the United States—mounted, and as the expected victory of the Axis powers failed to materialize, President Castillo began changing his position near the end of his term. He chose as his successor Dr. Robustiano Patrón Costas, a conservative sugar baron from the northwest who was linked to U.S. interests. The plan was to place Patrón Costas in power and realign Argentina on the Allies' side. The plan failed. The fraudulent and heavy-handed practices of the conservatives had isolated the government from the pro-Allies opposition parties so that it could not now expect their support for a change in policy. The army, on the other hand, was still convinced that the Axis powers would win the war. The corruption of the conservative civilian regime, the impotence and lack of prestige of the opposition parties, pro-German prejudice, and the power rivalry with Brazil prompted a military takeover. The officers wanted, by this act, to assure Argentine hegemony over the subcontinent, and wished to launch a program of rigid political control and heavy industrial investments.

This bismarckian project was hatched by a military lodge that resembled the Japanese militarist cliques of the same period: the GOU (Grupo de Oficiales Unidos, or United Officers Corps). In the event of a German victory, this group had fantasies of transforming Argentina into a Latin American sub-Reich. When fascist Germany collapsed in the war, the officers decided that Argentina should become its own Prussia, through domestic repression and foreign expansion. The members of the semisecret lodge were officers of the rank of colonel, major, and captain, that is, the younger strata of unfulfilled ambitions. The fascist inspiration was unmistakable: In their first public statement they asserted that "as in Germany," their government "would be an inflexible dictatorship" that would "inculcate the masses with the spirit necessary to travel the heroic path in which they will be led." The main instruments of the GOU were General Ramírez, who was minister of war in Castillo's government, and General Rawson, the commander of the Buenos Aires garrison. General Ramírez ousted President Castillo as the army marched on Buenos Aires on June 4, 1943. General Rawson was proclaimed president, but he only lasted two days because he wished to transfer power to a civilian government. The GOU deposed Rawson and proclaimed Ramírez president, thus frustrating the hopes of civilian politicians and establishing a direct and permanent dictatorship.

The 1943 coup was unique in that it represented military autonomy—rule "above politics." The officers set out to construct a sufficiently powerful bureaucratic apparatus, including the agencies of repression, the military and the police, in order to free themselves from the influence of both extreme reactionary and popular or radical pressures in the society. The government was to become separate from society. Such phenomena emerge when there is a general political exhaustion of all classes and factions in society, as Marx showed in his analysis of the class struggles in nineteenth century France. And indeed this was the case with Argentine society in the forties. The new character of military rule emerged in 1943 and 1944, when for the first time in Argentine history officers were placed in most administrative and political posts. The constitution was suspended indefinitely and open dictatorship was proclaimed.

But autonomous dictatorship does not last long. It soon finds itself engulfed again by social conflict. If it does not express or instrumentalize a viable coalition of social interests the omnipotence of pure military rule becomes empty and stupid. This is what happened to the officers of the 1943 coup. Isolated from political life, their professional puritanism gave them no guidelines for effective action. Thus, they fell back on the massive generalities of Catonism (Moore, 1966, 491–496): religion, patriotism, and discipline. They attacked professional politicians as grafters, and they persecuted Jews. They brought under church control thousands of children of city workers and middle-class parents who were not among the church's most faithful flock; they spoke of "the movement," the "will of the people," and "national unity," of "social peace" and good morals. But in terms of economic policies and social strategy they moved blindly.

In foreign policy they were grudgingly forced to break with the tottering Axis powers. The forced declaration of war on Germany cost Ramírez the presidency, but there was no turning back. Before his replacement, Ramírez had launched vicious attacks against communists, socialists, and Jews. He attacked the unions and placed labor leaders in concentration camps. All political parties were dissolved. Indeed, by October 1943 the officers had managed to punish virtually every class and political group in the country, using fascist methods at the exact time when fascism was on the defensive everywhere else. In 1944, when General Farrell assumed power, the Axis powers were already crumbling and the Argentine middle class became increasingly belligerent against the military regime. It seemed that the days of that regime were numbered—were it not for an episode that had taken place in October 1943, the full significance of which only became apparent a few years later. An officer in the ministry of war, an important member of the GOU, Colonel Juan D. Perón, had asked for and obtained the job of running the labor department.

Perón was intelligent enough to realize that the military project could not survive by force alone, isolated from different political groups and social interests and against overwhelming pressure from abroad. Perón was responsible for ending the assault on the workers' organizations, and he proceeded to reverse labor policy. He achieved this end with remarkable skill. The unions were well organized and well run when Perón began his work. Despite splits and demoralization after a decade of repression, they had withstood the vicious attacks by conservatives

and militarists and continued to uphold demands that had been sys-
tematically denied by successive administrations since 1930. We have
already seen how the working class had borne the full weight of industrial
accumulation during the thirties and early forties. By satisfying the pent-
up demands of the workers' organizations, Perón easily gained the upper
hand over left and center parties that had been rendered impotent by
the previous regimes. His approach was eminently reasonable, though
opportunist, and the workers' support for Perón was eminently rational.
To interpret Perón's appeal as exclusively charismatic, that is, as the
irrational attachment of miserable, undereducated, unorganized masses
of migrants from the countryside to a Latin *caudillo* is to forget the
important role played by older, mature worker organizations and leaders
in the initial phase of Peronism. It is my impression that during the
initial phase of Peronism there was an objective advance of the Argentine
working class as a whole. Under Perón's leadership the Argentine labor
movement experienced a phase of liberation and growth before passing
under his control in later stages of the regime, when cross-pressures
and contradictions turned it into a stagnant and reactionary system.

Perón's first step was to raise the labor department to full ministerial
status. He then persuaded his military friends to join with him in
meeting some of the trade union leaders. He managed to convince the
latter that he meant business when he spoke of satisfying the demands
of the working class. He thus obtained the support of a number of
leaders and organizations. But many workers were not organized, and
many were, because of rapid industrialization, recent arrivals in the
Buenos Aires labor market. These were shirtless ones, the *descamisados*
about whom Perón and his companion, Eva Duarte, often spoke. The
packing plants, to take an important example, had long resisted attempts
at unionizing the workers. The meat workers were subjected to wide
wage differentials and to seasonal unemployment. There were many
other workers in a similar position, seasonally unemployed, ill paid,
and hard to organize. Perón helped them. He got union leaders out of
prison and tried to win their support. He organized the unorganized.
He opened government posts to union men. In short, he provided many
short-run benefits to the workers and added a large welfare dimension
to the activities of the state.

The support Perón obtained as a result of these measures was not
too different from the support Roosevelt's social security legislation won
from the American poor. Social welfare went deep, and transformed
Argentine politics. In 1946 the welfare colonel was able to win the
presidency in free elections against a solid block of privilege ranging
from large conservative landowners on the right to the socialist and
communist *politicos* on the left. Perón's success should be understood,
however, in terms of his opponents' weakness and serious political
mistakes. Peronism came to fill a vacuum created by the debilitation of
the different social classes and the weakening of the political fabric in

the previous decade. The crisis of the thirties had dealt a serious economic blow to the landed bourgeoisie, who responded to economic weakness with political usurpation and in so doing corroded and corrupted the entire political system.

Industrialization, however, could not be prevented, even though it took place haltingly, was kept contained, and was initially designed as a mere import-substitution device by the agrarians. Industrialization had produced a new bourgeoisie that was politically timid, ethnically segregated, and above all dependent for its prosperity on exceptional international circumstances and on the often reluctant protection of the state. Industry had also given birth to a large urban proletariat—exploited and repressed, which found its demands unfulfilled and its struggles frustrated. From 1930 to 1935 high unemployment and political repression had weakened the power of the unions. After 1935, rapid industrial expansion reduced unemployment and brought masses of rural migrants into the cities. The union movement began to grow again, but under the severe repression of the conservative regimes, strikes did not produce gains for the workers during this period. These pressures undermined the leadership of socialists and communists in the unions. The General Confederation of Labor (CGT) split into two rival factions in 1942, one controlled by socialists and the other by communists. The frustration of those years finally led workers away from political activity and from union participation. After 1943, Perón's labor policies offered the workers an opportunity to regroup and advance their position in society.

The political fragmentation and the inconclusive conflict of classes in Argentina had their counterpart in the conflicts between the imperialist powers that impeded any metropolis from controlling the country. World War II exacerbated these trends. In brief, no single class within, and no major power without, could control Argentina. This conjuncture made political action decisive. Perón's strategy was to use the state apparatus in order to forge a new coalition of classes from above that would support a program of national capitalist development.

From Militarism to Populism

During 1945 the military authorities searched for a constitutional way out from the impasse in which they found themselves. That was very difficult because the different political parties—until recently victimized by the army—were reluctant to respond to the new solicitations of the regime. Their capacity to strike any deal with the military regime was limited by their zealous middle-class constituencies, who had been encouraged by the Allied victories in the war, and by the suspicion of the upper classes, who were becoming increasingly alarmed at Perón's labor policies. Perón's attempts to improve the lot of the rural workers and to change tenancy regulations were considered an attack on the landed bourgeoisie. Thus, conciliatory moves failed. Negotiations between the military and their civilian opponents broke down and gave way to a frontal clash.

After seeking unsuccessfully to obtain support from traditional parties, Perón launched his presidential candidacy relying almost exclusively on the political forces he had managed to mobilize from above. These forces, aided by the political mistakes of Perón's opponents, proved sufficient to propel him to power, and in 1946, to the presidency. The military were by then as divided and confused about their own goals as any body of civilian politicians. In August 1945 they lifted the state of siege, trying to placate their opponents. This opened the gates for massive civilian demonstrations—mostly by the middle and upper strata—in favor of the restoration of the constitution and of liberal freedoms. The state of siege was reimposed and repression resumed, at which point an army faction rebelled and marched on Buenos Aires. After some hesitation, they managed to have Perón removed from his office as minister of labor and arrested. Not content with the arrest of Perón, civilian politicians demanded the immediate overthrow of President Farrell and the transfer of power to the supreme court. Simultaneously, the employers' organizations announced their intention not to give their workers a paid holiday on October 12, 1945, which was traditionally celebrated as Columbus Day. Thus, it became clear that the liberal struggle for constitutional guarantees was at the same time an attack on the proletariat. This was not lost on the workers. When Perón was arrested he was with his companion, Eva Duarte, who immediately rushed to tell union leaders what had happened. Packinghouse workers then organized a counterdemonstration. Rioting began on October 15. During the next days, workers from the industrial suburbs (Avellaneda and Berisso) began to move into central Buenos Aires. By October 17 they had taken over the city without the opposition of either the police or the local military garrison, which were well disposed towards Perón. Nobody knew exactly what to do but there was the feeling that this was a turning point. Perón was released from prison and appeared on the balcony of the government house, the Casa Rosada, with President Farrell. He gestured in victory to the thousands of workers cheering him in the Plaza de Mayo. Then the labor confederation (GCT) declared a general strike in support of Perón. His military opponents were arrested. Perón won the day.

October 17, 1945, was a turning point in Perón's career also. It marked his transformation from a military man of fascist proclivities into a new sort of civilian politician—a democratic populist. From then on he worked for the restoration of the constitution. He retired from the army and accepted the challenge of open elections. He began organizing a new party to give expression to the new coalition of forces behind him. This was the Labor Party, which was patterned after its British counterpart. This is not to deny Perón's personal opportunism or his heavy-handed attempts at controlling the working-class movement by having his military friends in the government issue special regulatory laws to deal with unions that were cantankerous or by forming parallel rival unions. But the bulk of the working class was solidly behind him. Nor did Perón rely solely upon the workers. He had already won over decisive sectors of the armed forces. He now began courting the favor of an institution that had deep roots in Argentine society and reached across class lines: the Catholic Church. He made several concessions to the church—among them his marriage to Eva Duarte and promises of blocking legal divorce and lay education. The bishops—with sound political instinct—began praying for Perón's victory. Perón also established some rather tenuous links to the traditional parties. He secured a second-rank radical politician, Hortensio Quijano, as his vice-presidential running mate.

Arrayed against Perón was almost the entire Argentine establishment: the Conservative Party and the landed elite, cattlemen and grain farmers of the littoral, the Industrial Union representing big industrial capital, the middle-class radicals, and even the socialists and communists, providing a left-wing embellishment to the conservative conglomerate. It was an establishment coalition parading as a popular front—the Unión Democrática. But two ingredients were missing from the conservative coalition: the army and the church. They had joined the new alliance of classes: workers, national industrialists of recent vintage, and scattered middle sectors.

Most observers agree that the election which followed was one of the few free and honest elections in Argentine history. The victory for Perón was clear, if not overwhelming: 1,479,517 votes for Perón-Quijano, the candidates of the Labor Party, and 1,220,822 for Tamborini-Mosca, the candidates of the Unión Democrática. In the congressional elections the result was even more favorable for Perón. His Labor Party won substantial majorities in the Senate and the Chamber of Deputies. All but one of the provincial governorships went to *peronista* candidates. There were several amusing episodes in the situation. The U.S. ambassador, businessman Spruille Braden, threw himself into the election campaign against Perón with an enthusiasm worthy of a better cause and sharper judgment. He produced a Blue Book exposing all the political sins of Perón, especially his alleged connections with Nazis and fascists (but carefully deleting the names of fascists who were now opposing Perón). Perón's answer was a Blue and White (the Argentine national colors) Book denouncing the imperialist intervention. "Braden or Perón" became a favorite campaign slogan of the Labor Party.

5
Populist Reform

Argentina Justicialista: The Equivocal Revolution

When Perón was elected to the presidency in 1946, he came to power under exceptionally favorable circumstances. He was elected by a majority in open and free elections. His support came predominantly from the urban working class and from sectors of the lower middle class, but not exclusively so, nor was it limited to only one region of the country. Industrialization had already made strides and Argentina had the resources to develop autonomously. There was plenty of money in the banks: The sale of supplies to the Allies during World War II had produced sterling and dollar balances worth $1.5 billion. International prices of food and agricultural raw materials were rising relative to industrial goods. Perón's development plans aimed at strengthening and extending basic industrialization, at spreading its benefits throughout the country, at improving education, renewing immigration, improving social services, and finally attaining an independent "Third World" position—before the term was coined—in the community of nations. Yet despite these auspicious beginnings, the Peronist revolution failed to materialize. After ten years of rule the international conjuncture was no longer favorable to Argentina; its resources had been misapplied and dissipated; its economy was stagnant, its political system more rigid and hidebound. Perón was ousted from power and his successors did worse. Argentina has since been underdeveloping at a steady pace. Perón constructed a hybrid social and political system that he did not run successfully. Those who inherited that system could neither dismantle it nor run it better than Perón. The populist facade concealed a tremendous amount of tugging and hauling among competing interest groups unable to purge each other. In recent years this stalemated pluralism has increasingly assumed the character of a latent civil war.

The Peronist victory signaled a change in the balance of social forces: The working class now formed, together with the army and the church, the political base of the government and became one of the principal beneficiaries of postwar prosperity—which lasted until 1949—and of Peronist policies. The new social policy consisted of welfare measures and income redistribution organized along semipaternalistic lines by Perón, and even more sincerely and efficaciously by Eva Duarte de Perón. This remarkable woman did more than Perón to upset the class structure of Argentina and to disturb one of its most insidious syndromes—male chauvinism.

It was above all Evita, as she was called, who presided over the participatory revolution in Argentine politics. She prepared a place for the uprooted and the excluded in the new social order—or at least made them feel welcome. Eva Perón was impressively dynamic and beautiful. She had made her way through a class-bound and male-dominated society from the bottom of economic and sexual exploitation to the top of political leadership. She was an illegitimate child in a society that protected the sanctity of marriage by treating children born out of wedlock as outcasts. She was poor in a society dominated by wealth— a woman whom males would only reward for the crafty use of beauty. Her life was bound up with ambition and pride that sought vengeance upon the masters of superior fortune. Suffering had made her "an enemy of (bourgeois) society." Her life is fascinating precisely because it embodies the moral essence of an age. She rose above her predestined lot in a time of social decomposition: She knew how to gain power, how to use it, now with ruse, now with violence, while championing the cause of the underprivileged. Twenty years after her death she was still a symbol for the poor and her memory still haunted the bourgeoisie.

The Phases and Contradictions of National Populism

Peronism also innovated in matters of economic policy. The mechanisms of control over the economy that Perón inherited from the previous conservative regimes were now used to transfer economic surplus from the primary export sector to the industrial sector. Imports of raw materials and capital goods for industry were kept at low prices. The potential earnings of agrarian exporters were sacrificed in order to finance industrial growth. The state gained increasing control over the economic system through the monopoly of external trade, the nationalization of the central bank, and concentration in that bank of most reserves from the private banking houses. Railways, telephone and gas companies, and urban transport were all nationalized, thus increasing the capacity of the state to affect the course of economic development.

However, foreign exchange earnings were spent in costly compensations to the concerns that were nationalized. A big chunk of earnings accumulated from foreign trade during World War II was invested in the equipment of light consumer industries. By and large, the creation of a heavy industry remained an unaccomplished project. There was limited investment in the infrastructure of transport and public services. A state-sponsored mixed enterprise was set up to produce steel, and the industrial enterprises run by the armed forces were expanded. Even a state-owned aviation industry was set up, but these more ambitious projects did not produce impressive results. Insurance was also nationalized. Although noises were made suggesting the possible nationalization of land, agrarian reform was not instituted. The main export business in grain and meat was not nationalized, but a state marketing agency took control of the export of all major commodities—the Institute for Exchange Promotion (Instituto Argentino de Promoción de Intercambio, IAPI)—with power to fix prices to producers and consumers. The differential between the internal and external prices of the meat, grain, and other products that were thus traded gave the government a handsome profit, used to facilitate credit to the national industrialists. At the same time the pension system was expanded to all industrial workers, so that 25 percent of the workers' wages (10 percent from the worker and the rest from the employer) was funneled into state pension funds. Pensions were set for the low age of fifty-five—more suitable to a postindustrial than to a developing society—and adjusted to wages at the age of retirement rather than to payments made into pension funds. This pension system was eventually extended to rural workers as well.

The relative standing of the working class improved remarkably. Since 1945 Argentina had attained conditions nearing full employment. The marginal work force was being absorbed by industrial expansion. Thus, the solid position of the workers during the first half of Perón's regime was the combined result of a favorable economic conjuncture and of his prolabor policy. Workers' earnings rose sharply during the years 1946/1947 and 1947/1948, rising 17.7 percent and 11.7 percent respectively. After a new rise in 1949, they stood 24.3 percent above wages in 1945. Real wages in industry rose much more rapidly than total wages per worker (Silverman, 1969, 244). From 1943 to 1949 labor's share of national income rose from approximately 45 to 59 percent. Most of this shift occurred from 1947 to 1949, reflecting the implementation of new social security programs as well as rising wages (Silverman, 1969, 243). Perón's policies tended to favor the industrial sector. The few available studies indicate that there was also a continued rise of entrepreneurial income through 1950. Rentiers (landlords and landholders) and agricultural producers bore the brunt of income redistribution. The rentiers were hit the hardest on account of rent controls and inflation (Silverman, 1969, 243–244).

A large proportion of investments went to nonproductive activities that produced, however, high political dividends: housing and public expenditures in social, administrative, and military services. In this way an enormous new complex of interests was created that on one hand supported Perón and on the other constituted a political obstacle to any deepening or radicalization of his "revolution," since that process would of necessity have entailed the sacrifice of immediate rewards to long-term and self-sustained development. In short, the initial political advantage of Peronism became its long-run handicap. Any step toward a serious transformation of the economic order beyond income redistribution and consumer-based industrialization implied tightening the political controls and most likely the transformation of the populist regime into a progressive but more rigid dictatorship. Perón tried on occasion to follow this road, but his moves provoked other supporters— notably the army—to balk. So Perón was confined to reformism—a political formula only suited to times of prosperity. Economic policies became conditional upon the political requirements of populism, and these in turn depended upon prosperity and official largesse. Caught in that circle, Perón became incapable of making sound choices and establishing the priorities necessary to make any system effective. Despite five-year plans, the political style of populism made nonsense of plans in general and of the details of their effective execution. As long as the postwar boom lasted, Perón could manage his system by simultaneous and large payoffs to different groups. Even the much maligned landed oligarchy was not seriously hurt by redistribution and industrial credit. For a while, real wages continued to rise and with them popular euphoria. But the Peronist revolution had a serious flaw: Nothing really guaranteed its continuation.

In this, Perón succumbed to an old Argentine illusion born in a previous epoch of prosperity—the liberal export period—namely, the mirage of endless good fortune, typical of a once-pampered colony. But the lean years arrived in 1950, and Perón was faced with a difficult choice: either to unleash radical social changes, or to preside over the liquidation of his revolution. Either path was fraught with dangers for the regime. Perón chose to move backwards. During his second term as president (he was reelected in 1952) Perón went conservative. He turned increasingly towards right-wing authoritarianism, but he did not survive his self-imposed Thermidor.

The favorable economic circumstances of the postwar period had allowed Perón to follow haphazard policies that, though inducing mass support, failed to sustain economic development. His populism was not radical enough to change the basic structure of society. His compromises, labeled by some as his economic "bonapartism," were not skillful enough to produce a viable "revolution from above," an Argentine version of bismarckism. After 1948 economic deterioration and political reaction took hold of the regime. Per capita GNP steadily declined. Stagnation set in, at which point Perón frantically attempted to change the direction of his policies. These negative trends set in as a result of economic conditions largely beyond the control of the Argentine regime, but they were also caused by policies that stopped short of radical structural reforms.

First, the low prices paid by IAPI to the agricultural producers tended to discourage agricultural production. Acting as a disincentive to agro-pecuarian productivity, it caused the meat and grain output to decline. In the haste to industrialize, the government failed to make sufficient foreign exchange available for the purchase of new farm machinery. At the same time, the 1950s witnessed a serious decline of international prices for agricultural products, which, coupled with a series of bad droughts in the *pampas*, cut export earnings and consequently limited the country's capacity to import. Thus, as the volume of exports declined and the terms of trade moved against Argentina after 1948, the country soon found itself in serious foreign-exchange difficulties. The decline of agriculture was strikingly revealed in 1952 when, after a succession of droughts and bad harvests, Argentina actually had to import wheat from the United States! The problem underlying these difficulties was the regime's decision not to alter the agrarian framework. In the absence of agrarian reform, no incentive had been offered to agricultural production. The country's most strategic productive activities were in fact penalized under the operation of the state trading and multiple-exchange-rate systems, which denied the producers—that is, the landowners—the benefits of high external prices without crippling their capacity to rebound as a pressure group either, and without diversifying agricultural production. In consequence of this, and also as a result of the significant rise in the standard of living of the urban masses mobilized by Peronism, a steadily increasing domestic consumption of meat and other foodstuffs inevitably reduced the country's exportable surpluses.

The specter of dependency arose once more, even though the *nature* of dependency had changed. The development of consumer goods industries had reduced consumer imports. But the ability to maintain existing industries depended upon the import of indispensable fuels and raw materials and imports of capital goods for industry and transport. As a result of Perón's policies Argentina had an established "light" industry but was not in a position to promote its development without outside aid. One thing then became apparent: The utilization and direction of investment had been Perón's worst blunder. Nearly 74 percent of the total increase in fixed capital had gone into nonproductive activities (Silverman, 1969, 251). To give a striking example: Between 1945 and 1946, over 50 percent of real investment of the national government was applied to national defense. Between 1947 and 1951 defense expenditures were reduced, but they still represented an extravagant 23.5 percent (Silverman, 1969, 252). The cost of living began to rise more rapidly than money wages, so real wages began to decline. At this time, Perón began to rely more on the redistribution of income between industries and occupations, thus reducing wage differentials between skilled and unskilled workers. Political patronage caused wages to rise substantially above output per worker. Government policies resulted in a redistribution of the labor force into the least productive sectors of economic activity.

All these developments had serious implications for economic growth: It was simply a failure. At the end of Perón's regime, per capita gross product was only 5.9 percent higher than in 1946. Perón tried to salvage what he could. There was a shift in agricultural policy in the fifties. Perón made friendly gestures toward foreign investors. He began sacrificing the two pillars of the regime: social justice and economic independence. When the internal contraditions of his experiment forced an option between radicalization or reaction, he opted for the latter, but could not escape the political and institutional pressures he had created. Opportunism proved self-defeating. When hard times arrived Peronism revealed its deepest conservative impulses. It had after all attempted to develop a populist labor policy within the institutional framework of capitalism. Strong labor policies, the strategy of its revolutionary phase, had provided Peronism with working class support. But it contradicted the requirements of capitalist accumulation, which Perón had not once challenged. Perón had now to stabilize the hybrid system he had created. He began instituting repressive controls and freezing the class struggle by setting up corporativist institutions. In brief, he tried to build a power apparatus in order to free himself from the reactionary and radical cross-pressures in the society.

Thus, the Peronist administration increased its political control over the country. The supreme court had already been purged in 1947. Later, the administration had closed opinion weeklies and taken over radio stations. Then the government secured from congress the power to mobilize the nation for war, which involved the power to break strikes. These measures amounted to a serious attack on political opponents and constituted a large buildup of presidential power. These early repressive measures had been compensated by a large payoff program: large wage increases for the workers; large budget appropriations for the armed forces; new jobs for political supporters in the new nationalized enterprises; tariff protection for national industrialists. When the economy began to show signs of incapacity to support the strategy of redistribution and payoffs, when the crisis began to manifest itself in the form of inflation and in the lowering of real income, Perón responded by strengthening and extending the political controls. The constitution was reformed—largely to allow the reelection of Perón. The more independent labor leaders were arrested on trumped-up charges. The Labor Party was attacked and a new Peronist Party was formed. The labor movement was further bureaucratized; the CGT became dependent on the leader. In other words, power was centralized and coordinated in the hands of Perón. An Argentine version of the Stalinist "cult of personality" was instituted—balanced only by a generous dose of homespun McCarthyism: An anti-Argentine activities investigating committee was set up.

Despite these features, the regime lacked most of the distinguishing traits of totalitarianism. There were only halfhearted efforts to establish control of the political process, to institute a program of political socialization, to positively control the media. There were increased repression and police brutality but no ubiquitous terror. The regime became stronger and more rigid as time went by, but it was not totalitarian—clearly not a variant of fascist totalitarianism as it is sometimes depicted. In fact some analysts insist that throughout the regime, the relationship between Perón and his followers was basically rational as opposed to the relationship of European fascist leaders to their followers, which is described as irrational (Germani, 1965, 245–252). In short, Peronism was not "effectively totalitarian" (Silvert, 1963, 362–366). There was censorship, and an atmosphere of intimidation and harassment, but the opposition was not crushed. In the presidential elections of 1946 and 1951 Perón was opposed, and most observers agree that the elections were quite free and honest. One thing is clear, however: By the time Perón entered his second term in office (he was reelected in 1951, securing 4.6 million votes against 2.3 million for his radical opponents Ricardo Balbín and Arturo Frondizi), his economic failures had begun eroding the bases of his support, and forcing him to become more dictatorial.

In August 1951, a great gathering of Perón supporters proclaimed the candidacy of Perón for a second term as president, and the candidacy of Eva Perón as vice-president. This was an important departure from political norms. Perón's constitutional reform of 1949 allowed the reelection of the president and the candidacy of a woman, for women had been enfranchised due to the efforts of Evita. The conservative flanks of the regime—the army and the church—balked at these prospects. To them, Perón was going too far. The possibility of a woman succeeding to the presidency especially outraged the chauvinism of the officers. They demanded her resignation of the candidacy. Perón bowed to military pressure, and Evita was sacrificed. Perón ran for a second term and won the elections. The people were still on his side, but it was the beginning of the end. The economy was stagnant. Almost simultaneously there was a severe drought that revealed how thoroughly Argentina was still dependent on the products of the countryside. In order to feed the people grains had to be imported in the country of wheat. Meat production declined alarmingly. In September 1951 there was a military revolt that was put down partly by pro-Perón officers and partly by the mass mobilization of the workers. Eva Perón contracted cancer and died in July 1952—lucid and fierce to the last. Her funeral produced an outpouring of popular grief as had not been known in Argentina before.

Unbeknownst to the mourners, it was also the funeral of Perón's reformist populism. The army was wrought by dissension. The navy was solidly against Perón. There had been tension between the regime and ecclesiastical interests since the regime had usurped the church's role in the welfare and charity movements, and the enfranchisement of women was seen with disfavor by the skirted hierarchy. The students also began to move against the regime. By handing over the direction of the universities to incompetent goons, Perón made a serious and rather silly mistake: He created an opposition among the very people who could have easily and generously supported him.

By 1953 the Argentine economy was in such bad shape that Perón decided to change his economic policy. This period marks the reactionary phase of Peronism. Politically he was not yet in a position to turn the screw on the workers, and to find in stepped-up labor exploitation the funds needed for industrial investment. The landed bourgeoisie and the farmers had been hit hard by drought and by the process of decapitalization to which Perón had subjected them. There was one source of capital to which Perón now turned: U.S. investments. In August 1953 he opened negotiations with Standard Oil of California. Petroleum extraction was now opened to "imperialism." Then U.S. and West European firms began taking over major sectors of Argentine industry. With tariff protection now working in their favor, U.S., German, and Italian firms developed high-cost automobile plants and chemical complexes. The nationalist pretensions of the regime were simply thrown overboard.

By 1954 there was a new alignment of forces in Argentine politics. Perón found himself in alliance with the workers—still loyal to him, foreign capitalists, and government officeholders and hangers-on. Against him stood the oligarchy as always, sectors of the army, the church, and increasingly both the industrial bourgeoisie and the urban middle strata. The industrialists found it hard to reconcile their interests with Perón's labor policies. The middle sectors, which had been outflanked in their quest for power in 1945, were increasingly adopting a pseudo-aristocratic contempt for the plebeian style of the regime. The middle sectors were characterized by false consciousness and political ambivalence. And Perón's unnecessary attacks upon these sectors exacerbated their opposition. Nevertheless, some middle-class organizations began adopting political programs that purported to complete the unfinished work of Peronism: land reform and a transition to socialism.

On the other side of the political spectrum, some conservative politicians tried to approach the regime and negotiate with Perón. But Perón chose to free himself from these opposing pressures by beginning to mount corporativist structures in order to control the different social interests—workers, industrialists, and agrarians—from above. Side by side with the docile CGT, a General Economic Confederation (Confederación General Económica, CGE) was created to deal with capitalists. Then came a CGP (Confederación General de Profesionales or Federation of Professionals), a CGU (Confederación General Universitaria, or University Federation), and even a corporate organization of high-school students, the UES (Unión de Estudiantes Secundarios). At the same time, the state ceased to be a champion of the workers and became instead a neutral arbiter in labor disputes. Several strikes were suppressed. By 1954 it was clear that Perón's revolution had completed its cycle and was entering a reactionary period. The hybrid system created by Perón was becoming ossified and promised to last indefinitely as a corporative status quo. The opposition was hamstrung and divided. Perón had made his peace with big capital and Argentina was now solidly in the orbit of U.S. power. Yet Perón failed to make the transition to a new conservatism.

Hitherto Peronism had consisted of an uneasy alliance of trade unions and secondary institutions like the church and the army. Prosperity kept them together through a policy of simultaneous and large payoffs. The economic debacle of the fifties made payoff impossible and forced instead a different set of political maneuvers that proved fatal to the regime. Perón could not turn against the working class—as the new political situation demanded—without first weakening the conservative institutions of society: the church and the army. Otherwise he would rapidly become their prisoner. His new political strategy was to attack the conservative secondary institutions while he kept control of the labor movement and was still popular with the workers; then turn the screw on the wage earners. Such maneuvers, combined with the realignment of Argentina on the U.S. side and the opening of its economy to foreign capital, lured Perón to the prospects of many more years in power as a tamed strong man—a friend of the West. Unfortunately for Perón, his attacks on the secondary organizations backfired. In 1954 he hammered the church with a law making divorce legal, he authorized the reopening of brothels, and downgraded religious holidays—Christmas and Good Friday included—to secondary status. The opposition managed to capitalize on these attacks. In 1955 there were mass demonstrations against the government by middle- and upper-class individuals. Perón took the bait: He replied with further repressive measures. On June 16, navy planes attempted to kill Perón by bombing the presidential house. They only managed to kill several hundred city workers in the heart of the business district of Buenos Aires just after lunch hour. That night several churches in downtown Buenos Aires were burned by Peronist sympathizers. There were rumors that Perón was arming the workers. Perón orchestrated his public resignation on August 31. Masses of workers gathered in Plaza de Mayo, asked him to stay in power, and he graciously conceded. But this was the end. In Córdoba the military garrison, under the leadership of General Lonardi, rose against Perón. There were popular demonstrations of support among the middle and upper classes. This time the proletariat was quiescent. The army hesitated at first but did not come to the rescue of the president. Perón boarded a Paraguayan gunboat and was taken into exile.

The Peronist government collapsed as soon as he departed. It was the end of what probably was the first instance of a political phenomenon that later became common throughout the Third World: nonaligned developmentalism in a mixed economy. In Argentina this phenomenon had taken the form of a pseudorevolution: a coalition of different classes and institutional bureaucracies within a capitalist framework, under-written by the large funds accumulated by Argentina during exceptional years when the bonds of dependency were relaxed. The alliance collapsed ten years later, when the funds had run out and import substitution could no longer sustain an independent industrialization process. After the fall of Perón, the different components of society turned upon each other in sharp conflicts that to date remain inconclusive—exacerbated by the increasing vulnerability of Argentina to foreign penetration. After nearly two decades of internal strife and social crisis one secondary organization and one social class have proved durable: the military and the proletariat. Other groups and institutions have been weakened perhaps beyond repair.

When Perón came to power, Argentina had witnessed the slow disintegration of an inherited conglomerate of dependency and mis-development, still very far from complete. With Perón, many Argentines experienced a momentary sense of liberation, marked by advances in social justice. They were for a moment confronted with the prospect of a society much more open and independent than anything previously known. But they soon began experiencing something else—the unmis-takable symptoms of a recoil from that prospect. There was hesitation before the jump, and then a flight backwards. Peronism rode to this jump and refused it. Was it the horse that refused, or the rider? Perón's personal flaws are too great and too many to be dismissed. But the coalition of social interests that supported him and made his experiment possible was fragile and unstable. Perón could not control them. Argentine rulers after him have made the fatal mistake of thinking they could ignore them.

6
Political Seesawing

The Restoration

At the end of Perón's rule, Argentina was passing through one of the worst economic crises of its history. The failure of the Peronist program of autarkic industrialization, coupled with the policies of mass mobilization and social welfare that had characterized the regime, had left a sequel of inflation and misdevelopment, changing the nature of, but not abolishing, dependency, and reinforcing the pattern of "superstructural" modernization typical of Argentine social change. Perón himself had already been faced with the dilemma of either unleashing a social revolution—a qualitative change in the relations of production— or stabilizing the system he had created through the enforcement of not only economic but also social and political deflation. He had chosen stabilization but failed to survive the strains of the transition. The military leaders that overthrew Perón in 1955 set out to complete with new zest the unfinished task of reaction. The so-called Liberating Revolution of 1955 was designed to contain the class tensions unleashed by Peronist arbitration, to restrict political participation to the "respectable" parties representing the middle and upper classes, and to stabilize the economy by strengthening the traditional export sector, curtailing secondary sources of inflation—wages, public expenditures and services, the state bureaucracy—while seeking to attract foreign loans and direct investments.

The program of the regime of 1955 was at the same time a policy of stabilization and of denationalization. This restrictive and in many ways backward-looking enterprise was fraught with grave risks, for it entailed among other consequences nothing less than the disenfranchisement of the bulk of the urban working class. This was a drastic devolution in the process of political modernization and democratization, and it was accompanied by considerable economic hardships for the lower classes. The program of stabilization in economics and regression in political participation was rendered particularly unrealistic by the liberal commitment of the ruling group to the formal mechanisms of pluralist democracy. Upon the repression of the most significant political phenomenon in twentieth-century Argentina—namely, the incorporation of urban and rural masses into the structure of national political participation—the anti-Peronist regime wished to rebuild the old skeleton of pluralism, this time restricted to the parties of the middle and upper reaches of society. This could not but result in political cheating, since by no possible stretch of the imagination could the regime hope to infuse the old parties with representativeness and legitimacy among the large Peronist electorate. In the long run, this tutored, conservative pluralism of semiliberal stamp jeopardized the stabilizing policies of the government by making them inconsistent, by fostering a demagogic jostle between unrepresentative parties in a scramble to hoodwink Peronist voters, by strengthening the self-fulfilling prophecy among the military that civilians were corrupt or at best inept in leading the nation, and eventually by generating a cycle of political instability and military intervention that ended with the demise of all liberal semblance *tout court* in 1966.

It is therefore possible to treat the eleven years from 1955 to 1966 as unitary and continuous. Four basic features are worth noting. First, a ruling elite with military and landed upper-class components tied to foreign interests emerged. The new coalition agreed on the need to curtail and suppress Peronism, to return to traditional patterns of dependent growth, and to seek foreign aid and investment as a decisive instrument of policy. Second, a defeated Peronist mass, divided and plagued by the inner contradictions of populism, began a "long march" underground. Third, a formal democratic structure of parties of the middle and upper strata developed. "Restrictive" or repressive pluralism may be adequate descriptive terms for these arrangements. Fourth was an economic strategy designed to dismantle the hybrid system created by Perón by encouraging the export sector and foreign investments and instituting policies of monetary stabilization.

This cursory outline of the sociopolitical system installed in Argentina after the fall of Perón shows that its various components worked at cross-purposes, and especially that, under conditions of restrictive pluralism, economic stabilization could not but generate political turmoil. No wonder, then, that the main political forces during this period proved unable to develop a common framework or any consensus capable of sustaining a coherent program of economic growth. Government policies were often illegitimate and unrepresentative. Thus, the more the system of restrictive pluralism was corroded by its inner contradictions, the more it became vulnerable to military intervention. And the more frequently military intervention occurred, the weaker the political fabric became. This stalemated pluralism blocked all the ways out of economic stagnation: Every one of the potential victims of alternative solutions to the economic impasse—the working class, the middle sectors, the landed bourgeoisie, the industrialists—was still powerful enough to veto the execution of any coherent development strategy.

We have seen how the response to crisis and war had produced an unintegrated industrial system and with it a fragile balance of social forces. Peronism capitalized on these processes and attempted to institutionalize them in a hybrid system. The experiment failed: Social equilibrium was not consolidated, and from 1955 onward Argentina entered a period of increased social tension and political confrontations. These strains had deep economic roots, internal as well as international. But other episodes and factors added to the stress: The Cold War, and the emergence of Cuban socialism in particular, imposed a new sense of urgency upon the exhaustion of previous political experiments. Not only the survival of particular governments but the very existence of capitalism and U.S. hegemony were at stake. National and international interests rapidly moved to stabilize the status quo.

By the mid-fifties, the signs of economic decay were unmistakable. Inflation reached intolerable levels. The state could no longer prevent the drift of the economy. The groups in power responded to the critical situation with a set of neoliberal policies that clearly betrayed class loyalties. Faced with a continuous deterioration of the terms of trade, they promoted the concentration of benefits in the export sector, while the other sectors of the economy moved into recession owing to the curtailment of credit and the application of anti-inflationary policies. The aim was to produce a rebirth of prosperity through exports and then diffuse that prosperity through the rest of the system. It simply did not work. Moreover, the administration of such strong medicine caused unbearable social tensions, which were only assuaged by backtracking and reinstituting state controls and inflationary stimuli.

Increased external dependency was one of the clearest signs of the crisis. Argentina got deeper into debt: The balance of trade and the balance of payments yielded huge deficits. Its more complex industrial structure was in even greater need of credit than the old export structures had been during the period of outward growth under British hegemony. Without external credit there were neither raw materials nor essential fuels and parts to keep industry moving. Argentina appealed time and again to the international finance organizations that respond to the directives of North American capitalism. The International Monetary Fund now called the shots, both directly by channeling credit and indirectly by setting the pace of private investments. Thus credits gave temporary respite to the ruling groups of Argentina. In order to satisfy the pressures of different social classes, the elite launched periodic inflationary orgies that were subsequently checked by deflationary brakes and currency devaluations imposed by the international creditors. But deflationary measures managed to cause recession without necessarily stopping inflation. The stop-go cycle seemed hopeless. Economic crises were exacerbated in the dependent capitalist system of Argentina precisely when advanced capitalism seemed to have learned to stabilize its own cycles in the metropolis. Like addicts, the ruling circles responded to the existing morass with a stronger dosage of the poison: They pinned their hopes on ever-larger flows of metropolitan dollars and plants. The country was flooded with proposals, plans, and theories of development. But every one of them was successfully vetoed by the social sectors that would have had to bear their respective weight.

In 1955 Argentina had reached the full employment of its labor force, fed from the peripheral regions of the country. Industrialization had placed the manufacturing sector ahead of the agrarian sector in the share of GNP. Yet the concentration of industry in the production of consumer goods made it dependent on imports of raw materials, fuels, and capital goods. The stagnation of agro-pecuarian production and the rise in the internal consumption of that produce had depleted exportable surpluses. The consequence was a steady disequilibrium in the balance of trade. Therefore, any attempt to continue economic growth produced inflation. And policies designed to correct inflation halted growth.

When the Peronist administration had tried to break that vicious circle by adopting conservative measures (strengthening the export structures, transferring income from urban to rural sectors, appealing to foreign capital, disciplining the labor force), it was overthrown by a military coup. The new regime restored the pre-Peronist political arrangements. The two wings of the new restoration—a liberal conservative faction and a Catholic-fascist sector—agreed on one mistake, namely, to consider that Peronism had died with the fall of Perón. They wished to dismantle the system created by the latter by favoring the policies already instituted by Perón himself in the final hour of his regime. External trade was liberalized and the peso was devalued as measures in favor of the primary exporters. Public expenditures were curtailed and workers were denied wage increases. These policies—sponsored by the head of the United Nations Economic Commission for Latin America (ECLA), the Argentine economist Raúl Prebisch—aimed at replenishing the stock of foreign exchange that Argentina needed in order to revamp its mining and industrial structures. But the economic plan was only halfheartedly executed, on account of two main factors. On the one hand, the new economic measures risked popular unrest. Therefore investment was often sacrificed to the maintenance of the wage level for the sake of social peace. On the other hand, the agro-pecuarian interests—who had an important role in the post-Peronist governments—were not disposed to surrender the advantages they had recently obtained for the sake of further industrialization. The net result of economic policy was thus to increase the profits of the landed bourgeoisie, to raise the internal prices of foodstuffs, and thereby create more inflationary pressures by raising the cost of living. Development remained an unfulfilled promise.

The Opposition

While the government teams attempted unsuccessfully to dismantle the web of affiliations inherited from the Peronist era, new political groups wished to operate that system better than Perón had done. The most important of these groups was the left wing of *radicalismo*, led by Arturo Frondizi. Frondizi wanted a renovated *radicalismo* to supersede Peronism. The latter, however, proved more durable than was expected, or wished, by its rivals and would-be heirs. In 1957 the military authorities—under the leadership of the provisional president General Pedro Eugenio Aramburu—called a constitutional convention designed to revamp the constitution of 1953 and scrap the more recent Peronist constitution of 1949. The elections for the Constituent Assembly revealed the strength of Peronism. The *peronistas* cast over 2 million ballots, representing about 20 percent of those voting. These protest votes took the lead, followed by the votes for the traditional wing of the Radical Party (Unión Cívica Radical del Pueblo, UCRP). Frondizi and his faction (Unión Cívica Radical Intransigente, UCRI) came third.

Frondizi was forced to change his political strategy. Instead of replacing Perón he tried to become his ally. He made a secret deal with Perón in which he promised to readmit the *peronistas* into the political process in return for Perón's support in the presidential elections prepared by the provisional military government for February 1958. The result was an easy victory of Frondizi over his radical rivals. The Peronist support also won for Frondizi the mistrust of the military and the conservatives. As soon as he assumed the presidency, however, Frondizi turned his back on his popular support and sought instead the backing of the industrial sector, which he invited to struggle against the landed interests. Frondizi thus pinned his hopes on leading the national bourgeoisie, and secondarily, the Peronist proletariat along the path of *desarrollismo* (developmentalism). Despite endless wheeling and dealing, this task proved more formidable than Frondizi had expected.

Two considerations were mainly responsible for his failure. On the one hand, the Peronist experience had produced an urban proletariat that was organizationally more advanced than the industrial bourgeoisie. Only sectors of this industrial class had supported Perón, and had done so timidly (Freels, 1968). Dependency on state protection and social segregation had kept this class relatively weak in a country in which the traditional hegemony of the landed bourgeoisie had constantly discouraged the investment of capital in industry and induced it into land purchases—the early antioligarchic gestures of Perón notwithstanding. The end of Peronism had caused the landed bourgeoisie to rebound politically and to resist the imposition of any sacrifice for the sake of industrial development and integration. This class vetoed different attempts to wrest funds for capital accumulation from the agro-pecuarian sector.

Frondizi then, in a classic about-face, turned to foreign monopoly capital to carry forward his plans for industrial *desarrollo*. He signed contracts with foreign oil companies, negotiated credits through the International Monetary Fund, and opened the sluices to the flow of foreign capital into manufacturing, energy production, and public transport. He thus avoided the real problems of internal accumulation and disguised the avoidance with a technocratic ideology of developmentalism. Every major political and economic decision made by Frondizi represented the betrayal of one or more of his previous planks. This maneuvering alienated different sectors of the electorate, multiplied suspicions, and left Frondizi with sheer political ruse as the instrument of government. The tricks did not work: Foreign capital left Argentina saddled with enormous debts. After a brief inflationary expansion, growth was halted by a new round of stabilization policies forced upon Frondizi by the zeal of international creditors. Economic austerity provoked the Peronist proletariat into a militant opposition that was met with strong repression. Frondizi's devious and shifting deals with different political forces raised the suspicions of the military. His attempted neutrality vis-à-vis the Cuban Revolution enraged the officers who looked to the Pentagon as a Mecca. But it was the durable Peronists who gave Frondizi the coup de grace. The provincial elections of 1962 produced unexpected victories for the Peronists, who retained the loyalty of one-third of the electorate, winning forty-five of the eighty-six seats up for election in the Chamber of Deputies and ten of fourteen governorships.

Meanwhile, the level of violence reached unprecedented proportions: There were guerrilla *focos* in the northwest and frequent clashes between factions of the armed forces. By allowing *peronistas* to run, Frondizi was belatedly fulfilling his end of the deal made with them in 1958, but the Peronist victories of 1962 convinced the officers that Frondizi was not worth all the trouble. They ousted him but stopped short of full dictatorship. As a compromise, the military placed Dr. José María Guido, the president of the senate and a colorless politician, in the presidency and instructed him to prepare for new elections.

The Guido administration was marked by two important episodes: the internal conflicts in the armed forces and the acute economic recession produced by the application of the orthodox economic policies sponsored by the IMF. The economic recession forced one-third of the available work force to remain idle. At the same time, a new currency devaluation transferred what little prosperity there was into the hands of the agrarians. Political confusion abated temporarily when the armed forces—wrought by serious factionalism as a consequence of their intense participation in politics—decided to retrench and discovered for themselves a new technocratic vocation under the leadership of General Juan Carlos Onganía, who became commander in chief of the army. The officers agreed to leave power to an elected civilian government acceptable to the establishment. Under those circumstances, the mantle of power fell this time to the traditional wing of *radicalismo*. Since Peronists were not allowed to vote for their own candidates, the *peronista* vote was dispersed in the presidential elections of 1963. Dr. Arturo Illia, a radical politician from the province of Córdoba, became the new president.

The Illia administration benefited from the expansion of rural production—the effect of economic policies applied since 1955. The activity of the export sector had been kept alive through periodic devaluations of the peso. Now, for the first time in several decades, foreign trade yielded positive balances and did so during three consecutive years. The foreign exchange thus obtained was manipulated by the government through a restored exchange control system. These sums, however, were not large enough to cover the enormous short-term debts inherited from the Frondizi administration. As a result, the Illia government had to appeal to international creditors, who once more managed to impose on Argentina a program of economic stabilization and austerity that interrupted the process of growth with manageable inflation of the mid-sixties. In brief, during the Illia administration, Argentina saw a temporary respite to the economic malaise but not the end of its troubles. The stop-go cycle of the economy managed to reassert itself in the end.

The political crisis was more serious than the economic difficulties. Just as with Frondizi before, the only hope for the party in power (UCRP) was to concentrate all non-Peronist votes in order to prevent a takeover by a unified Peronist movement in future elections—an event that would have taken place if anti-Peronist opinion remained split in different groups. But other parties adamantly refused to relinquish their electoral support to the *radicales* in the government. Meanwhile, Peronism was beginning to find support among sectors of the middle class. The latter had opposed Peronism when it became clear that Perón would postpone the satisfaction of its demands in order to attend first to the demands of the industrial proletariat. After the fall of Perón, the middle class did not see those pent-up pretensions fulfilled. Instead, the governments. that succeeded Perón increased the privileges of the landed upper class and added a new privileged member to the familiar constellation of Argentine society: foreign monopoly capital. As a consequence of this, sectors of the middle class began to redefine their relationship with Peronism. Thus, Peronism threatened to command an absolute majority in future elections. A return of Perón to power was more than the military could accept, despite the basically unrevolutionary nature of the movement and its leadership. But ten years of anti-Peronist blunders and economic stagnation had produced a peculiar result: Peronism became a treasure house of myth and legend for many Argentines, providing a source of political inspiration to a younger generation. In these metamorphoses, Perón's regime appeared as a golden age followed by periods of a baser ore in which all manner of greed and deceit broke out while prosperity and loyalty fled.

There were other changes, however, which the radical government planned to exploit in its own favor. These had to do with the struggle over the leadership of the Peronist movement. The restoration of 1955 had left many second-rank leaders of Peronism in positions of power and influence in both the unions and the provincial administrations. These leaders wished to institutionalize Peronism and incorporate it in the mainstream of political life as a respectable party in the post-Peronist era. They felt confident that they could accomplish this task by themselves. Their very resilience under hostile, often brutal, governments proved their point. Perón, on the other hand, wished to retain personal control over the movement from his exile in Madrid. He saw the new developments in Argentina as a challenge to his power. He therefore began to sabotage the unity of his own movement as a tactic to retain control. Through a policy of *divide et impera*, Perón pitted different leaders against each other so as to remain the supreme arbiter of the conflicts that he himself instigated. Powerful union leaders and Peronist politicians began to wish they could throw off the yoke of Perón's personalism. In short, they entertained the prospects of a *peronismo sin Perón*. They thought that a revamped, tamed, Peronist movement could be accepted as a major political force in Argentina without arousing the ire of the military and the fear of the establishment. Perón countered by sending his third wife—María Estela (Isabel) Martínez de Perón—to Argentina. The government welcomed this move, believing that it could only divide the Peronists further and thereby increase the radicals' own chances in important elections. Isabel Martínez managed, however, to wrest power from local *peronistas* and regroup the movement under the leadership of the exiled strongman. The provincial elections of Mendoza showed this trend very clearly: An obscure candidate sponsored by Perón and his wife easily obtained more votes than the official candidate of the Peronist Party, a seasoned politician of solid local prestige. The lesson was not lost on the military: It became apparent that in the next national elections, Peronism could win—with Perón still at the helm by proxy.

In June 1966, President Illia was ousted by a bloodless coup. The putsch encountered little if any resistance among the population at large: It had the tacit support of anti-Peronist groups and even the acceptance of some sectors of Peronism that preferred the arbitration of the military to the less productive arbitration of Perón himself. This time the military were unabashed about their intentions: They suspended the constitution, abolished all trappings of liberal democracy, vowed to stay in power *sine die*, and called their deed the "Argentine Revolution." Thus the liberal restoration of 1955 came to a precipitous end and nobody rose to defend it.

PART 3
Time for Evildoers

In the disorder of corrupted societies, the scene has been frequently changed from democracy to despotism, and from the last too, in its turn, to the first. From amidst the democracy of corrupt men, and from a scene of lawless confusion, the tyrant ascends a throne with arms reeking in blood. But his abuses, or his weaknesses, in the station which he has gained, in their turn, awaken and give way to the spirit of mutiny and revenge. The cries of murder and desolation, which in the ordinary course of military government terrified the subject in his private retreat, are carried through the vaults, and made to pierce the grates and iron doors of the seraglio. Democracy seems to revive in a scene of wild disorder and tumult: but both the extremes are but the transient fits of paroxysm or languor in a distempered state.

If men be any where arrived at this measure of depravity, there appears no immediate hope of redress. Neither the ascendency of the multitude, nor that of the tyrant, will secure the administration of justice: neither the licence of mere tumult, nor the calm of dejection and servitude, will teach the citizen that he was born for candour and affection to his fellow-creatures.

—Adam Ferguson, *An Essay on the History of Civil Society*

7

The Dictatorial Temptation

During the decade just reviewed, the landed bourgeoisie became once again a dominant political force in Argentina, in conjunction with allied sectors of society. The 1955 experiment was in this sense a second restoration (the first had occurred, as we have seen, in 1930), this time falling upon an industrialized society embittered by the failures of national capitalist development. Since 1943 the landed bourgeoisie had lost the capacity to exercise direct political power, but after the fall of Perón it could still manage to manipulate the apparatus of the state and the armed forces—a stronghold of the middle class—to its own advantage. The second restoration had two objectives: to abolish all protection to the accumulation of national industrial capital erected during the populist period, and to institute a new economic policy benefiting the agro-pecuarian sector. The first objective was accomplished by dismantling a whole series of institutions created by Perón. The Institute for Exchange Promotion (IAPI) was abolished; bank deposits were denationalized; exchange controls ceased to be enforced; credits to small and medium-sized industries were cut. The second objective was attained through successive devaluations of the peso, which meant massive transfers of resources to the exporters—a regressive redistribution of income in favor of the agrarians. A study of income distribution prepared by the United Nations Economic Commission for Latin America (ECLA) in 1969 clearly reveals the regressive trends in post-Perón Argentina. Detailed statistical estimates were made for three years— 1953, 1959, and 1961—so as to observe changes in the characteristics of the distribution. ECLA arrived at the following conclusions:

> . . . the earliest of the three years, 1953, was the one in which the distribution of income was least unequal. In 1959 the overall inequality was much greater. The top 10 percent of all families received over 42 percent of all personal income in the latter year, as compared to 37 percent in 1953, and all other income groups received proportionately less. Even

within the top 10 percent it was primarily the upper half of these families which benefited; the shift was almost entirely in favour of the 5 percent of all families at the top of the income scale. (UNECLA, 1969, 10)

Commenting on the consequences of post-Peronist policies, the same study goes on to say:

The net effect was a large shift in income in favour of profits, particularly in the agricultural sector, and the consequent rise in the degree of inequality noted above. . . . The more recent shift in favour of profits and toward greater inequality can to an important extent be regarded as a return to the pre-Second-World-War income distribution. (UNECLA, 1969, 10)

It is clear that such policies were antagonistic to the interests of the masses. Under those circumstances, the governments that followed Perón could not hope to retain power in an open system except by corrupting the very principles of democratic rule. They managed this by instituting political proscriptions, betraying electoral promises, making shady deals, trying to accommodate as many sectors of the dominant classes as possible and to deny access to government to the Peronists at the same time. In short, what emerged after the fall of Perón was a *consorteria* to which one could easily apply Pareto's notions of the alternation of elites. When cunning and the art of electoral combinations failed to achieve the principal goal of the restoration, namely, to keep the lid on *peronismo*, civilian governments were felled by military coups. Military regimes in turn became hidebound and rigid, or sometimes threatened— as in 1962—to degenerate into rule by armed factions, at which point they transferred power to new civilian governments, and so on—Ins and Outs, lions and foxes.

The liberal restoration of 1955 failed to return Argentina to the pastoral bliss of 1910. Instead it increased the role of foreign monopoly capital in industry to unprecedented proportions. The new economic sector gained in importance during that period and came to oppose the interests of both the agrarians and the industrialists, and to victimize every class beneath them.

In the 1960s, foreign monopoly capital became a powerful political interest group. In 1966 the cluster of interests around foreign corporations saw with pleasure the demise of the civilian government. The economic policies of the Illia administration had been in their own mild way obtrusive to these interests. More generally, the financial and political instability of the restoration decade was incompatible with the objectives of long-range multinational corporate growth. The military coup of June 28, 1966, placed in power a former commander in chief of the army, General Juan Carlos Onganía. Since that time, foreign monopoly capital, clustered around large North American subsidiaries, has had a decisive influence on the policies of the Argentine state. The new character of dependency under these multinational corporations has drastically modified the contradictions of the society and has exacerbated social tensions. Whereas during the Peronist period the principal line of cleavage was between the landed bourgeoisie and the nationalist state, which was prone to finance national industrial expansion with agro-pecuarian profits, the new pattern of conflict that developed during the restoration of 1955–1966 and that emerged full-blown after the 1966 coup opposed foreign monopoly capital and the popular classes affected by its expansion (Laclau, 1970, 5).

Gone forever were the days of outward growth conjoining the interests of British imperialism with those of the landed oligarchy. Gone, also, were tensions between the agrarians and a nationalist state that protected a weak industrial class and redistributed income in favor of the proletariat. Easy import substitution was exhausted. Autonomous industrial growth had come to a grinding halt for lack of investable resources. The class struggle had reached an impasse. Large North American investments in the industrial sector had come to predominate in the economy as a whole. Government rested on the naked use of force. The military regime of 1966 aimed at maximizing satellite industrialization and minimizing social change. The challenge was clear: The Onganía regime undertook to destroy the stalemated equilibrium of social forces, stem the tide of opposition that the destruction of the old order would produce, renovate the economic system with the aid of big monopoly capital, let the latter reconstitute the sundered puzzle of classes, and only then loosen the screws on the community. In short, the aim was to produce a new type of social integration on the basis of a dynamic industrial dependency.

Such was the grand project of the self-styled *Revolución Argentina* of General Onganía. Onganía did not, however, calculate the risks. In Argentina, the capacity of monopoly capital to promote a new kind of social integration proved much inferior to its ability to destroy the older equilibrium. It ended up creating mass opposition, narrowing the social base of capitalism, and it promised to rest on increasing, indefinite repression. The response of a wounded community was highly political, inspired by three years of insult and injury to economic well-being and political traditions. This response tore at the bland facade of bourgeois society: In May 1969, Argentina witnessed the first of a series of mass urban insurrections led by the industrial working class of the interior. The masses seized the city of Córdoba in episodes reminiscent of the Paris Commune of 1871. Other cities followed; the revolt became general. The steps leading to these episodes were of probably greater significance than those of the populist outpouring of 1945.

When the military seized power in 1966 they were responding to an immediate political crisis. Whether they were also under pressure from powerful economic interests—big monopoly capital in particular—is hard to know but easy to suspect. In any case, it was foreign monopoly capital that was destined to become one of the main beneficiaries of the regime through legislation and other official measures that allowed

transference of ownership and created conditions favoring denationalization of industrial and financial firms in many sectors of the economy.

The years immediately preceding the coup showed nothing unusual
in terms of the traditionally slow growth of the Argentine economy. In
fact, as we have seen, there was a somewhat higher rate of growth
than usual under the Illia administration. Good harvests and other
stimuli to the agrarian sector had strengthened the country's balance
of payments. The inflation rate was high—30 percent—but not unusual
for Argentina and tolerable in terms of past experience. Politically,
however, the situation was far more critical. There were unmistakable
signs of instability. The prevalent opinion in the governing party was
that, unless the Peronists were somehow incorporated into the political
system without unduly rocking the boat, it would not be possible to
lead the country toward any kind of consistent development. The
participation of Peronists was thus allowed in the provincial elections
in 1966, producing Peronist victories in some provinces. These victories
were less important per se than as a foreboding of things to come on
the national level. Observers began to predict that in the forthcoming
elections for congress in March 1967, the Peronists—still under the
control of the exiled Perón—would win and thus alter the fundamental
power balance. Those prospects produced acute anxiety in military
spheres and among establishment groups—the foreign monopoly sector
included. The military took power in order to postpone a solution to
the political crisis. The solution closest at hand, namely, the incorporation
of Peronism on its own terms into the political system, was deemed—
perhaps not incorrectly—incompatible with capitalist development, especially with the expansion of foreign monopoly capital. The exercise of
unfettered democracy under those circumstances would lead to basic
social change possibly beyond the confines of capitalist society. Democratic
government was therefore suspended until a vague later date when it
was hoped that—in the best tradition of the "free world"—politics
would legitimize but not alter the socioeconomic system.

The efforts of the military dictatorship were focused on creating the
preconditions for monopoly capital expansion. It wished to modernize
and streamline the system of dependent industrial capitalism, somehow
expecting that the application of the adequate economic measures in
that direction would eventually produce a new type of social integration
leading ultimately to new forms of political participation. Hence, the
overall strategy of the dictatorship consisted of three phases, or *tiempos*,
as they were called, in this order—*tiempo económico, tiempo social, tiempo
político*. The economic plan was executed: Foreign monopoly capital
took over strategic sectors of the economy with rapidity and precision.
But the social phase never was. Instead of a new social integration, the
economic takeover produced social dislocation, discontent, and finally
massive opposition. Social integration could only mean a better participation of the salaried groups in the share of national income, that

is to say, higher real incomes and better levels of employment. But this capitalist utopia was to come after a period of deprivation, during which real wages were lowered and corporate rationalization threw people out of jobs. The official dialectic did not work. For historical reasons that should by now be apparent, the social profile of Argentina is fairly integrated; the working class is characterized by advanced forms of organization and strong feedback capabilities. Therefore, the ruthless expansion of monopoly capital triggered a popular backlash that for a moment reached revolutionary proportions. Thus, the real dialectic of classes shattered the designs of the ruling groups and assigned a very different meaning to the three official *tiempos*: from monopoly capitalist takeover to social dislocation to revolutionary crisis. As a result of these circumstances, during the following years the military purged its leading ranks, shelved the former economic plans—at least temporarily—and frantically searched for a political compromise that could prevent the catastrophe of the status quo.

Social Regression

A detailed chronicle of the *Revolución Argentina* of 1966 is beyond the scope of these pages. Rather, the contours of its different phases will be sketched in terms of economic policies and social response.

The first acts of the military government of 1966 consisted of draconian measures of housecleaning. Those institutions deemed as obstacles to the economic designs of the ruling circles were simply destroyed. The basic framework of the economic status quo was strengthened and there were even some regressive concessions to the agrarian sector. The policies of the government managed to smash a number of institutions—political parties, the supreme court, the provincial governments, the national universities—that constitute the very fabric of bourgeoisie liberalism and the guarantee of juridical defense. Many of these institutions were damaged beyond repair. The General Confederation of Labor (CGT) was not affected at this stage of the dictatorship. Under the control of A. T. Vandor, leader of the powerful Metalworkers Union, labor organizations adopted a stance of wait-and-see. No coherent economic policy was implemented during the first months of the regime. There were only stopgap measures designed to rationalize some sectors of the economy and to curb inflation. Thus, an attempt was made to reduce the state deficit, to eliminate bureaucratic featherbedding, to make public services more efficient, making the trains run on time. An isolated effort was made to reorganize the economy of a peripheral province—Tucumán—with disastrous results: massive layoffs, hunger, popular resistance. The episode was a presage of things to come. The gross domestic product declined by one percentage point; inflation continued, and the rate reached a high point of 32 percent during the first year. The relations between the government and labor began to show signs of strain.

It is important to dwell on the cultural reaction that befell the country under this military regime. During a whole decade, from 1956 through 1966, Argentina knew the distortions and constraints imposed upon economic growth by the structures of dependency, suffered from the stalemate of social conflicts, and could not find a political formula that could translate civil tensions into orderly public life. Yet neither slow growth, social stalemate, nor political instability hampered intellectual development. Today, societies at the core of the world system are liberal in their practice. They experience a minimum of overt political or ideological repression, precisely because they are dominant. They thus become creative and innovating centers in the realm of culture. Semi-peripheral, or "advanced dependent," societies like Argentina are condemned to watch those developments like spectators itching to take part. The compromise that results encapsulates a burst of creativity in the intellectual milieu.

Argentines quickly developed the ability to learn, adopt, and adapt the most advanced cultural trends in the world; they became masters in the art of expressing in the realm of thought what others were practicing in real life, not without some spectacular results: Mathematics, theoretical physics, the social sciences, and arts and humanities flourished with panache, as if the mind had to make up within its ideal confines for the frustrations and failures of the economy, the society, and the polity. It was a fragile but proud achievement, a blossom in decayed soil. Buenos Aires could boast of being, in relation to South America, what late Habsburg Vienna had been in relation to Central Europe. Such flowers, however, do not last. It is well-nigh impossible to prolong indefinitely the rare moment when dependent progress, social stalemate, and political uncertainty converge to create a zone of cultural abeyance filled with the achievements of brilliant intellectuals. Political, as opposed to cultural, modernization would not take place.

Instead, Argentina embarked in 1966 on an authoritarian experiment whose first act was an episode of cultural brutality. The military regime attacked the universities, beat up deans and faculty, and forced the best among them, and not a few students, into exile. With the banished intelligentsia went the hope for a fusion between cultural innovation and political critique. In severing that potential connection, the military dictatorship prepared the ground for what would surge later in the wake of its own failures—when Peronism came back in force—as a massive mobilizing tide that was, however, culturally reactionary, prone not to creation and critique, but to Manichean sloganeering and anti-intellectualism.

The year 1967 marked the beginning of the economic phase of the regime. A new economic minister was in command. This man was Adalbert Krieger Vasena, director of National Lead Company and on the board of ADELA Company, a multinational investment corporation. In addition Alvaro Alsogaray, who had been minister of the economy twice before (during the Frondizi and Guido administrations) became ambassador to the United States. This man was associated with Deltec International Corporation, another multinational firm that had bought out International Packers Limited (a meat producer) and had on its board the Klebergs of the Texas King Ranch (Daniels, 1970, 10; García Lupo, 1972). This team launched a carefully prepared strategy of dependent industrialization based on the expansion of foreign monopoly capital. The paramount goal was first, to stabilize the economy and within that framework eliminate distortions and increase productive efficiency, and then generate industrial expansion with the aid of foreign capital.

The means applied consisted of income, exchange, and fiscal policies. Income policy consisted of a plan designed by large business interests to avoid inflationary pressures to facilitate corporate planning. Salaries were adjusted and then frozen. Social security contributions were reduced. The regime made it clear that hard times lay ahead for labor. The exchange policy was also heavy-handed. The regime produced an over-devaluation of the peso designed to "increase confidence" among foreign investors—they could now buy Argentine enterprises with fewer dollars—and to ease the balance-of-payments situation. The goal of the devaluation was to encourage industrial exports in the long run and to solve the problem of lack of reserves held by the central bank in the short run. To avoid the usual consequence of devaluations—an increase in the income of the agrarian exporters—a land tax was instituted. Fiscal policy in turn aimed at increasing the efficiency of the public sector. There was some large-scale reordering of the railways and the ports. These measures meant, of course, eliminating jobs while increasing the profits of business and using the state to stimulate private foreign investments. Other measures of economic rationalization included a reduction of tariffs, the elimination of rent controls and rural tenancy arrangements, and the modification of laws governing credit cooperatives that mobilized the funds of the commercial petit bourgeoisie. Just as the wage freeze repressed the working class, so these other measures were designed to break the economic basis of small and medium enterprises—a rather massive attack on the national and petit bourgeoisies. The unpopular character of these policies was perfectly known to the authorities, who were prepared to resist popular pressures by concentrating power in the army and thus guaranteeing the social control necessary for the influx of foreign capital. The ruling establishment believed the latter would rush in, restore adequate levels of employment, and create new bureaucratic middle sectors from the scattered fragments of the national and petit bourgeoisies. The workers' aristocracy might also eventually benefit from these developments, but the bulk of the proletariat was to remain exploited. Meanwhile, the institution of the land tax made it clear that this time the landed bourgeoisie would not be the main beneficiary of reaction; it too would have to bow before monopoly capital. In summary, this was the final satellization of Argentine capitalism. Argentina was supposed to become an industrial dependency in which stabilization is obtained at the expense of capital in the hands of foreign entrepreneurs and their local associates.

The results in the short run may have impressed the readers of the *Wall Street Journal* and the *Harvard Business Review*: The rate of inflation dropped from 32 percent to about 7 percent in 1967. GNP leaped forward at a rate of 6.6 percent in the same year. The foreign reserve situation was good, the fiscal deficit smaller; wages kept dropping. Argentina was a good spot for investing.

And foreign capital did flow into Argentina after 1967. By contrast to the period of British imperialism, the new imperialism was directed toward industry, accelerating the trend begun in 1955. In the period immediately preceding Onganía, U.S. capital investments in Argentina had already increased from $161 million in 1960 to $617 million in 1965. This flow of capital was less impressive in what it brought in than in what it took over and took out. Statistics reveal a marked discrepancy between the indicators of growth on the one hand and the increased activity of foreign monopoly capital in Argentina, on the other. Between 1960 and 1965, GNP increased at the low average of 2.8 percent a year, while industrial production grew by a modest 4.1 percent. However, during the same period, sales of branches of U.S. firms in Argentina recorded an increase of no less than 24 percent (Laclau, 1970, 7)! The process of takeover was greatly accelerated during the Onganía regime. By 1968 U.S. investment in Argentina totaled $1,148 million. Economically, this process can be described as one of massive denationalization of capital. Socially, it meant the liquidation of small and middle industrialists—the final solution to the national-bourgeois problem. Technically, the new investments were characterized by a high organic composition of capital. The logic of their drive was to increase the weight of constant capital with respect to total capital; that is to say, the part of total capital made up by machines and raw materials, but not in wages, tended to increase with the new advances in mechanization. The upshot was a decline in the capacity of the industrial sector to absorb labor: the marginalization of the working class that had been integrated into the system during a phase of labor-intensive exploitation.

The success of governmental policy hinged on the ability to compress wages, marginalize the proletariat, force the national bourgeoisie to sell out, destroy the petit bourgeoisie, and produce on these ruins a renovated economic system controlled by multinational corporations. Since the capacity of the latter to create acceptable occupational levels in a society like Argentina is limited, the regime could not promote a cluster of interests sufficiently large to provide a social base for the further expansion of monopoly capital and for the invention of a new political formula. As it was, the military dictatorship saw a rapid narrowing of support and the growth instead of a formidable opposition combining formerly antagonistic sectors of society: an indignant middle class, radical students, a militant proletariat mobilized by the unions. Even the oligarchy showed signs of displeasure at the impact of the plans of the monopolistic military regime. In this way, militarism and monopoly expansion became the unwitting unifiers of groups that previous decades had kept separate. The democratic middle class, the old left, and the student movement had been traditionally estranged from the proletarian masses that began their political experience under the banner of national populism and outside the democratic and socialist traditions. The decade that followed Peronism prepared the ground for transcending those cleavages. The policies implemented after the restoration of 1955 made the anti-Peronist petit bourgeoisie as much a victim as the Peronist proletariat. Monopolization and denationalization brought these two classes closer together. The military dictatorship of 1966 created further conditions that facilitated their alliance.

Popular Revolt

When the military regime of Onganía thought that it was reaping the first fruits of its economic policies; when foreign investors began to have confidence in a dictatorship that promised to make Argentina tranquil for capital for decades to come, major urban insurrections broke out in Córdoba, Rosario, and other cities throughout the country that had worldwide repercussions owing to their unprecedented scale and character. The Argentine working class was fighting back. The main feature of these mass political struggles was the alliance of workers and students with disaffected sectors of the middle class. This was something entirely new in Argentina and entirely outside the framework of established practices: the accumulated response to economic hardship and political grievance.

Several factors help to account for the historical radicalization and convergence of the working class and the middle sectors. During the initial period of the restoration of 1955, the middle classes were still part—as they had been in 1945—of the reactionary front. So was the traditional left. Socialists and communists received a share of the spoils after the fall of Perón (mostly university and union posts) while the regime welcomed foreign capital and applied terror to Peronist militants of the working class. *Peronistas* had to work underground and managed to attain a new political consciousness and new skills during those years. On the other hand, the rapid monopolization of industry undermined the economic base of the petit bourgeoisie, which became radicalized. At the same time, unemployment and punitive policies made labor more militant. As bread-and-butter unionism failed to produce tangible results, workers were forced to resort to direct and more political forms of action. They thus began to develop an advanced class consciousness beyond immediate economic demands.

These developments took place more rapidly in the cities of the interior, especially Córdoba, where industrialization had taken place after the fall of Perón in the modern, foreign-owned automobile plants, and where the proletariat was less inhibited by past traditions of populist paternalism to assume a radical stance. The bourgeoisie of the interior, on the other hand, was weak, satellized, and dependent on Buenos Aires for maintaining social control. The students of provincial universities were concentrated in compact communities. Recent patterns of urban settlement produced a constant intermingling of students, workers, and the petit bourgeoisie. The latter was offended by the policies of the central government and more generally by the internal colonialism exercised by the capital city vis-à-vis the interior. Similar situations existed in Rosario, Tucumán, La Plata, and Mendoza. These cities, and the workers within them, became the vanguard of mass opposition to the regime of Oganía.

The radicalization of the middle sectors was unmistakable. With the overthrow of President Illia in 1966, they were prevented from following traditional parliamentary access to decision-making. The economic hardships, the military and police repression, the ideological example of the Cuban Revolution and other events in the outside world—in short, exclusion from power and economic benefits as well as ideological curiosity—provoked first splits, then realignments, among different political groupings of the middle classes. Socialists, communists, radicals, and social Christians began dissociating themselves from past attachments, developed new radical sympathies, and eventually took a step that for many of them represented genuine self-criticism: a rapprochement to Peronism.

New forms of struggle emerged in May 1969 during the popular uprisings in the interior—what came to be known as the *cordobazo*. The exhaustion of conventional forms of political expression, the indefinite postponement of a solution to the political crisis that had surfaced in 1966, the economic pinch, and the punitive arrogance of the military authorities led the people to experiment with new and violent forms of protest. Moderate, economically oriented labor leaders were rapidly losing power to more politicized cadres. Young workers seized their factories and took to the streets to fight the police and the troops. They were soon joined by students who had acquired new experience in clandestine activities as a result of the military occupation of the universities in 1966—Onganía's contribution to culture. Students joined workers at the barricades, and defended their own neighborhoods in different cities with snipers. The middle classes joined in a supportive capacity. For the first time in Argentine history a classical popular uprising took place, linking the force of the urban proletariat with the middle sectors, the students, and significant sectors of the clergy. To regain the cities, the government had to send in armored columns with air support. Only the unity of the army and the spontaneity, the very surprise, of the revolt prevented the episode from causing the revolutionary collapse of the state. Out of these events grew a new sense of power: the belief that the organized uprising of the masses would eventually defeat the apparatus of repression. The events of 1969 were the popular veto of the military's attempt to service the needs of dependent modernization at the expense of the community.

The sequence of events, the patterns of behavior, the mistakes of the rulers, and the outrage they provoked among the ruled seem to confirm that political wisdom of the classics. What today, in sanitized jargon, we term "authoritarian rule" was once called cruelty. Of such cruelty applied to government Machiavelli wrote that it could be properly used by a strong man when he resorted to it at one stroke out of a need for safety and did not thereafter insist upon it, but sought instead to replace it with measures that are of the greatest possible use to his subjects. Onganía rarely applied violent repression at the start, but resorted to it with increasing rather than decreasing frequency as time went by. Instead of improving his circumstances, he lost his power as a result.

The situation of the Onganía administration deteriorated. It soon found itself harassed by the liberal-oligarchic opposition, on the one hand, and by militant general strikes and guerrilla operations, on the other. It reacted with exasperation. A wave of political assassinations swept the country. The union leader Vandor was gunned down at the office of the Metalworkers Union. Former President Aramburu, leader of the liberal restoration of 1955, was kidnapped from his home and killed.

The Role of the Military

Modern, professional armed forces only grudgingly consent to be cast in a policeman's role. Yet that was their predictable fate under President Onganía, who, imbued with messianic zeal, demanded from them a renewal of tenure as an absolutist ruler. Instead of granting him such powers, the chiefs chose to improve their waning public image by changing both their style and the course of policy. On June 8, 1970, the top brass deposed Onganía in a palace revolution that lasted only a few hours. Gone with Onganía were also the arrogant poise and the ambitious plans of the Argentine Revolution. They were replaced by the more modest goal of sheer political survival. After a week of consultations, a little-known officer, General Roberto Marcelo Levingston, was called upon to occupy the vacant office of the presidency. The new president was given less discretion than his predecessor: The junta decided that henceforth every major decision by the executive should be cleared beforehand by the joint chiefs of staff, whose chairman was General Alejandro Lanusse.

The original priorities of the Argentine Revolution were reversed. An eventual return to some form of civilian rule was considered in order to accommodate and contain mounting social pressures; a different economic policy was tailored to that end. Financial orthodoxy and monetary stability were abandoned in favor of other measures carrying nationalistic overtones and designed to appease the middle sectors— the agrarian, commercial, and national industrial interests. The second economic minister of the new administration, Aldo Ferrer, was an economist of solid credentials who favored limiting the role of foreign capital and sustaining that of national public and private enterprise. Unfortunately for the regime, the changes he introduced failed to win it new sympathies. The sugar coating came too late and was too thin to cover the bitter heritage of Onganía. The new president was not an authoritative figure; the armed forces were divided; the population at large was diffident at best and often hostile. Instead of winning new allies, the regime lost the only solid backing it ever had, namely the endorsement of the banking and big-business community. If anything, the new policies fanned the fire of inflation. On the political front, the attempt on the part of the government to organize a viable official party with the aid of second-rank politicians and provincial notables flew in the face of more solid realities such as the presence of Peronism and the endurance of old party and union structures. Very rapidly, the Levingston administration found itself at the mercy of fresh disturbances. A new *cordobazo* rocked the country, putting an end to Levingston's experiments. On March 22, 1971, the president was compelled to resign. The joint chiefs assumed direct control of the government. Their chairman, General Lanusse, became president and retained command of the army.

General Lanusse was a man of larger vision and greater political skill than his immediate predecessors. He seemed well aware of the iron dilemma facing the regime. Bluntly, the options were either a negotiated political retreat or a brutal dictatorship entailing unfathomable consequences. Lanusse chose the former course and proposed to all parties a patriotic covenant that he called the "Great National Agreement," under which everyone would solemnly pledge to reinstall democracy while respecting the original concerns of the Argentine Revolution. Ideally, such an agreement would have confirmed Lanusse as president, this time as the elected head of a transition government. It was a daring proposal, but had two serious flaws: It demanded of each powerful group the sacrifice of tangible political benefits, and required of all a leap of faith. Lanusse offered a political alchemy that would supposedly turn a bureaucratic authoritarian regime into an experience of democratic reconciliation and proposed himself as the high priest that would enact the mystery of that transubstantiation. But the ingredients were intractable, the omens unpropitious. Perón refused to negotiate on Lanusse's terms; only parties without followers heartily endorsed Lanusse's proposal. Popular discontent had, by then, a life of its own. To make matters even worse, the economy showed signs of rapid decomposition: Inflation and unemployment broke past records; by 1973 the workers' share of national income was at an all-time low.

It was hard to expect a persistently regressive redistribution of wealth to endear the responsible authorities to the populace. It was equally difficult to pretend that six years of authoritarian dictatorship and military neglect of civil life could be erased and forgotten by cosmetic changes of personnel. The isolation of the military was not remedied by Lanusse's schemes. Sometimes separately and sometimes jointly, the middle and the working classes took to the streets to voice their discontent. In the absence of legitimate channels to convey dissent in orderly fashion, with public authority unaccountable and aloof, a pattern of politics by riot came into existence.

In those troubled waters, several organizations of professional sub-versives began to fish. Guerrilla groups of various and sundry hues tried to capitalize on protest and ride the wave of discontent. Some were Marxist, like the ERP (People's Revolutionary Army) organization. Some claimed allegiance to Peronism, like FAP (Peronist Armed Forces). Still others followed the late Che Guevara in both vision and tactics, like FAR (Revolutionary Armed Forces). One of the more effective groups appointed itself the armed guardian of the Peronist left, although its origins could be clearly traced to the Catholic far right. This group, the Montoneros, named after the irregular *gaucho* armies that once harassed the Spanish regulars in the north during the wars of independence, claimed responsibility for the kidnapping of former president General Aramburu. This event had taken place in the waning days of Onganía's administration, under circumstances which remain still obscure, and had a public impact as shocking as that of the kidnapping and assassination of Aldo Moro in Italy years later.

In the meantime, popular insurrections exploded in the Andean provinces of Mendoza, Río Negro, and Tucumán; rural workers formed militant leagues in the provinces of Chaco, Corrientes, Formosa, and Misiones; the crisis of the sugar industry made the cane fields of Tucumán a powder keg. Confronted and stung by many challenges, the armed forces resorted to the one response for which they were professionally ready: counterinsurgency. Their fellow Argentines, whom they had long considered disorderly and corrupt, at any rate incapable of self-rule, would be treated, from then on, as potential "internal enemies." A vicious spiral of repression and insurrection ensued. To the terror of guerrillas, to their holdups, kidnappings, occupations of public sites, and political executions, the armed forces responded with kidnappings of their own, the routine torture of suspects, and the physical elimination of opponents. Towards the end of 1971 a secret dirty war broke out, without respect for legal norms, without scruples, without restraints. In that secret war all the weight of past political errors, the weakness of moral bonds, and the brittleness of institutions were exposed. Two worlds of intolerance and cruelty were brought face to face, wearing the badges of "order" and "revolution," mirrors of each other, terror and counterterror heaving with rival convulsions, and with the double darkness of death and madness. It began as a private war but it soon invaded the public sphere, until nobody felt safe, despite the fact that the officers claimed that they wanted law and order, the guerrillas justice, and the population at large peace. In the end, the main beneficiary of those yearnings would not be President Lanusse but Juan Perón, in whose leadership everyone would finally posit their hopes.

8

The Return
of the Proscribed

Perón was indeed the man whose analyses of the Argentine situation were being confirmed by developments and whose long-range strategy was bearing its first fruits. For several years he had presented himself, from his Madrid exile, as an arbiter and peacemaker. He had taken both a hard and a soft line, played both the right and the left. On the one hand, and thanks to the mistakes of the military, who managed to unite former antagonists in a front against the regime, Perón succeeded in overcoming the old cleavage between Peronists and anti-Peronists and in neutralizing the anti-Peronism of the democratic parties. To Lanusse's rejected compact he proposed his own agreement, which he called "The Hour of the People" and which was basically conceived as an understanding between the Peronists and four other parties to request free elections and to respect their results. *Peronistas* and *radicales* reconciled their differences in a tactical alliance against the armed forces: the final political upshot of six years of military rule—not precisely a tribute to military statesmanship. The experience confirmed the suspicion of many observers that the Argentine military find it much easier to seize power than to hold it with competence and leave it with grace. So much so that, thousands of miles away, an aging exile could play with them as a cat plays with mice.

Perón did not limit himself to demanding, together with the *radicales*, a return to democratic politics. Playing a more dangerous game, not only did he refuse to disavow the claims of several guerrilla groups that acted in his name, but he used these groups, which he euphemistically called "special formations," as a means of putting relentless pressure on the military regime. The officers and the business elite were led to fear a convergence of spontaneous urban insurrections with the guerrilla organizations and with important sectors of the Peronist movement.

Such apprehensions led them to believe that only Perón himself could steer and contain those dangerous trends. Perón finally managed to confront the military with the following alternatives: Either they allowed free elections, which in all likelihood would place the Peronists back in power, or they braced themselves for a national insurrection, not just another *cordobazo* but a wholesale *argentinazo*.

While Perón offered himself to the parties and the military as the man who could spare the country the social upheaval they feared most, the Peronist guerrillas intended to provoke, through the return of Perón to Argentina, a revolutionary tidal wave. The question was thus posed that would ominously weigh over Argentine politics in the years to follow: Who would be using whom? Most of 1972 was spent in a duel between Generals Lanusse and Perón. Beneath rhetorical invective and mutual public attacks they both moved steadily, along parallel paths, toward the same ground. Perón would be allowed to return to Argentina but not to run as a candidate in the forthcoming elections. In return, the Peronist party would be free to campaign and to present other candidates to stand in for Perón. The French system of elections in two rounds was adopted. The armed forces won assurances that their return to the barracks would not be the occasion for blaming or humiliating them. A date was set for the first round of general elections—March 11, 1973. There would be no need for a second round, for on that date the Peronist-led coalition, the Frente Justicialista de Liberación Nacional (FREJULI)—an electoral coalition of twenty-five organizations dominated by Perón's Partido Justicialista and including the party of former president Frondizi—won the contest with 49.5 percent of the votes. Héctor J. Cámpora, the Peronist candidate, became president on May 25. *Peronistas* and *radicales*, the two traditional groups that the military regime had originally sought to tame, if not eliminate from the political map of Argentina, gathered 70 percent of the votes. Altogether 82 percent of the voters backed candidates hostile to the armed forces. The candidate endorsed by the latter obtained 2.9 percent of the votes. When, on May 25, the new president was inaugurated, General Lanusse had to transfer the attributes of power to Dr. Cámpora in the presence of Presidents Allende of Chile and Dorticós of Cuba. Popular celebrations, the parade of guerrillas in the streets, and the storming of the jails to free political prisoners added insult to injury. The long-feared popular hour of reckoning appeared imminent.

The FREJULI platform, which became the program of the new government, was one of "national reconstruction" based on a social pact agreed upon by small and medium-sized businesses, through their representative organizations, the CGE (General Confederation of Entrepreneurs), and the powerful General Confederation of Labor, CGT. The program rested on well-known developmentalist proposals. It sought to implement reforms without challenging basic property relations, and by no means met the objectives of the more radical sectors of the

Peronist movement. In accordance with the program, as soon as Cámpora became president prices were rolled back, wages were raised by 20 percent, some controls were imposed on foreign investment, and bank deposits were nationalized. Plans were also drafted to establish state monopolies for the export of meat and grain. In foreign policy some important symbolic changes took place, most notably the establishment of diplomatic and trade relations with Cuba and other countries of the socialist bloc.

More important than such measures, however, was the manner in which they were carried out and the mobilization that built up around them. President Cámpora relied on representatives of leftist groups within the Peronist movement to carry out the reforms, and he encouraged mass participation. Popular mobilizations became frequent and were used as leverage by the new administration, which freed political prisoners and destroyed police records. Cámpora installed a Marxist at the head of the University of Buenos Aires and placed the political activity of the armed forces under the surveillance of a Ministry of War accountable to the government. The top brass were forced into retirement. On the provincial level, several Peronist governors pursued essentially the same tactics and policies employed by Cámpora on the federal level. The governors of Buenos Aires, Córdoba, and Mendoza in particular also sponsored mass participation and supported the actions of the Peronist left, especially the Peronist Youth, a merger of several extremist groups within the Peronist movement with ties to the guerrillas.

Perón at the Helm

The strength of popular mobilization under Cámpora alarmed officers, landowners, businessmen, and many moderates in the middle class. It put Perón, still in Madrid, under pressure to deliver on his promise to pacify the nation, and put the rightist elements within his movement on alert. The old leader announced his return to Argentina, and the first episode in the counteroffensive against the left took place during the welcoming ceremonies at Ezeiza International Airport, near Buenos Aires, on June 20, 1973. According to some estimates, some 2 million people camped near the landing strip waiting for his plane, which would actually touch ground at an air force base near the city. The Peronist Youth and the guerrilla organizations were notoriously present at the expected landing site. Suddenly, a fierce gun battle broke out between them and the security forces, leaving scores of dead and wounded. The crisis that ensued forced President Cámpora's resignation and opened the way for a purge of the cabinet. On July 10 Perón met with the commander in chief of the army and was reinstated as an officer with the highest rank in the military institution. Three days later, Cámpora was replaced by provisional president Raúl Lastiri, speaker of the lower house. Key positions in the government were then filled with old-line bureaucrats and politicians in the Peronist movement. An internal coup had been successfully staged by the right. New elections were called for September 23, with Perón and his third wife, María Estela Martínez, known as Isabel, as candidates for president and vice-president respectively. The ticket won by a landslide (62 percent of the votes), and Perón returned to the Pink House, the government palace, as president on October 12.

The triumphant return of Perón to power took place in an atmosphere of violence. Left-wing Peronists were almost entirely swept from posts in the universities and from local, provincial, and federal levels of the administration. Guerrillas stepped up their attacks on right-wing Peronists. In return, militants were jailed, kidnapped, tortured, or simply shot on sight in the streets. Repressive legislation was enacted that reproduced the security provisions of previous military regimes. On the labor front, conservative Peronist union officials launched a red-baiting campaign.

The rightist counteroffensive peaked with the violent overthrow of the governor of Córdoba in March 1974. Ricardo Obregon Cano, and his lieutenant, Atilio López, who would be assassinated later, had been elected in the general elections of March 1973 and were identified with the left wing of the Peronist movement. A year later, while Perón was president and they were holding office, they were placed under arrest by the former chief of the provincial police whom they had dismissed a few days before. While the governor and lieutenant governor were detained, bands of armed vigilantes attempted to terrorize the city population of Córdoba during several days and nights. From Buenos Aires Perón backed not the constitutional authorities under siege but the insurgents and the right-wing outlaws. He then replaced the arrested officials with federally appointed substitutes. This rather sinister operation, worthy of Benito Mussolini in style and substance, revealed the readiness with which Perón could make use of extremists from the right to consolidate and increase his power, just as he had made use of extremists from the left to acquire it. Indeed, from 1970 through 1973, on his way to power, Perón referred to the Montonero guerrillas as "that marvelous youth that struggles against military dictatorship with weapons in their hands and who know how to give their lives for the Fatherland." As president, on May 1, 1974, Perón disowned them as "stupid, smooth-chinned and mercenary youths."

As always, Perón's political maneuvers stemmed from a military conception of things, in which democratic methods hold nothing sacred in themselves and are but one item in a vastly larger and less humane arsenal. On this score too Perón was a quintessentially modern Argentine, a symbol and a symptom of the profound political disarray that has afflicted the nation for fifty years at least. In more fortunate countries substantial, sometimes radical, social and economic changes have been brought about through relatively peaceful and orderly means. In more tragic lands, change has come through violence. Argentines have, for their part, time and again resorted to unscrupulous methods in pursuit of modest goals. The gap between the savage political form and the mild social content, between criminal means and conventional ends, gives us a measure of the normative disorder, the political anomie that has seized Argentina.

If the political style was violent and uncivilized, indeed fascistic, the social and economic program of the government was moderate and reformist, middle of the road. On the economic front, national entrepreneurs to whom Perón delegated policy proceeded to renegotiate the terms of dependency with multinational capital. Transnational companies sponsored the much-celebrated Argentine breakup of the economic blockade imposed by the United States on Cuba. The "anti-imperialist" crusade of the Peronist administration in fact allowed U.S. automobile companies to circumvent the blockade by exporting to Cuba trucks, tractors, and cars assembled by their Argentine branches.

In short, Perón's government embarked upon a program of social and economic reforms with rhetorical overtones of nationalism and anti-imperialism. The basic elements of that program were similar to what Peronism had offered in the forties and fifties. But their meaning and function in 1973 were bound to be quite different from what they had been in 1946. Peronism could no longer be the same coalition of immature classes in pursuit of the initial benefits of industrialization. It was infinitely more difficult to balance the intersecting interests of labor and of national and foreign capital at such a late date, to house them all in harmony under the same political roof. But those structural strains did not by themselves warrant the conclusion that all-out internecine war was inevitable. Other societies have either managed or transcended similar and worse "contradictions" without the political cannibalism, the terror, the futile bloodshed of Argentina. Social structures and political institutions are arrangements that work themselves out through time—the accretion of "moves" by many actors, the result of constraints but also of creative responses to challenges, the heirs of mistakes, the creatures of accident as much as the consequence of iron logic. It is in this realm of under- and over-determination that we must seek both the origins and the consequences of what is the central problem in modern Argentina, namely, the extension and persistence of unprincipled public action.

Crisis Behavior

Forty percent of the Argentine population belongs to the middle class. Ever since Aristotle, the middle class has been considered a source of stability and moderation in politics. Argentina, however, seems to be a blunt exception to that notion, a strong counterexample. It is therefore important to explore the cultural malaise that has seized middle-class society in the country since the fifties and that gave rise to extreme forms of crisis behavior during the past decade. Whereas in many contemporary societies the class struggle has been deflected and sublimated into a struggle for middle-class status, in Argentina the visible recrudescence of class struggle has been in fact and to a large extent the result of heightened conflict within the middle class, a conflict that has pitted fraction against fraction of that class, generation against generation. The political episodes of the seventies bring to mind Turgenev more than Marx.

In 1973 the Argentines, given a chance to express their views freely after a long period of political proscription, chicanery, and dictatorship, opted for the wholesale rejection of that checkered pattern and placed their hopes once again in old Perón. As the political balance of an era of aborted projects and Paretian alternations between the lions and the foxes, the results of the 1973 elections were resounding, conclusive. That near plebiscite also discharged on the political arena a torrent of frustrations accumulated over the erratic and dammed-up course followed by the country since 1955.

A new group entered the scene at that precise point—the radical youth movement that had taken shape during the years preceding 1973 and whose irruption on stage set the tone of the second Peronist era. Looking back at the forces rallied around the Peronist banner in 1973 we find more than merely his traditional supporters, i.e., the working class and more generally the masses. Behind the impressive electoral victory of the Peronists stood also large contingents of middle-class sectors that had abandoned their former political loyalties to gather around Perón's return to power.

I will dwell here on this transfer of middle-class allegiance in favor of Peronism. The shift was highlighted by the role played by the Peronist Youth in the years preceding the political triumph of 1973. Recruited among university and high-school students, the Peronist Youth placed its hopes for political renewal in the leadership of Perón, thus making a complete about-turn from what had been the traditional political views of the sectors of society to which they belonged. The magnitude of this change appears clearly once we recall that the majority of middle-class Argentina was against Perón in 1955 and that at that time university students were the vanguard of a civilian opposition that contributed to the overthrow of the populist regime. We could say, roughly, that the children of those who had opposed Perón now turned their backs on their parents and embraced the very cause that the latter once resisted. Thus, whereas for the lower classes the return of Peronism signified the vindication of old political convictions, for the young newcomers to the movement it gave support to a gesture of political parricide. One does not need to belabor the importance of this last drama that enveloped Argentina in a wave of violence for which it was hardly prepared. The survival of Peronism among the laboring classes is understandable in the light of the social and political history of Argentina. In the forties Peronism presided over the incorporation of the workers into the political system and promoted their socioeconomic advance. As is usually the case with the formation of new social movements, that early and crucial collective experience left its imprint in the collective memory and therefore in the political consciousness of the Argentine working class. It was truly the birthmark of that class. Despite their repeated attempts at coercion and/or co-optation, the regimes—civilian and military—that succeeded Perón's could not erase that primary political loyalty. In fact, the policies pursued by those regimes over the course of eighteen years served to confirm that loyalty. But how can we account for the new youth movement that arose from the core of that reputedly cautious 40 percent of the population, the heart of middle-class Argentina, spread like brush fire, and progressively broke all ties with established political practices? What are the sources of that abstract and violent consciousness?

Perhaps the best way to tackle the question is to take a few steps back and trace the roots of this unprecedented break. A glance over the sociological map suggests that this violent form of radicalization appears in countries that, for quite dissimilar reasons, have experienced uncontrolled social development, with ensuing disequilibrium in the mechanisms of government. It is possible to attribute this deregulation to a general decline in socioeconomic rationality (exacerbated in dependent societies) in the West. In any event, for the specific case of Argentina a historical, retrospective glance may be an antidote to perplexity and disquiet, and especially to the simple exorcism of subversion through which people abdicate both understanding and responsibility.

Many have seen the emergence of radicalized youth in Argentine politics as a hurricane coming through the window of a peaceful home. The anger expressed by the youth and their abstract consciousness has been treated as a sort of *deus ex machina*. Yet despite such facile interpretations, we cannot deny that the attitudes and proposals displayed by the Peronist Youth were intimately linked to the avatars of Argentine development over a long span of time. Going back to the fifties (roughly the decade when this youth was born), we observe that Argentina was then undergoing a new wave of modernization affecting many institutions—among them education and the family—and resulting in the transformation of the cultural climate of the country. From 1943 to 1955, during the first Peronist era, Argentina had lived a culturally cloistered life. The Peronist regime had sponsored a return to the "autochthonous" and had spurned the "cosmopolitanism" that had accompanied previous periods of growth. Peronism had extended the social, economic, and political rights of citizenship to a relatively recent proletariat and to other popular strata of the population, but the mechanism of cultural diffusion had tended to bypass the educational institutions and to be lodged in the unions and the welfare apparatus of the state. In many instances, there had been severe tensions between the new mechanisms of redistribution instituted by the authoritarian welfare state and the citadels of knowledge in which the middle classes had already entrenched themselves. This situation had divorced the intellectuals from the masses (Corradi, 1979).

The demise of Perón's regime opened the gates to contemporary trends and fashions. The middle class eagerly embraced cultural practices and products that for long years they had been allowed to taste surreptitiously at best. The intellectuals who had been displaced by the Peronist regime devoted their efforts to updating the circuits of production and consumption of knowledge, in an attempt sometimes to imitate, sometimes to catch up with international standards of proficiency. Their project of cultural renewal coincided with the modernizing impulse promoted by such administrations as Frondizi's government, and which, as we have seen already, came to be known under the label of *desarrollismo*.

The wish to modernize culture seized the university milieu and from there radiated to the wider world of the middle class. Literature and the arts received a new boost, while entirely new modes of inquiry and expression were explored and then rapidly diffused. Psychoanalysis, not exempt from an aura of chic voodooism, signified best the experience of these groups—as a novel curiosity, as a symbol of change, and as an attempt to come to terms with the consequences of that change. After Los Angeles and New York, Buenos Aires was the city most addicted to the adventures of the couch in the Western Hemisphere. To grow up in such a climate meant, for the middle-class child of the fifties and sixties, to receive more fully the brunt of the new cultural trends, to face a wider set of choices, but also a more uncertain future, than any of his or her forebears. What needs to be added is that, like so many currents of reform in the Argentine past, the modernization that led this new generation into uncharted territory failed to encompass the whole society. Old traditions may have suffered serious setbacks, but they managed to survive, mixed with the new as oil mixes with water. Survivors and newcomers were thrown together in haste, geared for the dramatic confrontations and misunderstandings that would rock the country later on.

A second process to be noted that took place in the late fifties was the *disarticulation of political language* at the very heights of power. The political elites that at that time put forward the idea of development found the formulas inherited from the past largely unusable. It was thus in the register of official discourse that the political effects of modernization were first inscribed. Old words received new meanings; terms belonging to disparate universes of discourse were transposed and combined; former antinomies were wedded and welded. A bizarre discursive *bricolage* accompanied a no less daring act of political combinations—an art in which President Frondizi excelled and for which he came, eventually, to be almost universally distrusted. For the *desarrollista* elites, "liberation" was no longer incompatible with "dependency."

Frondizi—who once wrote a nationalist tract on oil policy—felt free to announce that, in order to rid the country of the tutelage of imperialist Big Brother, he would grant generous concessions to several of the Big Sisters. Small wonder then that this perverse dialectic would later find a fateful echo among those who would advocate violence as a means of attaining peace—*si vis pacem para bellum*. Such stretching exercises in political discourse puzzled an older generation of Argentines accustomed to hear the familiar sounds of separate ideologies. Frondizi, and others like him, introduced a new tension in the prevailing political style—a fundamental dissonance in the context of old cadences. Best intentions notwithstanding, neither he nor those who succeeded him in power provided a resolution, a satisfying synthesis of that conglomerate. Far from it: Political discourse in Argentina moved toward a dangerous freedom from all consonance, from the obligation to resolve the dissonance. Eventually almost any combination of notes was admitted, and the country moved farther and farther away from the possibility of releasing tension in rational ways. From this refusal of resolution came— ten years after Frondizi—the aptness of the discourse and style of the radicalized youth from the middle class for the enactment of anguish and the macabre, as in the example of General Aramburu's kidnapping, execution, and in the further kidnapping of his corpse.

The precipitating factors just reviewed should be placed in the larger context of Argentine global society, characterized by the weakness of social loyalties on the one hand, and by a protracted institutional crisis on the other. In words that others may find more familiar and congenial, this process can also be described as the inability of any social class to gain ideological hegemony over the entire society, and thus to assure its own legitimacy in the running of the affairs of state. These two features tend to reinforce each other and result in a vicious circle. Suffice it to say here that the rapid, inorganic development of Argentina has put side by side groups that failed to speak the same political idiom or include others in their own universe of discourse. Given such dissonance of political voices, a heavy premium has been placed on the distribution of resources, while social stability rests on the performance of institutions, on the reiteration of multiple payoffs; in short, on the fragile capacity to "deliver the goods." Where hegemonic values cannot cement the social order, only the perspective of a simultaneous satisfaction of concrete interests keeps the whole together.

It was precisely this capacity of institutions to satisfy a varied set of interests that began to falter after 1955, and in the following eighteen years the process eroded the credibility of those institutions as places wherein to pursue meaningful lives, as platforms from which to have an input in national life. From the days of Frondizi through the years of Onganía to the return of Perón, political disorder and economic crisis played havoc with the demands of a new generation and its pursuit of self-realization. The elders reacted to the general malaise by retreating to known and worn strategies of survival, to old political reflexes, to the narrow defense of acquired positions. They could afford to wait and see, or believed they could afford it.

But what rational strategies, what reflexes could the middle-class youth fall back on? Only the leap forward into the abyss became available to many of them. Repeated frustrations bred in them contempt for what society had to offer. In that situation they began blending the ingredients with which they would concoct a radical utopia. Whence the mythological treatment to which they subjected Peronist ideology at the very moment when the established political groups, including traditional Peronists, sought a form of conciliation. No such fallback or pragmatic accommodation was acceptable to the young. Cut from the past, greatly detached from both acquired interests and established values, the new generation refused all existing political proposals. To such plans they opposed their own radical design—one that scarcely took into account the actual composition of political forces. They formulated their great refusal in a language that sought to recreate and echo the tone of earlier, allegedly heroic, epochs of Peronism. They invoked the ghost of Evita as a champion of the uprooted and the excluded, and revived the figure of her old noble *descamisado*. The middle-class youth's retreat to a mythical past served as a symbolic shield against the prevailing climate of compromise that existed among other sectors of society. Distant evocations sought to preserve conflict in the face of a present that marched, haphazardly but visibly, toward the resolution of former discrepancies. The radical theme thus became "the revolution betrayed." While Peronists saw the possibility of obtaining historic reparation, the Peronist Youth perceived in that a loss of nerve that had to be ruthlessly combated. Whilst the organized working class was being accepted again as part of the political system and given a place in it after eighteen years of proscription, the young preached revolution in the name of the outcasts. To conciliation they opposed rupture; to accommodation, a struggle without concessions; to the disorderly and pragmatic, even messy, present, a purified and redeeming past. Such language ultimately exploded the rationality of political discourse, fixed its fragments in mythical essences, and redistributed the pieces in unbridgeable dichotomies until violence became the predominant communication strategy. The middle-class youth thus built an armed utopia with which it burst into the political arena, stunning the once-confident society that had nurtured it.

Argentine society found itself without any political answer to meet the challenge. Puzzled, unable to respond, politicians and intellectuals took a step back to watch in despair the invasion of the main stage by those whose only way to face the insurgent youth was retribution, whose only language was counterviolence. Fascism showed its horrible countenance and finally stole the show. Living through this drama has been an additional hardship for an already exhausted country. This may explain why those who visited Argentina during those years searching for visible signs of agony, or for the ferment of resistance, were often struck instead by a widespread wish to forget, by a passion for ignorance among large sectors of the population. The acquiescence—and sometimes even the outright support for abuses and outrages—among so many was connected to an immediate past that was perceived as wounding, chaotic, and unredeemed.

Governance

With the return of the military to the barracks after the formidable victory of the electoral front led by Perón in 1973, Argentines felt for a while that they might have reencountered their true political destiny. The wide consensus that developed called for leaving behind past apprehensions and recent animosities. It crystallized in a formula for political coexistence that seemed to fit the image enjoyed by the country among its Latin American neighbors—that of a nation socially democratic which should be, in consequence, politically articulate. On the one hand, *peronistas* and *radicales*, the two great national political groups, fraternized in parliament; on the other, unions and entrepreneurs rallied around a concerted incomes policy.

Backed by the indisputable electoral majority and holding the banner of coexistence, the old leader reentered the country. Thus culminated a long struggle that he had been waging since 1955 against those who now had to step aside and leave the path to power open to him. But if this Perón whom Argentines received after a long absence seemed capable of synthesizing his shifts in strategy and seemed able to redefine, from his new exalted position, policies that he had advocated from the opposition, could the same flexibility be expected from his own movement? That movement had grown over the course of eighteen years as a contesting force that was hardly committed to a political order that had persistently curtailed its participation. How then was Perón to impress the necessity of political agreement upon those in whom repeated proscriptions had instilled an acute sense of difference? How to persuade those who had seen the relentless diminution of their share of income distribution that it was prudent to make the demands of labor compatible with the general stability of the economy? Finally, how to wrest a commitment to peace from those whose violence Perón had previously endorsed?

The vast popular movement that the return of Perón convoked could barely hide a temptation for intransigence, the thrust of accumulated dissatisfactions, behind its proclaimed loyalty to the leader. In fact, the old *caudillo*'s calls for conciliation found a more favorable reception among his adversaries than among his followers. The former saw Perón's message as a promise of political order, while the latter preferred instead to listen to their own claims for political reparation. The political enterprise inaugurated in 1973 thus encountered its first serious obstacle in the breach between the spirit of conviviality animating the return of Perón and the mood behind the popular mobilization that carried him back to the government. In order to bridge that gap Perón would invest all the reserves of his charisma, which the distance of exile had preserved intact, shielded from the deterioration that by 1973 compromised the prospects of institutions. This reference to the state of the political system also throws light on another obstacle confronting the political design with which the old leader came back to the political scene.

The decision to open up the political game, taken by the military in 1972 after arduous negotiations with Perón, who was then in Madrid, sought to forswear the menace that emerging forces and conflicts in civil society might overflow the traditional brim of politics. The wave of regional rebellions that followed the *cordobazo* of 1969, the outbreak of multiple wildcat strikes in factories, and the spread of urban and rural guerrilla activities were developments that favored, within the armed forces, the ascendancy of officers like Lanusse, who counseled the importance of an urgent political way out. Thus, political institutions were suddenly convened to discipline the social struggle. But they had to be taken out of the closets where they had been kept in disrepair. The summons found those institutions with their structures in disarray, questionable and unrepresentative. The political parties and the trade unions that the Lanusse administration first rehabilitated, and that Perón subsequently invested with new prestige under his proposal for an "integrated democracy," had not withstood undamaged the onslaught of interdiction and punishment meted out under the authoritarian rule of General Onganía, from 1966 through 1970. Now that they left their forced passivity in order to sit at the table of negotiations, could they hope to retrieve the formidable portion of social power that, ever since the *cordobazo*, had been accumulating by their side and which remained in the periphery of institutions as a political residue intractable to compromise? Such was the ominous question hanging over political institutions, threatening the prospects of the political project that sought precisely to grow and consolidate itself around them.

For the enterprise to succeed Perón had, on the one hand, to channel the diffuse and virulent expectations of his followers and, on the other, to rebuild the battered political system. A curious paradox of history became apparent: He who once had been identified with one half of the country now came to be everything to everybody. The same man who had applied his remarkable skills to sabotage many a government from abroad was now called to the rescue of a drifting polity. At stake in 1973 was the very governability of the country. To this endeavor Perón devoted his remaining energies. The scene of Perón's last battle, symbolic of Argentine politics as a whole, would not be filled with the familiar cast of characters of yesteryear. He did not find himself leading a popular movement against established society. After the collapse of the *Gran Acuerdo Nacional* launched by General Lanusse, and with the Peronist triumph at the polls, the military and economic elites were in full political retreat. Thus, instead of confronting a strong social opposition, the populist veteran faced the harder task of taming the furies unleashed by eighteen years of discord.

Bearing in mind this last observation, Perón's return to the presidency and the retreat of his opponents have been interpreted as parts of a strategy, as cunning maneuvers on the part of the military, who presumably would wait in the wings for Perón's efforts to fail in order to step in again and end once and for all his political ascendancy. This conspiratorial hypothesis was no more than a rationalization introduced after the resounding defeat of 1973. In spite of its seeming confirmation by the events of 1976, it remains an argument of the type *post hoc, ergo propter hoc*. In actual fact, as we have seen already, in 1973 everybody placed their bets: The military regime sought to negotiate its own succession, and Perón offered himself as an alternative. Profiting from the armed forces' lack of political credibility after almost six years of an erratic exercise of power, and displaying his own political talent, Perón won the match, isolating his rivals and forcing them to grant elections unburdened by onerous conditions. Besides, an additional argument against the conspiratorial hypothesis is that the transfer of power to Perón created a situation so unforeseeable that it is hard to imagine a strategy that could count upon such risks. One may know how to start a war, but one can rarely control its upshot. It was precisely with this uncertainty about the future in mind that the military handed power over to the man that they had fought for so long, and left the scene.

The weakness of the outgoing regime was not supplanted by the strength of the incoming government. The skills applied by Perón to disband his adversaries proved insufficient to build a viable political alternative. The populist leader could not dissociate himself from the network of social and political arrangements that he had promoted. Everything rested on his shoulders to the point where he became, old and ailing, a system of politics by himself. Every group came to define its own position in terms of its relative access to the presumed will of the leader, and to couch its designs in terms of his political discourse. When a political system that transcribed social relations is substituted by a personalized system of politics, when society is expropriated, as it were, by politics and politics is embodied in one man, then social actors enter a symbolic universe characterized by the absolute and bizarre primacy of interpretation. This situation gave rise to the queer atmosphere of "political hermeneutics" that enveloped Argentina during much of this period. Every act of the leader carried a fateful meaning; every one of his utterances had to be deciphered. Driven to interpret, struggling over the words of the supreme Argentine oracle, every group in post-1973 Argentina strove to relate its actions to the expression of the subtle, shifting will of Perón. The compulsion to make their positions appear as manifestations of Perón's own was so deeply engrained that when the latter sought to repudiate the most extreme interpretations of his statements—notably those of the radicalized youth, those who were repudiated countered with the argument that the aging leader was surrounded and misled by a gang of evil advisers.

As Perón's politics became all inclusive, incorporating antagonistic forces into their fold, social conflict became entangled in struggles over the appropriation of his discourse. Side by side, traditional and new social oppositions complicated and confused the terms of political understanding. The fight against Perón's entourage—particularly against his sinister secretary and minister of social welfare, López Rega—was put on the same level as the opposition against big business; the war against the dissident youth was carried out with as much zeal as the effort to demobilize the masses. Thus, on the left and on the right priorities were perverted. Political life came to resemble a large, increasingly nervous Venetian carnival in which the masks, though hiding deep antagonisms, oddly resembled one another, for they were all patterned after the effigy of Perón. Political transvestism became the norm of public behavior. Propelled by the state of mobilization that embraced the entire country and fueled by the taste for violence cultivated within the Peronist movement, the social conflicts and the political struggles largely exceeded Perón's capacity to steer and contain them. They seized his language and stretched it to unimaginable extremes of disparate interpretation; they put his leadership to a severe test by blocking his decisions, and everything was done in his name, with his words. On June 12, 1974, one month before his death, Perón went for the last time to the scene of his past triumphs, the balcony of the Casa Rosada, and threatened to resign, in an effort to regain the political initiative over a society that had slipped away from his command.

With Perón's death, in July 1974, Argentina accelerated its pace towards political devastation. The countdown had begun, and nothing would stop deterioration. Perón had been unable to imbue political institutions with a life of their own. Instead, he had held the country together by virtue of his old charisma. But charisma cannot be transferred. Missing a core, even a fictitious point of reference, the precarious institutional arrangements collapsed like a house of cards. Brutally decentered, Argentina plunged into chaos. Whereas Perón had tried to be alert and responsive to pressures from below, his widow and successor, Isabel, and her entourage busied themselves with secret conspiracies and arcane intrigues. Isabel's close circle became remote from a political society that had, in turn, lost all regulation. The entrepreneurs' search for profits degenerated into an economy of sacking and plunder; the trade unions responded by pushing for enormous demands; and the devious manipulations of the presidential clique gave a tone of unreality to political life (Valenzuela, 1983). While existing social compacts and political understandings were blown to smithereens, people themselves also began to be blown up with depressing regularity. But despite the increase in violence, conflict did not result in an open civil war. The efforts of the contending groups—extremists of the right and of the left—to involve large sectors of the population in their crusades to redeem others against their will did not have the success expected by their promoters. Against a background of sordid struggles between armed camps, the established social groups preferred to continue their own bickering, trying to save their skins in the face of impending doom. The eleventh-hour attempts to find a way out failed because of the Peronists' sectarianism and because of the civil retreat of the *radicales* and other political parties. In the end, with the painful sight of wasted hopes before their eyes, there was nothing left for the majority of Argentines but to wait for the return of the military.

The Conundrum

It should be clear from the narrative in this book that Argentina has been built like a palimpsest of half-concluded projects. The country has lurched forward and then stopped, many times; its advances in time have been spasmodic. Each movement forward seems condemned sooner or later to recall. The social and political history of the country is marked by the recurrence of movements of restoration, and by inconclusive revolutions of all sorts. Such ups and downs are the counterpart of a society in which change has not taken place through the progressive incorporation of new actors and practices within an ongoing socioeconomic order. As in many other Latin American societies, here too the process of change entailed both the maintenance of old sectors and the creation of new ones. With the end of the prosperous society based on agrarian exports, a new industrial structure grew, and when it faltered in turn, modern enclaves of growth developed around transnational investments. As with the accretion of strata in the history of a geological formation, none of these societal forms managed to displace the others entirely. The old and the new remained juxtaposed in odd coexistence.

Neither this pattern of change by accretion nor the resulting fragmented, disarticulated society is a feature unique to Argentina (Touraine, 1976). It is a pattern constitutive of dependent social structures. The peculiarity of Argentina lies rather in the fact that each of the successive societal forms was able to give rise to a dense network of interests and to a deeply entrenched mode of life that vigorously persisted in obsolescent ways past its apogee. During the prosperity enjoyed by Argentina under the agrarian order, a dynamic urban society flourished that housed the most advanced middle sectors in Latin America at the time. Literacy attained levels hitherto unknown in the region, while secular modes of association went hand in hand with liberal ideas, shaping city and nation until World War II. The industrial development that started in the thirties opened the path for a new social actor—a powerful labor movement, the strength of which derived from the absence of large labor reserves and from the protection of the state. Unionization was fast and thorough, and the Argentine working class attained a level of sociological maturity comparable to that of advanced industrial societies (Goldthorpe, 1978; Torre, 1980). The evolution of organized labor provoked a dramatic extension of political participation, and from then on, the presence of the working class in politics could never again be dismissed. The productive and technological modernization that took place since the fifties remained encapsulated in industrial poles and lacked the extensive social impact of the previous waves of change. Nevertheless, it too contributed to the formation of a managerial elite wedded to foreign capital and carrying a decisive weight in national economic policies. Efficiency and growth became the catchwords of this sector as it sought in turn to steer the process of social change.

The social history of Argentina has thus resulted in a mosaic of groups juxtaposed in an uneasy, crowded collection. Each sector of society forms a strong cluster of interests and is firmly anchored in a set of institutions. Because each of these sectors is highly mobilized, each can defend its particular interests in an articulate manner against the others. The landed upper class both shaped and occupied a series of public and private strongholds from which it increased its wealth and exercised its influence. The middle classes used the educational institutions and the professions to lodge themselves as high as they could in the social hierarchy and in the apparatus of the public administration. Workers defended their wages and their rights through the formation of strong unions. Monopoly capital found its own bulwarks, with internal and external linkages. All busily promote their own projects, peddle their own wares, speak their own language. But no vision arises that proves large enough to reach out to the others, or sedimented enough to seek hegemony. The center remains forever elusive; no one finds a common ground.

In this volatile, active, articulate society, alliances, like fireworks, are as varied and colorful as they are ephemeral. Political fragility becomes the counterpart of all the hustle and bustle of an activist society. There are too many landlords for too many workers, too many shopkeepers for too many businessmen—the excess resulting from the fact that each and every actor is deeply entrenched and can be rapidly mobilized. To an observer, this sort of negative pluralism poses a fundamental problem of societal coexistence, a Hobbesian conundrum of order, a puzzle of passions that seek but cannot find an adequate political solution. Expectations are periodically directed toward the state to bring remedy and repair, to establish order and to unify a fragmented general will— to forge, in short, a single system from the disparate groups. Yet contrary to such expectations, state power does not seem to grow in Argentina at the expense of the competing institutions. Time and again the state does rise above the turmoil of civil society and seeks to assume the agency of this erratic historicity. But each time it seems to falter, to rapidly lose force, and then succumb to the tug-of-war between actors that cannot themselves rise to the level of social movements and that remain, strictly speaking, mere pressure groups. Thus no power appears that is great enough to unify the whole society. Too weak to lead, each group is still strong enough to prevent any other from doing so. Hence, though once intellectually brilliant and culturally creative, more emancipated than many other societies from the trammels of traditional authority, Argentina nonetheless easily falls prey to political decay. The state tends to rapidly lose whatever autonomy it may have attained vis-à-vis civil society and to become instrumentalized, not by a ruling class, as Marxists sometimes believe, but by a larger plurality of narrow groups. Things then return to where they started, namely, to the erratic behavior of a malfunctioning political system.

A political system that malfunctions is one that functions purely as a market. For political institutions to work best, they must be neither the simple translation of social interests nor a totally autonomous sphere. Between these two extremes, a political system is that space where negotiations can take place, where political succession is defined by rules, where change is institutionalized. To be viable such system requires a common framework of discussion—something more than a motley assortment of cogs and pulleys that each group manipulates for its own profit and pleasure—something more than a system of spoils. But what the state has been unable to guarantee from above, civil society in Argentina has been incapable of supplying from below. Instead of generally accepted rules we find mere drives; in lieu of political transactions we find a crazy quilt of deals. A tendency develops to exaggerate the importance of the political game for its own sake and to minimize the purposes for which the game is ultimately played—to lose sight of the larger societal stakes. Whenever the state formulates something resembling a national project, it meets derision. In a situation in which everybody knows too well what he or she wants and appears capable of the shrewdest insight into the intricacies of the opponent, the most pathetic of all actors is the one who ventures a general project for the nation. Where there is no largeness of aim, no breadth of political conception, only partial answers to blockage and reciprocal vetoes occupy center stage. Just as each group rushes to defend its particular interests and to prevent competing moves on the part of its adversaries, so each group clothes its demands in an autonomous discourse.

What results is not a debate, let alone an articulate class conflict, but a dissonance of independent notes played together or in haphazard sequence, as in Fellini's film *Orchestra Rehearsal*. The landed oligarchy—and to a large extent the middle classes—speak the language of order and propriety; the workers, the language of participation; the industrialists and technocrats, the language of efficiency and growth. The loudness of the parts only increases the cacophony of the whole. The society then does not make sense to itself and cannot interpret its position in the concert of nations and in its time. Viewed from the outside, Argentine society does not seem to find a sure—and certainly not a decent—place within a changing international order, the illusions of leaders and critics notwithstanding. Uncertain of itself, it drifts, it slides, it is pushed further to the margins. From within, it behaves spasmodically and seems to lack focus, not because there is a vacuum of power but because power is everywhere dispersed in explosive *quanta* throughout the social body.

Argentina puzzles to the point of exasperation those who expect a country seemingly modern and urbane to house a free, self-governing citizenry. It also disappoints those who, *faute de mieux*, believe that a modern, "efficient" form of despotism may bring remedy to disunion and license. Finally, it also frustrates those who would like to see a truly revolutionary alternative emerging, with lines of consciousness and organization clearly drawn. But no democracy ever appears, only disorder; no solid authoritarian state, but mere military regimes haunted by their lack of legitimacy and fearing retribution for their crimes; no revolutionary situation, but terrorism. A society that was once full of promise and is still young in age has entered a fateful spiral of decay that sometimes seizes much older nations. But in the latter, the strength of traditions, the respect for weathered and tested institutions, and the commonality of beliefs make decadence supportable and sometimes even genteel. For Argentina, decadence is hell. Without the appropriate moral, if not natural, resources to muddle through in an unsteady world, lacking the habits of conviviality on which to fall back and repose, the country declines frenetically, in ugly ways, tormented by the image of a past for whose disappearance no consolation seems possible. This vocation for nostalgia received a severe blow with Perón's death, the subsequent debacle, and the resulting punishment. The coming years will show if the Argentines are ready to face the challenge of looking toward the future, and not just to the past, when dealing with the anxieties of the present. Modern Argentina was born, as we have seen, in 1880. It looks old and exhausted today, and it is sinking fast past the centennial. It remains to be seen whether it will renew itself or stay instead mesmerized *in articulo mortis*. But our task is not finished yet, and what remains is most unpleasant, namely, to review and to analyze the events that have taken place in Argentina since 1976. It is a chronicle of sorrow and pity.

9

The Cult of Fear

But it has gone 7 in Argentina much longer, no?

"Fear," confessed Hobbes, "has been the one passion of my life." When they emerged from their self-inflicted holocaust, many Argentines uttered the same words. In foregoing pages I have reviewed the long phase of social and political instability that has beset Argentina since 1930. It is a phase of fragmented, discontinuous modernization. Economic, political, social, and intellectual movements that elsewhere have made their way by gradual stages and small increments of growth have been, in the Argentina of the last fifty years, in simultaneous ferment. Nationalism; the extension of social and political participation, first to the middle class and then to the workers; the onset of the industrial revolution, with the criticisms and aspirations that are its natural accompaniments; the partial dissolution of older habits and traditions—all these, and much else, have been crowded into the space of an individual's lifetime. The forces, as always, interact; the result has not been happy. No stable, satisfactory political formula has emerged from that checkered history. Fragile democratic experiments have been rhythmically superseded by authoritarian adventures that have not proven durable either. Institutional crises, crises of legitimacy, crises of participation, crises of distribution, de facto governments, an internal state of conflict bordering on war, states of siege and martial law, attempts at totalitarian or joint rule, experiments in corporatism, the enactment of repressive legislation, and particularly during the last decade, a steady crescendo of violence, terrorism of the left and of the right, and terror condoned or practiced by the government have been detrimental not only to democratic values and to the rule of law, but to the very existence of the state as well. From this pattern many actors and observers alike expected a regime to emerge that would finally possess a monopoly of coercive power, as an almost ineluctable response to the prolonged war of all against all. They thought that the new military regime established after the coup of March 24, 1976, against the government of Isabel Perón would accomplish that task. The military rulers believed so too.

The new president, General Jorge Rafael Videla, and his colleagues proclaimed that their objective was not merely to terminate the untenable disorder of the Peronist years, but to transform the very basis of Argentine society. The junta vowed to abolish terrorism, to revitalize the economy by freeing it from the trammels of state guidance, and to cut the Gordian knot of stalemated social conflict. To undo, in short, what had been built shoddily over the course of half a century. The vision was immodestly baptized a "Process of National Reorganization," echoing that other, founding process of national organization drafted by the political generation of 1837 and carried out by that of 1880.

Five years later, in March 1981, General Videla finished his mandate and conveyed power to a new president-select, General Roberto Eduardo Viola. Terrorism was abolished, but terror became part of the art of governing. The economy was not revitalized: It nearly went bankrupt. The different sectors of society started to protest again. If Argentina had changed, it was only in the sense of wholesale diminution: It had a smaller industrial base, a smaller working class, and a weaker middle class than before. Over the years, 2 million Argentines—including many of the better trained—had sought refuge abroad. Would general impoverishment and permanent dictatorship be the price of escaping the old political vicious circle? The administration of General Viola vacillated before that question, making gestures of détente toward the opposition, as if conscious of the need to start a gradual return to civilian democracy. But Viola's period of rule was to prove too short for that. Personal and military rivalries aside, this equivocation was probably the reason why Viola was forced to resign and was replaced by General Leopoldo Fortunato Galtieri, the army commander.

New winds blew from Washington that fanned different ambitions. Ronald Reagan was now president, and authoritarian Argentina was no longer the pariah it had been under Jimmy Carter. Reagan invited the Argentine generals to Washington to open up a new era of warm relations between the two nations. The man who seized the opportunity was Galtieri, not Viola. He visited the United States twice in 1981. He was wined and dined by the top echelons of the new U.S. administration: the secretary of defense, the White House national security advisor, the army chief of staff, the U.S. ambassador to the UN, and the assistant secretary of state for Latin America. He was called a "majestic figure," and someone likened him to Patton. Dazzled by the conservative euphoria, Galtieri saw himself as "the pampered child" of the United States and Argentina as a power in the hemisphere, with new roles to play in places like Central America, where the Argentine officers hoped to extend the dirty war they had waged against their own citizens a few years before. This new friendship between Buenos Aires and Washington was to have a decisive effect in shaping the Falklands/ Malvinas crisis of 1982 and therefore, indirectly, in producing the demise of the military regime itself. What was the style of rule that received the belated blessings of the queer convocation—the theologians of conservatism—in charge of the U.S. government?

Metaphors of Punishment

An important restructuring of power took place in Argentina in 1976, accompanied by significant changes in ideology. Both processes will be considered in this chapter. "Power" will be used in the conventional sense employed throughout this book of "political" or "state" power. What I have to say is concerned primarily with the acquisition and maintenance of centralized power and authority over the entire society. Nevertheless, many of my observations also apply to, or have consequences for, the exercise of domination in small-scale and day-to-day settings. Argentina in 1976 was a specially complex case in which internal decay produced a movement for the forced reintegration of society around new or partially new patterns of behavior. This reintegration can be studied also as a redefinition of the terms of meaning available to social actors, that is, in a broad sense, as an "ideological" process.

The military and civilian elites that seized power in 1976 had a draconian definition of the situation, rich in medical imagery: "diagnosis," "social pathology," "cancer," "surgery," "extirpation of diseased tissues," and so forth. To them, civil society was seriously ill. The disease that afflicted the country came "from below" and had to be met by decisive action from above. The explicit intention of the government of the armed forces was to close the historic cycle that Peronism had opened in the forties and initiate a new one. The political crisis of the seventies was perceived by both the military and some entrepreneurial elites as a basic threat to stable domination. Their critique went beyond the existing political regime that gave such a prominent place to Peronism: It focused on the social bases of the political system. Illness as political metaphor served to connect the two major components of ideology in the forced reorganization of society—to articulate the discourse of warriors and the discourse of free-enterprise conservatives.

The military rulers reduced the complex mores of Argentina to a simple dichotomy: friend or foe. Their negative reasoning was oriented to the past, a discourse of remembrance and avoidance. They substituted organized repression for past sins and diffuse violence. It was a doctrine of brute force in its most striking form. It articulated a limiting type of ideological interpellation that denied the subjectivity of its opponents, turning them into objects. By reducing political rivals to ideological nonexistence, the doctrine of national security framed them for "treatment." The construction and maintenance of this doctrine involved the deployment of sanctions that may be characterized as practices of abjection (expulsion, confinement, torture, "disappearance"—in short, varieties of extermination). The military rhetoric and the parallel deployment of abject sanctions sought to paralyze the critical will of the citizenry.

The strident rhetoric performed an ideological displacement by setting a spurious opposition between "violence" and "order." The opposition masked the real affinity between these two phenomena (as complementary modes of the disintegration of social relations). It also masked the true antithesis between violence (which belongs to the domain of strategic behavior) and conflict (which belongs also to the domain of communicative action). Civil society functions normally when it is not forcefully integrated, when it provides a public space for debate and negotiation, when social messages are not entirely clear and require constant reinterpretation by the actors. It is a conflict society. A forcefully integrated society such as the one imposed on Argentina after 1976 tends, on the contrary, to develop unitary mechanisms of control that collapse different orders of problems, reduce the public sphere, and distort and repress communication. Violence, not conflict, is a systemic attribute of that society. Violence and order belong to the same authoritarian equation, but it is precisely this connection that authoritarian ideologies seek to disguise.

In the contemporary world there are two types of systemic, generalized violence (understood as the destruction of civil societies): the violence of total state order, and the violence of unbridled economic competition. They roughly correspond to the global division of power between East and West. In the first case, the organization of violence is despotic: It stems from the will of an autocrat or from a party-state apparatus. In the second case, violence is a function of the commodification of life, stemming from market systems and their contradictions. In both cases, it penetrates deeply into the nooks and crannies of society. The originality of the authoritarian regime of Argentina rested on the conjunction of the two types, i.e., the articulation of a repressive state and an open market. To complete this picture, we must add other, less systematic types of political violence that—paradoxically—are more visible but also more sporadic, and yet function as the nemesis of established orders of violence. In this category belong the numerous social protests, popular revolts, and collective movements that have marked contemporary Argentina, that have sought to wrest space and recognition from established systems, either spontaneously or by recourse to their own organization of violence, including the fear tactics of the Mortoneros and the People's Revolutionary Army (ERP). These types of organic and inorganic violence interact. The rejection of social conflict, of open negotiation and debate, and the transformation of the country into an armed camp thus reduced order to violence, and provoked in turn the violent expression of dissent. At the same time, official ideology has used these violent eruptions— or, ideally, the memory of them after they were neutralized—as a rationale for reinforcing the established (violent) order.

The militarization of ideology and the redefinition of society as a war zone had, as one of its main consequences, the disorientation of preexisting mechanisms of ego and alter ego identification. The ideological couplets of chaos/order and foe/friend repositioned the subjects in a field that was at the same time extremely dangerous and utterly unpredictable. For beyond the stern generalities of ideology, who could be identified as friend and who could be pointed out as foe? Only the whim of the repressive apparatus, only the diktat of security personnel could produce that judgment. The public arena, the previous mechanisms of representation, and all free discursive exchanges disappeared. Subjects were no longer interpellated or recognized as belonging to a familiar central subject (class, government, party). The state withdrew from the public sphere to ensconce itself in the old *arcana dominationis* from whence it struck arbitrarily. To the underlying population, punishment arrived like the unfathomable act of a hidden God. Citizens had to work out for themselves, like latter-day political Calvinists, the rules, the signs, that distinguished a "good" from a "bad" citizen. All they were allowed to know was that their safety, their goods, and their lives were at stake. Argentines in those straits became not only obedient, but punitive of themselves and others. Fear acquired a life of its own; it became its own object.

The model of repression was simple. It included three actors: a source of punishment, a victim, and a target (Walter, 1969). The victim perished or "disappeared," but the target reacted to that destruction with some manner of submission or accommodation, initially by inhibiting his or her potential resistance. Depending on the whim of the authorities, the scheme remained simple or was complicated. Thus punishment could be ordered by the highest authorities or left to the judgment of autonomous paramilitary groups; the selection of victims could be random or according to specific categories—e.g., members of subversive organizations, their relatives, potential political opponents, professional categories, socio-economic strata, residential or ethnic groups. They were regularly selected and dispatched with variable rates of destruction. The terror process was applied continuously from the installation of the military regime in 1976 through 1979; from 1979 on, it went through phases of varying intensity, with the victims selected by specialized services or sometimes by other potential victims. In many instances, the population was made into an accomplice to the very acts perpetrated against it. This pattern of forced complicity was enacted widely in the armed forces. The involvement of the population at large was sought through the elaboration of a "discourse of summary justice" (Iestwaart, 1980) in the controlled or self-censored media. This discourse attempted to identify the "people" with security forces, on one side of the divide, and the persons who not only actively fought the regime, but who willingly or unwillingly assisted those who did, who sympathized with them in the past, or who even remained indifferent, with the "enemy," on the other side.

A striking feature of Argentine terror was the duplicity with which it was administered and suffered, ranging from the government's disavowal of responsibility to a split structure of consciousness and discourse among the population. During those years, Argentina was ruled by both a visible and an invisible government; by dignified military chiefs and also by secret terrorist associations whose hidden executioners were agents from an unseen realm that intervened in ordinary life at certain moments, holding sway by virtue of the widespread fear of their strange powers and through the violence of their acts (Constantini, 1983).

To wage war against subversion, the Argentine junta organized and armed many separate units within the armed forces and the police (Mignone, 1981). These units operated with total autonomy and impunity, having a free hand in the selection of their victims. This strategy had several advantages for the government: It became a very difficult network to infiltrate, precisely because of its decentralized, protean nature; it was largely immune to the influence of even well-placed relatives of the victims; and it allowed the central government to disclaim responsibility for violations of human rights. Terror went through an intense phase from 1976 through 1979. It then abated, although the repressive apparatus remained in place, in a state of latency. During the terror phase, somewhere between 10,000 and 30,000 persons were liquidated. The extermination was largely secret, which makes a precise estimate of the number of victims difficult. They rather belong to the category of non-persons, between the certified dead and the living, for which Argentina became sadly famous: those who were never heard of again, the *desaparecidos*. Although repression was presented as a war against armed subversion, terror spilled over well beyond the limited zone of counterinsurgency operations. It affected nonviolent opponents of the regime, and also potential and imaginary opponents. It threatened, for a while, to become total. The main categories affected were, in addition to members of guerrilla organizations, who were effectively decimated, lower and intermediate union cadres, students, civilian politicians, professional groups (lawyers, psychiatrists, artists, scientists, clergy, etc.), and relatives of the initial victims.

The terror process of Argentina served three main and two subsidiary functions. As part of the "dirty war" against armed insurgency, it eliminated those engaged in or suspected of active hostility to the power structure. It also functioned as a mechanism of deterrence, aimed at intimidating other opponents. It sought to destroy institutional alternatives and postponed the reintegration of the disorganized groups into new organizational patterns. Furthermore, it sought the prophylactic elimination of potential opponents, identified on the basis of an ideological diagnosis of the social "disease." Indirectly, the terror process helped the military bureaucracies to extend control across the country. This thorough penetration of the institutional fabric of society should not be confused, however, with the consolidation of a "bureaucratic-authoritarian" state (O'Donnell, 1982). It was a narrower and more particularistic seizure of the state apparatus by corporate groups. It was also part of a strategy to transform the country's economic structure without, however, strengthening the levers of bureaucratic command over the economy. Rather, the economy was streamlined and forcefully denationalized.

The dissociation of the invisible government from the social relations of ordinary life, the withdrawal of the state from the public sphere—a process reinforced by the abandonment of social regulation to the "automatic" mechanisms of the market—made systematic terrorism possible. By attributing their acts to the imperative of national security, the officials were freed from ordinary responsibility for repressive acts, although they were held responsible to the highest orders of military command. In essence, the state became a quasi-private and violent affair. To the privatization of civil existence under terror corresponded an increasing privatism of state power and violence.

Both friends and critics of the regime portrayed it as an authoritarian, though not authoritative, state, representing at the very least external power and internal social regulation—even if the latter was often reduced to mere police regulation, without the intrinsic bond of community among the governed. It is doubtful, however, whether a state even existed in Argentina in this restricted sense. The Hobbesian situation to which I have referred before did not issue in Leviathan but in Behemoth.

Something resembling a dual state existed in the country during the years of intense repression: one state within which two systems operated, one serving as a mask for the other. One operated under the remnants of the constitution—applied only with respect to those provisions that had not been amended by the military government—to which a new body of law was attached, comprised of laws and decrees, institutional acts and statutes, communiqués and specific provisions, and resolutions and instructions enacted since March 24, 1976. The other operated under individual measures in which expediency, arbitrariness, and considerations of military security overrode all law. The second system was contained in the first and acted upon it like a malignant growth. The seeds of that destruction were often contained in texts that had the semblance of law but none of its substance. For instance, by virtue of the Institutional Act of June 18, 1976, the military junta assumed "the power and responsibility to consider the actions of those individuals who have injured the national interest," on grounds as vague and ill-defined as "failure to observe basic moral principles in the exercise of public, political, or union offices or activities that involve the public interest" (OAS, IACHR, 1980, 19). The act led to the enactment of special laws and to the exercise of arbitrary power, designed to intimidate particular groups and individuals, on the basis of actions committed prior to the existence of such laws. The generic ground on which laws rested, the discretionary nature of the powers that they granted, the creation and functioning of special bodies to which they gave jurisdictional powers, the application of their provisions on a retroactive basis, the punitive measures they authorized—disqualification from holding office,

restriction against practicing one's profession, and confiscation of property—and the loss of liberty and life to which they led suggest, as in
the case of Nazi Germany, "a form of society in which the ruling groups
control the rest of the population directly, without the mediation of that
rational though coercive apparatus hitherto known as the state" (Neumann, 1966, 470).

A state can be said to exist when individual and group conflicts are
coordinated and integrated, within a given society, in a universally
binding fashion, by means of an abstract and rational legal structure
or at least through a rational bureaucracy. This state structure is common
to otherwise dissimilar political systems, however one wishes to classify
them. That is why an observer with many years of journalistic experience
in Argentina could make the rather startling but accurate claim that

> to consider the Argentine government authoritarian denies reality. If labels
> must be applied, Argentina could best be described as feudalistic and
> anarchic; it is divided by the rivalries of the separate fiefdoms represented
> by the armed forces, with their various free-wheeling intelligence services
> and the beleaguered, powerless Presidency. The tragedy stems from the
> fact that central authority, and the responsibility that goes with it, has
> never been established by the moderates in the military who have held
> nominal power since the March 1976 coup. (Cox, 1981)

In other words, under the umbrella of a stern military government,
armed bands were sovereign in many fields; powerful rival groups
roamed uncontrolled, having managed to conquer strategic positions.
Their antagonisms were not settled in a universally binding manner.
At best they agreed informally on certain policies. The state did not
stand above all groups; it was even a hindrance to compromises and
to domination over the ruled classes.

Argentina could only emerge from the morass if the compromise
between different social groups could be put on a binding universal
basis. Under the military, however, the opposite occurred. Many significant groups had been disenfranchised. Among the few that ruled,
few common loyalties existed. The glue that bound them together was
shameless profit, arbitrary power, and fear of those beneath them.
Sometimes one group seemed on the verge of absorbing all others; at
other times, it appeared that compromise structures would arise. Finally,
the system lapsed into further anarchy. The lesson of those tragic years
seemed to be that it was as strenuous to develop the potentialities of
Argentina on a dictatorial as on a democratic basis.

In 1976 the military groups that seized power benefited from the
disappointment of large sectors of the population with a nominally
democratic system that delivered them to internal war. Yet after six years
of rule, a majority longed again for structures of representation and
binding social compromise, and for deliverance from the executioner's
method. Coercion and fear appeared to them, in retrospect, as another

form of disorder. As previously mentioned, the operating metaphors of official ideology were medical, and more precisely, surgical. They staged the self-presentation of the regime as punishing definite acts of subversion and breaking up seditious organizations, on the one hand, and establishing the bases for "sound" economic behavior, on the other. These metaphors provided a common definition of the situation for the military and technocratic elites; they bridged the vision of national security with free-enterprise utopias. Yet behind the manifest discourse, a culture of fear developed. This culture was mostly produced and circulated in nondiscursive circuits. It has been likened to a chemical process— specifically, to a process of corrosion of social networks. The adoption of ultraliberal economic policies by the power holders produced similar effects. In their hands, economics became a self-conscious attempt to dissolve previous social loyalties and identities. Whereas in classical liberalism the emphasis on the market was associated with a denial of the relevance of authority, in the Argentine regime, the "invisible hand" was essentially a piece of political technology.

By 1982, these strategies were exhausted, and it was clear that the military had won their dirty war but not the peace. They had achieved neither social consensus nor economic solvency. Their alarums over territorial sovereignty camouflaged the weakening of real national sovereignty through disastrous policies. The military power holders offered the Argentines external war as the bitter substitute for national consensus, but the war would merely postpone the question: Would Argentina achieve freedom without chaos, and order without fear? Defeat would bring this very question back with a vengeance.

The solution had been there all along—known to all, undramatic, but eluding Argentines as if it were a supreme task for which they were singularly inept: the acknowledgment of their social complexity, the commitment to democratic processes, and the acceptance of perhaps a modest but steady level of economic performance. In time, such reasonable prospects would dawn again, but not before other riskier and demented visions were followed to their bitter end.

Life on the Tightrope

Only in some occasional episodes did the military regime in Argentina come close to fascism. For most of the time it preferred to combine nativism with an emphasis on discipline in a more quiet manner, avoiding organized mass mobilization. On account of its predominantly diffuse style, the regime may be called pseudoconservative rather than fascist. Under the military regime, the central feature of state action was neither compromise nor mobilization, but withdrawal from the pressures of organized social sectors and immunity from popular demands. Liberal economic policies and free-enterprise ideology were pieces of that political strategy. They were designed to destroy preexisting patterns of economic behavior and political alliance (Canitrot, 1981).

Two years after the junta seized power, democracy had become a bad word. Perón had been dead for four years. Guerrillas were being decimated in a bloody campaign that claimed many innocent victims. The country had moved from terrorism to state terror. Mass silence reigned—except on one occasion. In the winter of 1978, Argentines were allowed to pour out on the streets again, to celebrate the world soccer championship, which the Argentine team had won. The event was studiously exploited by the regime to make citizens forget their ordeals. The flag-waving fans that filled the streets with cheers were the country itself proclaiming a jubilant "Here I am." No sense of communion was more resonant in Argentina, more unanimous, than the simple sense of communion with the favorite sport. Soccer came to mean fellowship on the cheap. In the awesome stadiums the junta and the masses feigned working for a common cause. An illusory bond was established between a people whose enthusiasm could not find worthy political expression and a regime whose policies were anything but popular. Fear was not the enemy of enthusiasm. Together, they were formidable enemies of reason.

Only Jorge Luis Borges, the aging writer, a stubborn elitist and old-time conservative, dared to comment on the pathetic nature of the episode. A writer of truly universal stature, Borges had placed himself squarely in the line of Yeats, Eliot, Pound, and perhaps even Wyndham Lewis, making the same leap in the dark when he attempted to connect his own kind of conservative traditionalism with the politics of a Pinochet or a Videla, patronizing these dictators when he thought that they expressed rather crudely certain ideas already in the mind of Borges, then taking his distance again when they concurred in unspeakable practices. In the end, Borges too spoke out against the terror and corruption of the military regime. For many other Argentines, however, politics and culture were mortal; only the cheering in the stadium seemed eternal.

During those days in the winter of 1978, while the regime acknowledged that it held nearly 3,500 political prisoners, when the armed forces had penetrated Argentine society more deeply than ever before, having seized command of all major institutions and not a few minor ones, public life returned to a primordial state, a state that comes after every attempt to build a true community has failed, a state that seems to follow history. Without batting an eyelid the military rulers let doctors, lawyers, directors, scholars, poets, workers, physicists, architects, journalists, and painters go into exile, jail, or to their death, but they decided to pay homage to soccer players.

The farce of 1978 seems, from hindsight, to have been a prelude to the tragedy of 1982 in the South Atlantic. It may therefore be fitting to dwell on the social-psychological dynamics of those years. The sportive-jingoistic fervor of 1978 was short-lived. Coming home from the stadium, citizens had to face the chores of daily life, the uncertainties of the week ahead. When the junta came to power, it had promised to put an end to the confusion and disorder brought upon the country by the decomposition of Peronism. An iron fist, a no-nonsense approach to dissent and subversion, the definitive uprooting of terrorism, were supposed to bring relief to the law-abiding, peace-seeking Argentines, to restore their faith in work and progress. Repression was thus endorsed by many a philistine. The government made clear that the economic measures it intended to apply—inspired by contemporary schools of market freedom—would restore a lost productivity and an eroded work discipline. The labor unions and their leaders were put back in their place. The legal and institutional arrangements that had in the past allowed the collusion of "inefficient" industrialists and oversized unions had to be dismantled. Capital would be capital again, and labor labor. The cost would be austerity and recession. Nothing would shelter the national economy from international market forces.

Only landowners and bankers enjoyed governmental leniency and the prospects of vast fortunes. While real wages were rolled back a hefty 40 percent, exporters of grain and beef cashed in on record sales, bankers and financial operators of all sorts paid interest on deposits that outran the phenomenal inflation rate, promising savers a windfall. Grain went to the Soviet Union; capital was channeled into speculative ventures; foreign goods flooded the local market; and the government bought sophisticated weapons.

Military security and economic speculation soon got out of hand. Both further sapped the public spirit. On the one hand, state terror confined citizens to looking after themselves. The arbitrariness of security procedures, the tales of disappearances, the fear that anyone could be picked up, the rumors in one's neighborhood or in the office that someone's relative had vanished or been tortured soon made denial, rationalization, and mere self-regard the outstanding social norms. Everyone became security conscious, reproducing in the microcosm of the job or in the intimacy of the family the brutal thrust coming from above. Meanwhile, the people's strategies to cope with inflation turned them into speculators and moonlighters. The carrot was no less demoralizing than the stick. Imagine individuals who run with their paychecks and a pocket calculator to study the day's posted interest rates, then place their earnings in thirty-day, even seven-day, certificates, while inflation and interest yields race each other on the three-digit lane. Collective pressure urged the individual to secure maximum value for money for himself or herself. Everything conspired, from the police state to wild market forces, to turn a person into a maximizing consumer rather than into a cooperating citizen, eroding feelings of social obligation. Traditional social conventions gave way to a pervasive cynicism (Asis, 1981). Anxiety seized all alike—those who did poorly and those who did well, those touched by the terror and those graced by the paper boom.

In the liberal West, there is tendency to think that the inhabitants of repressive societies are massively "brainwashed." If the Argentine experience is any guide at all, this does not seem to be the case. The brains of the repressed are not washed at all: They are full of clever tricks and dirty little secrets. A U.S. worker may believe in the superiority of private enterprise and in the evils of socialism, even though those beliefs often run counter to personal experience and good sense. In an extremely repressive atmosphere, this kind of false consciousness is absent. What usurps its place is something different and worse: a form of torn consciousness, what may be termed a "debased consciousness," the main feature of which is cynical despondency. Thus, an Argentine citizen under military rule did not necessarily believe with passion in the validity of the "Western Christian" ideology force-fed by the regime. What he or she passionately believed in was the influence, desirable or undesirable, that the display of a positive or a negative attitude toward the doctrine could have on his or her personal fate.

In the circles close to power, the sense of ideological war was strong. Moral crusades were launched against the specter of subversion. The values of the military were an amalgam of small-town morality, religion, and national security. The rulers possessed the zeal and self-righteousness that such values endow, not precluding the behavior, in some of their official dealings, of scoundrels. They believed in an alleged "Argentine style of life" that was the supposed antithesis of "communism." The simplicity of official ideology was, however, paradoxical. The ideas of those moral crusaders were reactive and antimodern—yet Argentine culture is nothing but the product of modern enlightenment. In consequence, right-wing Argentina offered the spectacle of a young country defending mythical old values, of a modern melting pot worshipping traditions it never had, of conservatives with little to conserve. The ideology of the officers was a universe plagued with demons, ill-digested values, and a sense of intellectual siege. On this level, Argentina was not merely a "dependent culture"; it managed, after all, to autonomously develop its own madness. Many Argentines became critical of Western culture in the name of a myth of that same culture—a myth that harried authoritarians construed in solitude and resentment, feeling besieged by countless and abstract enemies and betrayed by imagined friends. It is hard to see how such a mentality could produce anything but internal and external catastrophe.

Dangerous Fictions, Sobering Facts

The central Argentine problem has not been eminently economic or strategic, but political. Argentina has developed into a complex society, but it has not achieved the political sophistication and self-restraint that could make participation and freedom compatible. It has repeatedly denied itself what it has needed most: a properly functioning "bourgeois-democratic" system. Because of this lack, economic policies have been inconsistent and economic crises, in turn, have been rapidly translated into wild social tensions and political disruptions. In comparison with most developing countries, Argentina's basic predicament has never been too grave. Per capita product and income have traditionally been the highest in Latin America. The economy has had a sluggish rate of growth, but the population has also grown at a very modest rate. Moreover, Argentina continues to produce attractive surpluses of food-stuffs and is self-sufficient in energy. But social disarticulation, political fragmentation, and galloping expectations have outpaced the capacity of the economy to please everybody. Argentina has become—in the words of a distinguished economist—"a country underdeveloped largely through its own efforts." This frustration has led to attempts to "salvage" the economy, whenever political circumstances have allowed it. Those circumstances have been periods of the lowest ebb in politics, coming generally as a result of previous failures.

And so the economic remedies have come to depend on political dictatorship. In general, they have lasted as long as authoritarian rule has managed to keep civil society on a short leash. In every cycle of this spiral, dictatorship has become more savage and the economic medicine more bitter; but instead of approaching a definitive solution, both have only increased the danger of disintegration and explosion. In the end, one is left with the unequivocal impression that what Argentina has always needed and seldom had is a solid team of political craftsmen, not an assortment of stuffy officers—mostly murderous—and economic wizards—mostly fake.

The novelty of the economic program applied by the military in 1976 was twofold. On the one hand, the program was adopted in the wake of an unprecedented political devastation, and therefore enjoyed a measure of autonomy that no other liberal program ever had. On the other hand, it was designed to eliminate, again more radically than any previous attempt, bottlenecks in the productive structure. The program sought to rationalize the economy to the point of deindustrialization. Economy Minister José Martínez de Hoz, a veteran of past efforts, was determined to resocialize Argentines in the discipline of the marketplace, making them live by its rules both externally and internally. In his mind, this required the elimination of competitive politics, so his brand of economic freedom went hand in hand with the suppression of liberty so dear to the generals. Martínez de Hoz's tenure was one of the longest on record in a country where instability and inconsistency in policy had been the norm. The average tenure of an economy minister during the previous thirty-two years was eleven and a half months. Martínez de Hoz held sway for five years. During that period he had virtually carte blanche to destroy the balance of a productive structure built haphazardly since the forties, and beset by the vagaries of the "stop-go" cycle. Economic intervention was freed from the normal constraints of deadlines and from the necessity to negotiate with antagonists.

Martínez de Hoz and his technocratic associates seized the opportunity to launch what promised to be a liberal revolution, a capitalist counterrevolution against even some capitalists, but mostly against organizations and mentalities "below." The faith in a renovated free market as the medium of social, political, and ideological change was clearly stated in the discourses of the minister (Martínez de Hoz, 1976, 1977, 1978a, 1978b). They reaffirmed the role of private initiative and the free play of competition; they raised the banner of more balanced growth; they launched a campaign against inflation; they warned against the dangers of a reckless redistribution of wealth; they expressed confidence in the ultimate expansion of employment as a result of future growth. These tenets were no different from the style of economic thinking that has found its way to policy in many Western countries in recent years, and had similar results: Monetarist strictures were enveloped in what John Kenneth Galbraith has termed "theology, wishful thinking, and a modest resort to necromancy" on the part of the high priests of economics (Galbraith, 1981).

For five years, Argentine economic policy belonged to the idiom of Thatcher and Reagan. The distant gods of the cult were Walras and Pareto; the proximate deities von Hayek and Friedman. Yet the stereotypes and shibboleths of this brand of economic liberalism cover a wide variety of national situations, and the consequences of its policies are bound to be different in core and peripheral societies (Ferrer, 1979). In the case of Argentina, hidden in the agenda was the hope to dismantle the structures inherited from the early days of Peronism. For Martínez de Hoz, the structures forged under Perón and never seriously reformed had several fatal flaws: an overextended, inefficient, and arbitrary meddling by the state; a habit of protectionism in whose shadow the most bizarre anomalies took place; an archipelago of powerful labor union with extensive financial, social, and political influence in the life of the country; and finally, interacting with the rest, the vices of sloth, demagoguery, and speculation. Together, those features constituted, for the minister, a "Peronist syndrome" that was at the root of more visible problems like stagflation.

The minister's remedy for this "syndrome" was a four-pronged strategy of attack. The remedy against the hypertrophy of the public sector was the reduction of public employment and the sale of state-run enterprises to private investors. The state would play, at best, a "subsidiary" role. Against protectionism and its nefarious consequences—industrial inefficiency and the misallocation of resources—the minister proposed "opening" the economy to the strong breeze of international competition. Against the abuses of unionism, he would apply the force of fact and the force of law. In other words, he would see to it that labor was disciplined by the reorganization of enterprises and by a new legislation designed to disarticulate the Peronist-controlled system of unions. Finally, Martínez de Hoz's solution to sloth and demagoguery was the application of the technocratic calculus and a new emphasis on productivity.

The junta in charge of the government wanted to change the country along similar lines. The officers were there to stay. They made it clear that their commitment was "to objectives, not to deadlines." For those purposes they counted on, if not the active support, at least the acquiescence of a populace that had grown weary of anarchic social and economic conditions. Besides, political parties and labor unions had been reduced to silence. Given those ingredients, many expected a thundering bolt to descend from the heights of power and assumed that methods would be applied in the field of economics no less brutal than those tried out in Chile after the coup of 1973, with the help of blueprints from Chicago. But the policies of Martínez de Hoz would be, in many ways, significantly different—never going, as in Chile, swiftly to the bitter end. Important for this difference was the concern among military officers—then still engaged in their total war against subversion—not to produce massive unemployment through measures of stabilization.

As a result, economic policy proceeded at a graduated pace, following several phases (Ferrer, 1980) and seeking to avoid some of the consequences of the strictest monetarism. Thus, the hard line in repression was not accompanied by an equally spectacular economic blitz. Instead, Martínez de Hoz unfolded his plans and measures over a four-year period, altering them as he deemed fit. The results were mediocre in terms of the avowed objectives. His policy had severe effects on the existing structure without establishing new bases for a durable recovery. It was, moreover, mortgaged to the eventual backlash of many special interests that were hurt but not crippled. After five years, Martínez de Hoz stepped down under a volley of criticism hurled from different and often opposite standpoints. Keynesians and Friedmanites, agrarians and industrialists, labor and capital, civilian politicians and military men— each had a different diagnosis and a different complaint, but all agreed that something else should be tried again.

The policies pursued by Martínez de Hoz should be reviewed in terms of their stated objectives and their mode of implementation to gauge how consistently they were followed and how far they went, to measure the gap between purpose and result, to distinguish their manifest and their latent functions, to consider who benefited and who lost, and to ponder, finally, both premise and achievement in the light of a vision of society and in the context of both local and international realities. A detailed review is beyond the scope of these pages; I will limit myself instead to a general description (for more thorough accounts see Ferrer, 1979, 1980; Botzman, Lifschitz, and Renzi, 1979; Canitrot, 1979; Rocca, 1980).

At the heart of these policies lay the premise that the government had to be streamlined. Martínez de Hoz sought to devise a better system for the collection of revenue on the one hand, and to restrain spending on the other. In Argentina, where the public sector has traditionally absorbed a sizable portion of the national output, the claims of the state have weighed heavily on the economy. According to the new policy, they were both to be significantly reduced and better financed. But to cut government spending was to try to put the lance into hard-shell institutions that had their own interests to protect, a formidable task even under authoritarian rule. Although welfare funds were cut and labor unions disciplined, it was still difficult to disconnect government from the ownership and operation of industry, and harder still to restrain the appetite of military bureaucracies, now in full command of the state. Anyone who cared to look just a short stretch beyond the rhetoric of budget cutters would not fail to detect a contradiction within the political and economic amalgam of the Argentine regime—something for which terms like "liberal militarism" or "market fascism" seemed appropriate.

Dismantling the public sector was therefore problematic. In 1979, the government announced that it had reduced public employment by 100,000, but the state continued to account for about half of total investment. Plans to sell some 700 state-run enterprises to private buyers met with resistance from military officers. The gross public deficit in the end remained extremely high, despite slashes in the budget. Modern military hardware was significantly more expensive than other items; its procurement was, curiously, not touched by austerity. In these matters, the advice of the sociologist to the economist could have been helpful: The country was not an economic abstraction, something that could be separated from its classes, its institutions, its history, and the bulk of its population. To persist in this illusion was to place the cart unerringly before the horse. Over the course of those years, Argentine society taught that lesson to an entire lineage of self-appointed saviors. The pending task would be to incorporate the lesson in a humane democratic project.

The goal of lightening the weight of the state on the economy was only partially attained. If the government deficit was reduced between 1976 and 1979, it was due to increases in the scope and enforcement of taxation, not to any significant reduction in expenditures. Thereafter, the deficit resumed its growth, and so did the monetary supply. Paradoxically, it was public demand that propped up the economy between 1976 and 1980. The state was never reduced to the much trumpeted "subsidiary" role promised by the economic authorities. With few exceptions—notably in the fields of energy and communications—the combination of laissez-faire doctrine and state intervention made an awkward amalgam.

In the battle against inflation, which in the waning days of the previous Peronist administration had reached astronomical proportions, the military regime first utilized the usual weapons, such as wage and price controls and monetary policies, but without much consistency. Until December 1978, it avoided the use of harsher methods. Prices continued to climb, at a rate of 175 percent in 1977 and 170 percent in 1980—surely a dramatic reduction from the staggering 738 percent that marked Isabel Perón's last year in power, but still the highest in the world.

At the beginning of 1979 a new course was charted, consisting of a combination of measures. The economic authorities fixed, in advance, a decreasing rate of devaluation of the peso vis-à-vis the dollar, on a level purposely lower than the inflation rate. As a result, internal prices faced a stiff international competition, a situation that was eventually expected to cause both sets of prices to converge. Policy was thus designed to stabilize inflation as a function of currency devaluation and international price trends. In order to reinforce these measures and to increase the pressure of external competition on domestic economic activity, the authorities accelerated the schedule of reductions in import tariffs. But the expected convergence failed to materialize. Between December 1978 and July 1980, the peso was devalued 87 percent in relation to the dollar, but wholesale prices rose 212 percent and retail prices 256 percent. The gap between the rates of inflation and devaluation only started to narrow in the course of 1980. But the mechanism that had been set in motion still did not produce the desired results. Moreover, the monetary efficiency of the system continued to depend on a sizable reduction of the budget deficit, which, as we have seen, proved intractable. The main objective of Martínez de Hoz was to bring inflation down from three to two digits—an objective that for a while seemed attainable (from September 1979 to September 1980), only to become elusive once again during the last quarter of 1980.

If these policies were slow to bear the expected fruit and if the fruit was somewhat sour, they did have other, more dramatic consequences. The inflow of imported goods at competitive prices drove local goods out of the market and pushed many enterprises to bankruptcy. The currency, kept artificially strong in relation to other currencies, fostered speculation and stimulated the flight of wealth abroad. A mirage took place for the lucky stratum of the population whose increased revenues also turned into good dollar values. A bleeding economy appeared for a while as a bonanza, behaving very much like a patient who experiences blissful moments as a phase of a terminal disease and brightens up with visions of remission and good health.

"Opening" the economy to international market forces was an explicit objective of the authorities. But an international economic policy can mean quite different and sometimes contradictory things. It may be an end in itself or a means to an end; it may be active or passive; it may pursue the conquest of foreign markets for national goods or, in reverse, the surrender of the home market to foreign goods. Martínez de Hoz's policies were designed to combat inflation and expressed a passive view of the comparative advantages of the Argentine economy within the international system. The overvaluation of the peso and the reduction of import duties logically led to a spectacular rise in imports—75 percent in 1979 alone—and a drain of $1.2 billion for the same year in expenditures by voracious Argentine tourists, who suddenly found prices in other countries affordable or cheap. Martínez de Hoz's policies were also responsible for a slowdown of exports. While traditional exports were adversely affected by the economic policies, nontraditional exports suffered even more. Capital that could have gone into productive ventures was deflected to more lucrative but unproductive money-market games and to the import trade. Private and public debt rose to the skies.

In the midst of these distortions, many Argentines believed that the fruits of advanced civilization were, once again, within their grasp. The political by-product of those economic policies came down to a demagogic payoff to the higher income groups. But the price was high, both in the short and the long run. The balance of payments was bound to show a growing deficit that could be dissimulated only for a while by the inflow of large amounts of short-term speculative capital from abroad, lured by sumptuous interest rates. This infusion would later destabilize the external financial situation of the country and further depress economic activity. The external debt incurred by both the public and the private sectors rose to $19 billion by the end of 1979, exclusive of interest. The debt was by then the equivalent of the volume of exports over two and a half years. The debt service bill for 1980 came to $6 billion—the equivalent of eight months of exports. When the regime finally collapsed, in 1983, the external debt had risen to $45 billion.

Martínez de Hoz had expressed a will to free Argentina from the scourge of speculation, to steer its economy through an era of productivity and efficiency. He succeeded in reconstructing savings (placed, however, in short-term notes) through measures that put interest rates at a higher level than inflation. However, as inflation remained high, interest rates climbed to dizzying heights in order to stay positive, fostering precisely what the authorities said they wished to avoid, namely a frenzy of speculation. Financial institutions—not all of them solid or serious—multiplied like toadstools after the rain, under the protection of the central bank. Laissez-faire meant unchecked freedom, and it drove four banking groups—including the largest private bank—to irresponsible adventures and finally collapse. The entire financial system had the solidity of a house of cards, eventually requiring the massive intervention of the very same state that, according to official doctrine, was to stay out of business.

Policies of stabilization entail recession, a severe reduction of purchasing power, and increased unemployment, consequences that are more or less severe depending on the intensity of the treatment. Argentina bore those costs, but without the technocratic consolation of "success." The Argentine economy remained stagnant, and inflation was held to acceptable levels only temporarily, while lowering real wages. The social and political implications of the policies became more onerous with time, while economic results, even in the narrow sense, were wanting. Between 1976 and 1980, annual GNP growth barely kept pace with the growth of population, and in two years (1976 and 1978), the growth rate was negative. In 1980 the level of industrial production was below that of 1974. The most disturbing aspect of the policies applied during five years of the harshest dictatorship within Argentine memory was the seemingly futile deindustrialization they spawned. All the measures just reviewed were justified in terms of "efficiency"—an expression dear to technocrats. But the balance was negative: Many poorly managed enterprises survived because their services and products could not be easily substituted with imports, while many enterprises that played the game of rationalization went under as the result of reckless exposure to foreign competition. The overvaluation of the peso and the absence of a true export policy had the ironic consequence of damaging that sector of the economy—the agrarian and foodstuff sector—that had static comparative advantages in the world market. Every day enterprises closed down; industry was either moribund or dead; new ventures were stillborn.

Marxists—prone as usual to impose a reconstructed logic on events—asserted that behind the policies of the military regime lay a master strategy to adapt the Argentine economy to the requirements of a new international capitalist order. Yet beyond the obvious rewards to international banking houses (David Rockefeller eulogized Martínez de Hoz to the very end), the policies did not satisfy major interest groups—not even transnational corporations, some of which abandoned their operations in Argentina. The one major change in Argentine trade patterns, namely the spectacular rise in foodstuff sales to the Soviet Union in the late 1970s, is difficult to square with that interpretation. One is hard put to fathom the commonality that might exist between the Argentine military and the Soviet regimes, aside from simple expediency and a silent complicity in the sordid violation of human rights.

Martínez de Hoz left his country in a most difficult predicament, entering a recession of great magnitude. He left behind an economy that, when subjected to inspection, kept the observer in doubt as to whether the proposed renovation ever got beyond the stage of demolition. In the rubble it was hard to distinguish the new building blocks from the old debris. Partisans were disappointed, outside observers remained unconvinced, and foes were poised to take revenge.

The officers who succeeded Videla in the presidency after March 1981, Generals Viola and Galtieri, inherited a very delicate situation. The timelessness of terror, the high velocity of monetary speculation, and the disorienting abstraction of political and economic processes explain why, by then, traditional social conventions such as fellowship and conviviality had given way to a pervasive cynicism that not even psychiatric treatment could heal. Economics had had a powerful desocializing impact; civil society had reached its "degree zero." Ironically, the very collapse of civilian life under the boot left the military rulers dangerously exposed. Once their first repressive objectives were untidily achieved, and once they proved no more competent at running the economy than those they had berated, political dissension began to affect the ranks of the services themselves. But this time the military rulers could not simply hand power back to the civilians. Blood had been spilled, and no civilian party could or would protect them against retribution. Anxiety became the driving force of their endeavors, and whatever elements remained of reason in their leadership were placed in jeopardy.

10
Authoritarianism Undone

Power Deflation

The preceding chapters have described and commented on the acquisition and management of power by various military groups in Argentina. In them, I have tried to take into consideration both internal and external elements. In Chapter 9, I sketched the power strategy employed by the last military regime, a strategy based on physical coercion, socioeconomic disorientation, and during one of its phases, the use of terror. I have also described some of the effects of this strategy on institutions and ideology. It is now time to mention the growth of checks on authoritarian power holders. In order to do so, it is helpful to organize the developments reviewed so far into a sequence of partially overlapping crises.

The first order of crisis, lasting from 1955 to 1976, involved the decay of institutions preceding the seizure of power by the last military regime. The essence of that crisis was the failure of political institutions to satisfy the expectations put upon them by a complex web of organized groups. The crisis came about through damage from external and internal sources to the social and political structures and through changes in the level of consciousness.

The ultimate consequence of institutional failure was an added flow of power to military authorities and an attempt by the latter to extensively overhaul the status quo. At this juncture the rulers imposed a draconian model of what in their eyes was a better system and sought frantically to prevent other groups from developing alternatives. The model was based on a charter myth—a theory of what is wrong and how to change it—combining the doctrines of national security and free enterprise. It had clear totalitarian elements, notably the recourse to terror, the attempt to pulverize old structures of participation and collective identification—albeit through market mechanisms, and the use of ideological controls to dissolve previous identities. These policies constituted a second order of administered crisis, what Barrington Moore, Jr., has called a "vested interest in confusion" (Moore, 1965).

Yet the project of the power holders also contained a number of contradictions and self-checks. First, there was a tension between the economic and the military "logics" of the regime. The corporate interests of the officers often clashed with the designs of the free-market technocrats. Moreover, the radical and autonomous nature of policies deprived the regime of stable alliances among crucial economic sectors. Second, the combination of physical coercion and economic disarticulation managed to stifle organized social and political opposition but failed to provide substitute structures of participation and isolated the regime from society. Society became increasingly opaque to the rulers, making potential opposition less predictable. The lack of early feedback signals from society compounded rather than corrected the strategic and tactical errors of the authoritarian regime. When these errors were perceived, it was late. At that point the regime changed course in a fitful manner, trying to escape from one crisis by jumping into another. When the indications of economic malfunction became clear, the rulers switched channels and prepared a mass mobilization for a war that, much to their own dismay, actually took place—and that they lost. This opened a Pandora's box of resentment, retribution, old populist myths, and alternative ideologies. These subsidiary dysfunctions of power management constitute a third order of crisis that finally brought down the regime.

The growing checks on the authoritarian rulers of Argentina had little to do with the processes that develop in mobilizing systems (e.g., Soviet-type societies) after they have gone through a terror phase. In the latter, the checks are associated with the emergence of a more "mature" complex society following a developmental breakthrough. The checkered pattern of Argentine development has meant instead that in the end, a vicious but weakened regime ruled over a weakened and craven society. In this respect, the Argentine terror phase seems to have been an episode in the general decomposition of the social system.

War

By early 1982, the military regime had landed itself in a terminal paradox: At the very moment of total victory against its enemies, pure irrationality suddenly prevailed. After years of uncontested power, the officers possessed all the cards in the deck but one: They had nobody left to blame if everything went bad. And everything turned bad. The country was experiencing a frightful economic crash. Unemployment mushroomed and inflation went back to three digits. The currency was devalued several times. The wail of labor, business, farmers, and even political parties became louder. The right of the regime to stay in power was called into question in a significant way for the first time, and by established groups. The junta was faced with several unpleasant alternatives. If clean elections were held, the likelihood of a Peronist return to power was high. If restricted elections were sponsored, a weak government would only inherit the pressing problems. If, on the other hand, the officers remained in power and did nothing, sooner or later serious divisions would appear within their ranks. If the harshest hawks prevailed, another bloodbath might ensue. In April 1982 the military administration of General Galtieri chose a classic and suicidal nonsolution: the flight forward into war. In the Malvinas/Falklands adventure, they counted on the nationalist loyalty of the population. They were not wrong. But disaster in action convinced the same people that they had been led into a cul-de-sac by incompetent opportunists, and the hour of reckoning arrived.

During the spring of 1982 (autumn in the Southern Hemisphere) the world watched aghast as a crisis gathered around a remote archipelago in the South Atlantic. The conflict finally pitted Great Britain against Argentina in a brief but intense war. The archipelago consists of two large islands and a number of smaller ones, with an area under 5,000 square miles. In the language of the day when they were first sighted by an English captain (1592), they lie "50 leagues or better from the ashore east and northerly from the Straits [of Magellan]" (Calvert, 1982, 5).

Since 1592 the archipelago has had a tangled history, involving contested claims and seizures by the great European powers of the seventeenth and eighteenth centuries—Britain, France, and Spain—and by the newly independent nations of the nineteenth—the United States and Argentina. Despite anarchic conditions throughout the land, the government of Buenos Aires established a convict settlement there in 1820. In 1826, a French merchant was appointed governor on behalf of Argentina. Disputes with U.S. ships, eviction, mutiny, and even murder marred the life of settlers on the isles. But Britain ruled the seas, and was determined to hold the islands as a strategic base along the route round Cape Horn. In January 1833 they were seized and henceforth ruled as a colony by Britain until 1 April 1982. The British settlers—Scots for the most part—introduced sheep, which rapidly became the mainstay of the economy. The population remained small (some 1,800 in 1982, including those on short-term contracts), the herds numerous, and the wool excellent. The Falkland Islands Company, which developed this simple economy, has dominated life in the islands since 1851.

Argentina has objected all along to British rule, basing its legal claims—as a successor state—on the original rights of Spain and on the argument of geographical proximity. Early in this century, Britain placed its other possessions in the South Atlantic and Antarctica under the jurisdiction of the Falklands/Malvinas. Argentina also made claims on a portion of Antarctica and some of these other South Atlantic islands. The Malvinas versus Falklands conflict thus reached, in principle, the South Pole.

For the greater part of history the argument was theoretical, and for Argentina especially, an issue of discarnate right. For Britain, the importance of the islands was proportionate to its fortunes as a power. The days of schooners seeking repairs after rough weather round the Horn came and went, and so did the coaling stations for steamers and the threatening battleships of Admiral von Spee. The empire languished and waned. On the other side, the resources of the archipelago were insufficiently impressive to impel Argentina to action, especially in light of its proclivity to merely skim the resources it already had. It had all along been almost exclusively a matter of national honor. In 1982 it was also a matter of expediency and professional prestige: Patriotism was the last refuge of the junta.

Plans for the seizure of the Malvinas/Falklands were developed in the early days of the military regime, as part of interservice rivalry. Pressure for intervention came from the navy, which had long been hawkish on the issue. In 1977, the ambitious and unscrupulous navy chief, Admiral Massera, insisted on an invasion of the islands as a way to challenge President Videla. Massera lost his gambit, but nevertheless commissioned Admiral Anaya to prepare a plan, lest his bluff be called by rivals inside the junta. The detail is important, not only because Anaya—a mystical hard-liner—would himself later become chief of the navy and principal actor in the conflict, but also because it revealed the paramountcy of warmongering over sober considerations of diplomacy, balance of forces, and logistics in the Argentine decision to invade.

The crisis that the Argentine military finally provoked in 1982, and that led them to war, would confirm once more the historic correlation between authoritarianism and incompetence (Dixon, 1976). As several studies have repeatedly shown, authoritarians are less likely than nonauthoritarians to make good social leaders. In war they are less likely to comprehend enemy intentions and to ponder information that runs counter to cherished preconceptions. They have greater difficulty than nonauthoritarians in recognizing threats. They guide themselves through stereotypes (Kogan, 1956). These characteristics had a compound significance for the planning and execution of the Malvinas fiasco. The ideological zeal of the Argentine military rulers and their persistent introduction of metaphysical variables into decision making biased their decisions away from realism and toward wishful thinking. It is no exaggeration to suggest that every plan they made failed to envisage properly what might happen after the seizure of the islands (Cardoso, Kirschbaum, van der Kooy, 1983, 65ff.).

The invasion was the brainchild of a fanatical officer whom the avatars of military politics eventually placed in a strategic position during the crisis of the Viola administration. It seems that at that time, Admiral Anaya made a pact with General Galtieri (Cardoso, Kirschbaum, van der Kooy, 1983, Ch. 1). The admiral agreed to help the general reach the presidency in exchange for a carte blanche for the admiral's pet project. When other circumstances intervened, Galtieri made Anaya's Malvinas scheme his own. These circumstances were the failure of economic policy; the need to find a political solution to the ensuing social crisis; and the encouragement that the regime began to receive from Washington—in particular the prospect of joint ventures in Central America. The other main issue in Argentine foreign policy over that period was the sovereignty dispute with Chile over three islands in the Beagle Channel. At stake were territorial waters and continental shelves. Argentina was opposed to any extension of Chilean sovereignty into the Atlantic, and the two countries had almost gone to war over the islands in 1978. The Pope's mediation thereafter calmed things down. Nonetheless, the dispute was likely to go in favor of Chile or reach deadlock.

The conflict with Chile spurred the quest for a compensatory success in the Falklands/Malvinas. Galtieri's dream was that the occupation of the islands would be hailed as a historic achievement by the Argentines, condoned by the Americans, and—with the latter's sweetening influence—swallowed by the British as a fated pill. Such an outcome would turn Galtieri from a circumstantial president into a popular strong man. He was conscious of the need to revitalize the "Process," to seize the initiative. Galtieri placed himself at the center of power in Argentina, and, in his mind, placed Argentina near the center of the world. He produced an international incident with tools appropriate for a coup de main. The international tantrum epitomized the distemper of the authoritarian republic, which placed an entire nation at the mercy of the errors of generalship. Military organizations had attracted a minority of individuals who were a menace at top levels of command, and the nature of militarism accentuated traits that could prove disastrous. And, alas, there was no civilian counterpoint. In a democracy, even the most inept governments come up for dismissal every so often. This was not true of a country in which there was absolutely no public control of government, no constitution: The only recognized division of power was among the army, the navy, and the air force.

Galtieri enthusiastically endorsed the projects with which the Reagan administration sought to realign Argentina. These ranged from Argentine participation in an international peacekeeping force in the Sinai—a proposal that would eventually be dropped—to Argentine "fronting" for the United States in El Salvador, Honduras, and Nicaragua, on behalf of the forces of reaction in those countries. The lobbying efforts undertaken—without much success—by such personalities as Jeane Kirkpatrick and Vernon Walters before the Viola administration soon bore fruit under Galtieri. But the enthusiasm for friendship exempted the partners from examining the actual commonality of their assumptions. Seen in retrospect, the *quid pro quo* was not favorable to Argentina. In exchange for a commitment to act as a proxy in Central America, Galtieri obtained a rather vague expression of U.S. interest in a joint venture leading to the eventual formation of a South Atlantic treaty organization. In that case, the Falklands/Malvinas might become a military base—an arrangement patterned after the U.S.-UK deal in Diego García. The Argentines apparently mistook these discussions as a "green light" for their plans to wrest the islands from the British. While Reagan persuaded Congress to lift the sanctions imposed on Argentina by the Humphrey-Kennedy amendment of 1978 due to gross violations of human rights, Galtieri streamlined the top brass of the Argentine army and poised himself to storm the presidency. Viola was forced out and Galtieri replaced him in what amounted to a quiet, bloodless coup.

Galtieri's style of rule was boisterous, aggressive, centralized. He intended to win for the military a new lease on political life until about 1990, when a plebiscite would confirm him in power. For that, he needed spectacular achievements, and he chose foreign policy as the arena. He appointed a hard-line nationalist, Dr. Costa Mendez, as minister of foreign affairs. He made Costa Mendez his adviser and accomplice in the centerpiece of his strategy: an invasion of the Falklands/Malvinas. An ardent Anglophile, Costa Mendez believed that the British were too genteel to respond with force. The sesquicentennial of British occupation was almost upon them, and the timing seemed perfect.

The junta's first explicit discussion of the invasion took place, *in camera*, on December 29, 1981. The discussion initially involved only the triumvirate of service chiefs. Later, the circle was extended to only a handful of trusted collaborators. The cabinet, the bulk of the armed forces, and the population at large were kept in the dark until the very last moment. On January 6, the chiefs decided to go ahead with the invasion if the forthcoming negotiations with the UK—scheduled to take place in New York on the last two days of February—did not yield new and significant results.

A perusal of transcripts and reports from those days (Cardoso, Kirschbaum, van der Kooy, 1983) reveals the authoritarian naiveté of the commanders: their childish assessment of the international balance of forces, of the priority of issues, and of the power structure and decision-making process of the industrial democracies. The Argentine leaders apparently had ingested the ideological drivel meant within some influential circles in the West as an item of public consumption, not as a guide to policy. Secrecy, the absence of correcting feedback, lack of reliable information, and a messianic sense of purpose left the commanders isolated. They distrusted civilian collaborators, notably the diplomats, expressed contempt for the citizenry, and had a callous disregard for their troops. Their authoritarian bent made them deal not with real enemies and issues, but with phantoms and narcissistic projections—the windmills of Don Quixote. For instance, in the early stages of the conflict, they attempted to remove one of Argentina's ablest diplomats from his ambassadorship in London and replace him with a naval officer, on the assumption that the latter would know better what to say in the event of an action of arms.

From January through March, three simultaneous processes converged: (1) a rapid rapprochement of Argentina and the United States, (2) Galtieri's determination to strengthen his leadership and seek popular support, and (3) negotiations with Britain. As everyone supposed on the basis of precedent, these negotiations produced only tepid results. London's strategy was to postpone significant decisions, to maintain the impasse on the whole affair. The Falklands/Malvinas issue had the lowest priority in the British government's agenda. It had been raised countless times in the course of seventeen years, and the diplomats on both sides were resigned. Much to their surprise, their bland communiqué was greeted with an angry salvo from the regime in Buenos Aires. The junta threatened to take unilateral action if diplomacy bogged down. The British and Argentine negotiators did not know what the generals had secretly hatched, and the official broadside from Buenos Aires embarrassed the diplomats. Nonetheless, the episode was interpreted in London as an Argentine attempt to gain concessions, and as a "get-tough" stance for the benefit of the Argentine home front.

Meanwhile Thomas Enders, the U.S. undersecretary of state, visited Buenos Aires. He was sounded, on the occasion, about possible U.S. reactions to a hypothetical seizure of the Malvinas. It is most unlikely that the question was put to him bluntly, and Enders had less exotic preoccupations at the time. The United States wanted assurances that no war would be initiated against Chile before lifting the arms embargo sanctioned under Carter. Chile was beyond the pale, and if Argentina was to be helped, some balance had to be preserved. The U.S. gesture had, as mentioned already, an ulterior purpose: to secure Argentine participation in the Central American crusade. If that was in fact the undersecretary's paramount concern, then a vague and hypothetical question on the Falklands/Malvinas could easily have prompted—as was reported—the debonair suggestion that the U.S. response to escalating pressure on the issue would probably be "hands off." At any rate, the probing was sufficiently vague, and the response sufficiently noncommittal, to leave each party to its wishful musings.

Misunderstanding was rampant on all sides. The U.S. administration, lured by prospects of help from Argentina in Central America, took signals about the Falklands/Malvinas lightly. Their attitude was in turn misread by the Argentines as a complicitous wink. In London, British diplomacy was not duly alarmed by pressure that it mistook for a bargaining ploy. The juggernaut was set in motion while on all sides the exercise of judgment acting on experience, common sense, and available information failed to function. The nations belonged to the same block; they all had conservative rulers in their prime; yet they pursued policies that were contrary to their respective and collective interests. Their interaction in 1982 placed the West in a rather dismal light. Poor judgment stemmed from misgovernment, which was then of several kinds: tyranny combined with incompetence in Argentina; decadence and compensatory ambition in Britain; sheer folly in the United States. It is of course impossible to totally disentangle the problem from individual rulers, but nonetheless the erroneous policies were those of the groups, not the personalities, involved. In the context of this discussion, the questions are: Why did the military rulers drag Argentina, after 112 years of uninterrupted peace, into a war they had no chance of winning? Why, during successive stages of the crisis, did they toughen their stance though repeatedly advised that the harm done would be greater than any gain? Why did they refuse to heed the voices of advice or alarm until they woke up to find that power had completely slid from under them? Why did they choose, in a lunatic spectacle, to hear no voice other than their own, amplified by propaganda? Why did their role models and masters allow them to nurse fatal delusions until it was too late?

Galtieri picked General Menéndez as future governor of the islands. When he broke the news to the flattered but perplexed nominee, the latter ventured a sensible query: What would the British do? He was told not to worry and that, in any case, such a concern was none of his business. Thus was launched the ill-fated Argentine campaign. The strategy was simply to increase pressure in diplomatic negotiations until a breaking point was reached, whereupon the "military option" would be exercised, counting on celerity and surprise. The aim was to produce a fait accompli with the help of British reluctance, U.S. benevolence, and widespread support in the Organization of American States (OAS) and the UN. Under such assumptions, the Argentine armed forces were adequate for the task, and it mattered little that their command structure was marred by interservice rivalries, that they were suited primarily to the conduct of counterinsurgency operations, that the bulk of their forces were raw draftees, that they relied heavily on hardware rather than on fieldcraft and motivation, that an immense effort was required to supply a large number of conscripts although these soldiers were of little value on the battlefield. In sum, for the junta's gamble it mattered little that the armed forces had no conception of how to fight a war against a major enemy. The Argentine rulers were after glory—fast and on the cheap. Theirs was not real power, but the cowardly flattery of strength.

The military regime was wrong on every count. The junta's chief diplomat misjudged the willingness of the British prime minister to meet force with force, miscalculated the extent of the U.S. government's predisposition to abet the misconduct of occasional Latin friends in detriment of more solid Atlantic bonds with old allies, and overestimated the support for repressive Argentina in the fora of the world. As the Argentine diplomats stumbled in move after move, their military superiors in Buenos Aires simply scorned them and disbelieved the evidence. They thought they had an ace up their sleeve. Actually, they were narrowing their options to the very worst one: an all-or-nothing showdown. Their morale and determination on the front, and ultimately their grip on power in the capital, never recovered from the realization, in May, that the British proposed to fight.

The war should have never taken place. Argentina had pressed its claims for a century and a half. In 1964 it put the matter before the UN, which prompted the British and the Argentines to negotiate on terms, though they dodged the important question of self-determination. The negotiations dragged on unproductively for seventeen years. They could have led, in principle, to a settlement based on the formula of a "leaseback," acknowledging Argentine sovereignty while preserving the *modus vivendi* of the islanders. The goal on which both parties could have converged, had they been willing, was a symbolic redefinition of the status quo. The main culprit, on this historic score, was British dereliction. There simply was no interest in, or political support for, a compromise with Argentina. The Foreign Office had been perfectly ready to solve the issue for years, but the public and the politicians were utterly indifferent. British diplomacy was first-rate, but in this particular case, it had no clout. As diplomacy drifted unsupported, decisions made outside its purview reduced the credibility of Britain's interest in the islands. Proposals for economic development and resource exploitation, such as the Shackleton survey (Frank, 1983, 9), were shelved, and Britain bestowed second-class citizenship on the islanders. Given the fitful nature of Argentine politics, such contemptuous sloth invited aggression. Once aggression occurred and the British fleet sailed from Portsmouth, leeway for negotiation was much reduced. In London and Buenos Aires, hawks raised the stakes to a point of no return.

A succession of mediators were drawn into the dispute, but they all failed to avert the war. The most notable failure was that of U.S. diplomacy, under the stewardship of Secretary of State Alexander Haig. Washington divided its loyalty, wavered, became frustrated with the junta, and finally sided with Britain—to nobody's satisfaction, and with severe damage to U.S. interests and prestige. The U.S. mediation produced some disturbing revelations, from which some lessons may—one should hope—be drawn. It suggested an administration torn by bickering between key figures (Haig, 1983), blinded by the simplicities of anti-communism and inept at understanding subtler issues, wrong about the dynamics of Latin American politics, amateurish in the UN, and ill-prepared to confront, as should befit a great power, the intricacies of international relations. If the United States had from the beginning thrown its weight firmly against the Argentine regime it is quite likely that a peaceful settlement of the dispute could have been achieved without the bloodshed. The Haig mission left no role for the UN to play and actually helped escalate the conflict. The row between Secretary Haig and Ambassador Kirkpatrick became a competition to determine who would make the worse mistake.

Mediation was made especially frustrating by the junta's delusions of grandeur and inability to deliver consistent decisions, on the one hand, and by Margaret Thatcher's firm attachment of her political destiny to a close-knit war machinery. To her, "the Falklands spirit" was a single-minded (but politically expedient) fight for abstract value that with tenacity should and could be won. As is often the case, the staggering disproportion between the objective of reconquest of odd rocks on the fringes of a bygone empire, and the human and economic costs to be incurred (probably 1,500 dead and three times as many wounded on both sides; 2 billion pounds spent by the British treasury alone)—indeed, the deep absurdity of it all—made high principle seem more, not less, glittery.

It took a trivial episode to trigger the sequence of events that would lead to war. On March 19 a naval support vessel delivered an Argentine contractor and his workmen to Leith Harbor, on South Georgia, where they were to dismantle an old whaling station. They raised the Argentine flag. A diplomatic protest by London ensued. The majority of Argentines then left, but a small group remained—probably to probe British reaction. Other Argentine vessels were dispatched to give them "protection." Meanwhile, the rest of the Argentine fleet was due for joint maneuvers with Brazil. It could therefore sail in full view of all. An order from Admiral Anaya diverted it, at full speed, towards the Falklands. They landed at Port Stanley at 6:30 A.M. on April 2. They overwhelmed the small local garrison and took command. Three days later, the first elements of a British task force sailed from Portsmouth. When it arrived in the vicinity of the Falklands, on April 29, it was an impressive fleet. Less than a month after the invasion, British commandos landed on the islands.

In the interim, all diplomatic efforts failed. The last chance for a mediated settlement (through the auspices of Peru) was lost when the Argentine cruiser *General Belgrano* was sunk by a British nuclear submarine on orders from the war cabinet. The previous U.S. effort at mediation had come to a standstill at the end of April, and Washington had sided openly with Britain. From that point on, a rather spectacular naval and air action captured the headlines of the world press. The bulk of the British landing force was then dispatched. A landing site was chosen in San Carlos, and the actual landing began on May 21, amidst great fracas. It took the various British groups twenty-four days from the initial bridgehead to Port Stanley. The troops won an important battle at Goose Green and suffered a disaster at Fitz Roy. On June 11 they reached the heights surrounding the capital, broke through Argentine defenses in various battles, and captured the city. The Argentine commander surrendered on June 14. The war had lasted seventy-four days. Argentina had started it. Britain won.

The British final sweep made the whole campaign seem, in retrospect, of textbook quality. In fact, it had been fraught with uncertainty and danger. One should not forget that both nations had drifted almost unintentionally into hostilities, that the crisis began with a collapse of communications, that intelligence was poor, that air superiority was difficult to achieve, that troops were sent regardless, that the ships lacked point defense, that carriers might have been sunk, and that after the landing, the British troops could have been bogged down in a stalemate by less timorous defenders determined to do more than hold fixed positions. Launched 8,000 miles from home, the British assault was a gamble as reckless as some of the most compromised operations of World War II, requiring its quota of luck to succeed. It was helped by the fact that the Argentines planned poorly, withdrew their fleet, were ill coordinated, overwhelmed themselves with supply problems, and massed and immobilized a large force of unprofessionals. Except for the pilots, they fought little and not well. So much seems reasonably established from a lay viewpoint. The rest is better left to the experts. The point so often made that any civilian who meddles in military affairs is guilty of presumption is surely one that I accept. In this chapter, I have merely sought to illustrate the obverse: to show the dire consequences of the military presumption in usurping functions proper to civilian government.

The war was rich in paradox. It demonstrated that ideological affinity was no guarantee of security, that staunch "anticommunism" was a poor guide to North-South tensions, that Ambassador Kirkpatrick's influential theses—to wit: that authoritarian regimes Argentine-style were responsive to liberal pressures and devoid of expansionist ambitions—were bogus (Kirkpatrick, 1979). "Thatcher's war" was supposed to show the world that "aggression does not pay." But Britain's superior aggressiveness did pay—although it was very expensive. Besides, Britain won the war but not the argument. The islanders were defended, but in the process their life-style was destroyed forever. By granting them full citizenship after victory, Britain undermined its own defense of self-determination at the UN. Albion's prize was restored pride—for victory in a long-lost colonial cause (Barnett, 1982). The defeat had, on the other hand, a salutary effect on Argentina, where it brought an abominable era to an end.

A New Start Toward Democracy

By a peculiar ruse of history, the same arrogance of power that had left many Argentines bereaved, others ashamed, and the majority poorer caused the ruin of the dictators. The war was the straw that broke the camel's back. After the surrender at Port Stanley, the generals' days in power were numbered. But if the junta's self-destruction was unmistakable, the orderly passage to democracy was much less clear. Tyranny had left a legacy of fear. The party system seemed battered, and new political actors had not yet emerged. Old ghosts were being revived.

Argentines could look back only to a tradition of intolerance and opportunism, and many seemed kindled by the spirit of revenge. Under such sorry circumstances, democracy appeared as the ineluctable imperative, since other solutions had proved disastrous. Past mishaps made it seem, however, a choice by default.

No orderly transition to democracy took place after the war, nor had there been a vigorous one in the making before it. The process was rather one of power deflation (Cavarozzi, 1983; Fontana, 1983) and decay. The increasing fragmentation of military rule produced a momentary opening, followed by a failed attempt at forced reintegration, followed in turn by an almost total abandonment of control over social, political, and economic processes.

Only once—in 1981, under the presidency of General Viola—had the regime made some moves towards democratization. But the worsening state of the economy had cast that strategy into doubt and raised the suspicion of conservative officers. The opening allowed, however, the formation of an alliance between the five principal civilian parties. The strategy of the multiparty alliance was based on the belief that the regime would be affected by internal divisions, economic woes, and an evaporating legitimacy. It would need, sooner or later, to appeal to the main parties, and especially to the Peronists and the radicals. The latter agreed on three restrictions: They would not collaborate with the government; they would not lend their consent to a tutored or partial "democracy," or to a civil-military government; they would oppose the creation by the state of an official party. It was an abstentionist, not an assertive program. The political parties did not want to provoke a return of the military hard-liners. They were equally concerned to avoid a "repeat" of what had happened in 1972, namely, an abrupt withdrawal from power accompanied by popular tumult.

The parties were timid, fearful of the military, and ambivalent about economic management. On the one hand, it was clear to them that the military government was losing control of crucial variables (foreign debt, inflation, unemployment, bankruptcy, and the balance of payments). On the other hand, they also knew that the same facts provided ammunition to hard-liners seeking power. Despite this deference from the civilian opposition that it sought to court, the Viola administration succumbed to the reluctance of the parties to partake of the deteriorating process, and to the gathering storm inside the armed forces. At the very most, the deterioration of the government's position created opportunities for some political groups to reestablish a long-lost public presence, but did not encourage them to negotiate seriously.

The Viola administration declined fast and was displaced by the hard-liners, represented by Galtieri. The first attempt at democratization had yielded a disheartening spectacle: weakness in government—by then fully absorbed by crisis management, lack of serious negotiations between the government and the opposition, vagueness and moderation on the part of the political parties, factionalism within the armed forces, lack of organic ties between the parties and social groups or movements. In short, there was an acute disarticulation between the state, the parties, and civil society.

When Galtieri wrested power from Viola, he and his associates sought to reestablish authority, reimpose stern economic controls, and redefine the political opening that had taken place under Viola in the direction of forming a pro-authoritarian civilian support group. The goals were contradictory: The economic measures alienated whatever support the military hoped to woo. Protests soon surfaced. In March 1982 one of the two labor federations called on the population at large, not just the workers, to demonstrate against official policies, and the government responded with repression.

Then came the Falklands/Malvinas crisis to create a temporary rally behind the flag. The unions conditioned their support on that occasion; most of the parties endorsed the invasion unconditionally. It seems clear that success in that operation—by any definition, short of retreat or surrender—would have consolidated the regime and weakened the opposition. Defeat favored democratization, as it had favored it in Greece in 1974 (Diamandouros, 1984; Cardoso, Kirschbaum, and van der Kooy, 1983). As Raymond Aron remarked during those days, the Argentines would have to search for their own Caramanlis.

The political aftermath of the defeat was swift and heady: There was a rapid deterioration of power, further fragmentation and bickering inside the armed forces, and the will to govern collapsed. Galtieri resigned and was replaced by General Bignone, whose mandate was to preside over a difficult but inexorable transition to civilian rule. The only issue that tormented the power holders was the mode and the timing of their exit. They tried, unsuccessfully, to negotiate retreat; to obtain, at the very least, some assurances that they would not be held accountable for their past acts of terror. But there was no response from the parties. The church sought to mediate, and also failed. The regime was left to rot by itself, in pathetic isolation. The parties did not, however, take strong initiatives. They only focused on consolidating their respective organizations. The labor unions were more active in public opposition, but they did not engage in debates about the future. Nobody actually dared to touch the burning issues: repression, debt, civil rights. These became "wild" themes wielded by more or less spontaneous social movements and, whenever possible, the press.

During the Argentine winter of 1983, the country was seized by a collective sense of defeat. The reasons for such despondency had deep roots in the past. As noted throughout this book, the haphazard development of the country placed side by side diverse pressure groups, conscious of their special interests but oblivious of the common good. Power had accumulated outside institutions, in a sort of political wild market, whence it burst in wild actions and reactions. The ballot had been only one weapon among many. The main political movement had behaved undemocratically, the democratic parties had not commanded majorities, and the vacuum had been filled by authoritarian minorities. Argentina had rarely been governed by law. Authority had decayed to a point where life became a war of all against all with pockets of order under strong men waging vendettas against each other. Clearly, the only way out of this jungle was a solemn democratic covenant. Whether Argentina would arrive or not at such a covenant was contingent on two factors: the balance of constraints and opportunities, and the formation of a new collective will.

What were the obstacles and opportunities for democracy when the campaign for general elections started, in mid-1983? Peronism seemed still the major political force. Its legacy was mixed. It had been both the vehicle for the organization of labor and a heterogeneous charismatic movement. The working class was mature, but the labor organization was pyramidal, had a single political allegiance, and weighed massively on the political process. Strong, unified labor organizations are not per se barriers to democracy. Nobody would make this claim about labor organizations in Sweden, Great Britain, or West Germany. Why then, had Peronism not become a social-democratic force? Partly because of three internal reasons: the domination of unions by authoritarian labor barons; the integration of labor and nonlabor sectors of Peronism not in a modern party structure, but in a populist movement under a *Führerprinzip*; and a corporatist style of negotiation with other political and social forces. Changing these features would not be impossible, but it would be a project for the longer run, falling on a new generation of labor leaders and Peronist politicians.

The other answer lay outside Peronism. Argentina has lacked cohesive center and center-right parties as effective counterweights to labor. Since 1930, a rather fragmented Argentine establishment has lacked the will and imagination to organize itself for democratic politics. Faced with the Peronist onslaught, these groups have tended to secede from competitive politics and knock at the barracks door. Without the reconstitution of the political center, unions and regiments would continue to act as surrogates of parties. Only if the political campaign that was hurriedly improvised in 1983 revealed, after seven years of political silence and social opacity enforced by the dictatorship, a strong reconstitution of the political center, would democracy have a chance in Argentina.

As soon as elections were announced, the traditional political parties started a process of internal reorganization. Affiliation to the two major parties reached record proportions, indicating a strong thirst for involvement on the part of the population. The platforms and proposals of the major parties were not, however, substantially different. The difference was rather in the style, in the shifting involvement of such sectors as the middle-class youth, and in the emergence of a new and younger leader, the radical Raúl Alfonsín. Under Alfonsín's leadership the old Radical Party turned the tables on the Peronists by projecting an image of change and renewal. Still, many observers doubted that this new momentum would suffice to overcome the long-standing handicaps of the *radicales*. They recalled that, in the two presidential elections of 1973, the *radicales* had obtained 21.3 percent and 24.4 percent of the vote.

Before October 30, 1983, any Americans who took their news from the elite press probably inferred that Argentine political habits had not changed—that Perón, dead, still continued to command the political destiny of Argentina. Those were the very words used in commentaries and editorial columns. To others who were watching the weekly polls from Buenos Aires, three trends suggested a more nuanced and hopeful picture.

1. For the first time in almost forty years, the outcome at the polls was not a foregone conclusion. Since its appearance in 1946, Peronism had been the principal electoral force. Every time free elections were held, it had vindicated that title. This time, the polls showed a parity of strength between Peronism and the Radical Party. The latter, under the leadership of Raúl Alfonsín, became a serious electoral alternative. This trend indicated that even if the Peronists won, Argentines now would finally have surmounted a period of overwhelming Peronist domination.

2. Almost ten years after Perón's death in 1974, the effects began to make themselves felt. The polls suggested that Peronism was losing the multiclass support that had accounted for its strength as a popular movement. Instead, it was becoming the political expression of a narrower though still important constituency, based on the organized working class. A sign of this change was the internal reorganization of the party, with union leaders seizing key positions, while reserving a symbolic place for the political cadres represented by the presidential candidate Italo Luder. Therefore, one could conclude that a more labor-centered Peronism might not be credible enough to present itself, as it had done, as the embodiment of the whole Argentine nation.

3. The sense that a traditional political mold was about to break was confirmed by the election campaign. Despite the relatively peaceful Peronist reorganization, there were strong tensions within that party. The union leaders preferred an aggressive campaign, but their candidate Luder tried to project an image of order and civility, hoping to dispel the memories of the Peronists' disastrous performance in power under Isabel Perón. Luder wanted to draw votes from the middle sectors, without whom he could not win. This search for respectability, which was not shared by noisier populist sectors of the party, seemed in line with the trend that was pushing Peronism into becoming another, albeit still important, political force. The campaign showed that the political initiative had shifted.

In sum, far from being a new rendition of the past, the situation in Argentina now seemed close to a major political change. And this seemed reason enough to sound a note of cautious optimism: It was possible to begin thinking of an end to a forty-year cycle of disruption and despair. To be sure, the election outcome would not dissipate the pressing problems facing the country: the need to refinance a staggering foreign debt, the legal and moral imperative to account for the rate of thousands of *desaparecidos*, the necessity to institute civilian control over the army, the challenge to find an honorable solution to pending international conflicts. But it seemed that a condition for tackling these problems was to recreate democratic conviviality in a country that had long suffered from its absence.

In the presidential race, Alfonsín won by an unprecedented margin (for a party other than the Peronist) of 52 percent. Such a feat was made possible by the maintenance of the traditional middle-class radical constituency, a massive swing of undecided voters in Alfonsín's favor, by a significant portion of "borrowed" votes from the right and center-right, and last but not least, by a good number of *peronistas* deciding not to vote for their party this time. In all likelihood, it was the switch in allegiance of this last group that produced such a pronounced difference in favor of Alfonsín.

These considerations fail to capture the intense sense of relief that the outcome of the elections produced in Argentina's collective consciousness. The exercise of formal democracy no longer meant repeating a feared and tattered script. For many a month of shame and bitterness after the defeat in the South Atlantic war, with the sudden realization that the country was near bankruptcy and the slower awakening to the crimes and corruption of the military leaders, Argentines felt condemned—not destined—to democracy, largely because they could not see it as anything but a new turn of past failures. As the campaign gathered momentum, however, many acted against this dark self-understanding and broke the spell.

Until it looked at itself in the mirror of elections, the new majority had thought it was a minority. Thus the elections represented not only a reconstitution of political forces in terms more favorable to democratic politics but also a profound symbolic break with the past. What makes an event stand out in the history of a community is the realization—by the actors and after the fact—that they have crossed an invisible threshold. It is still early to say if this was a temporary or a permanent shift in Argentine politics. It was, at the least, an important occasion.

Peronism has not vanished. It has survived the debacle of 1983, but with clearer and more restricted boundaries. Barring a dramatic reorganization, it may in fact become a traditional ethnopolitical subculture. Some Peronists who banked, in the past, on the almost automatic capacity of their movement to win elections may seek other watering holes. But a hard core endures, impervious to change. Like the French workers who remain loyal to the Communists—despite Poland, the Gulag, and "democratic centralism"—there are popular sectors in Argentina that continue to tolerate the vices of Peronism, that feel represented by populist and authoritarian leaders, and that even see in the abhorrence of union bosses among democratic and progressive sectors (an attitude sometimes blending easily with middle- and upper-class prejudice) a confirmation of their proletarian authenticity. A popular subculture fed by an undercurrent of resentment remains an important component of Peronism, and the Peronists remain a dominant political force, especially in the less-developed provinces of the vast, uneven country.

While Peronists seek, with difficulty, to adapt to the new situation, the Radical Party is also being tested. Peronists argue that at least they have a reliable political base, whereas Alfonsín gathered around him a disparate constituency. They have a point. President Alfonsín faces the hard task of satisfying the crisscrossing demands of a motley alliance. The 52 percent of the vote that swept him into office may dwindle as he governs. Many who cast their vote for him did it in repudiation of the Peronists, not out of confidence in Alfonsín. His chances could well lie in following a strategy that he successfully pursued as candidate, which consisted of raiding the margins of Peronism. He might then lure into his fold an important bloc of skilled workers who still voted Peronist, through an active policy of social reforms. Yet the economic crisis imposes severe restraints on a judicious reactivation of the productive apparatus. Antidepression measures could transform a temporary plebiscite into a durable political coalition. Yet the country is restive and choked by a gigantic debt. The bloc of votes (19 percent) cast in the national elections of 1973—the last before the military interregnum—for right-wing candidates went in 1983 to Alfonsín. In the parliamentary elections of 1985, this bloc will again range itself behind its natural candidates. The *radicales* will have to counteract this centrifugal trend by a stiff competition with the Peronists for the white-collar vote. The political future of the Radical Party and the country may depend on that effort.

Present conjectures may be confirmed or may dissipate. But the significance of the present moment in Argentina shall remain: It represents the opportunity to enforce and guarantee a truly democratic covenant, based on the conviction that accountable statesmen must prevail over soldiers and technicians at the helm. The risks are many, and the opportunity could easily be lost. But ahead lies the promised land of common sense. In the end, Argentina may well contemplate these pleasing prospects: the taming and containment of authoritarian populism; a more balanced political party system, a greater role for skilled political brokers in various parties; a diversification of working-, middle-, and upper-class political preferences; and the appearance of a new democratic left. Some steps have already been taken: The military has been made to submit to both civilian control and to the justice of the constitutional regime. An independent judiciary, transpartisan commissions, and religious leaders have been given a large role as custodians of civil society. Underneath, however, the *sottogoverno* of particularism and strife still rages.

Time and again I have insisted in these pages that corporate groups, strong in Argentina, are prone to bypass the official political process and to enter into deals outside and around representative institutions. If this conception is correct, then some of the most formidable obstacles to democracy in the country stem from civil society. The authoritarian state presently undone—or in abeyance—was a particularly bleak compromise solution, not the deep source of the difficulty. Argentina's clumsy dictators have been, after all, only a piece in a complicated social machinery that has traditionally worked against democracy. Factors working against democracy move quite fast, whereas those supporting it take more time. Crisis management and civilized political compromise work at cross-purposes.

This book closes with a question that in Argentina seems perennial: Will the unruly, impatient society grant the present democratic regime enough time to learn and muddle through? Conflict will not cease: What remains to be seen is whether it will be carried out within the boundaries of law and around rational principles. If Argentina is to count anywhere, it must begin by counting at home, as an entity both livable and lovable that is more—and not, as hitherto, less—than the sum of its parts.

Selected Bibliography

Alfonsín, Raúl (1981). *La cuestión argentina*. Buenos Aires: Editorial Propuesta Argentina.

Altamirano, Carlos (1982). "Lecciones de una guerra," *Punto de Vista* 5, No. 1 (August-October).

Aparicio, Francisco, and Difrieri, Horacio, eds. (1958–1963). *La Argentina: Suma de geografía*. 9 vols. Buenos Aires: Peuser.

Argentina (1958). *Memoria: Gobierno Provisional de la Revolución Libertadora, 1955-1958*. Buenos Aires.

Argentina (1979–1980). *Anuario estadístico de la República Argentina*. Buenos Aires.

_____. Banco Central de la República. *Memorias* (Yearly). Buenos Aires.

_____. Banco de Crédito Industrial (1944–1956). *Memorias*. Buenos Aires.

_____. Banco de la Nación Argentina, Oficina de Investigaciones Económicas. *Revista económica*. Buenos Aires.

_____. Dirección de Estadística Social (1943–1945). *Investigaciones sociales*. Buenos Aires.

_____. Dirección Nacional de Estadística y Censos. *General Censuses (Censos generales de la nación) of 1869, 1895, 1914, and 1947*. Buenos Aires.

_____. Dirección Nacional de Estadística y Censos (1936). *Censo industrial, 1935*. Buenos Aires.

_____. Dirección Nacional de Estadística y Censos (1954). *Censo nacional minero, industrial y comercial de 1954*. Buenos Aires.

_____. Presidencia de la Nación (1955). *Producto e ingreso de la República Argentina en el período 1935-1954*. Buenos Aires.

Argentina 1930–1960 (1961). Buenos Aires: Sur.

Asis, Jorge (1981). *El Buenos Aires de Oberdan Rocamora*. Buenos Aires: Editorial Losada.

Bagú, Sergio (1969). *Evolución histórica de la estratificación social en la Argentina*. Esquema: Instituto de Investigaciones Económicas y Sociales de la Universidad Central de Venezuela.

_____ (1952). *Estructura social de la colonia*. Buenos Aires: El Ateneo.

———— (1949). *Economía de la sociedad colonial*. Buenos Aires: El Ateneo.

Bailey, Samuel L. (1967). *Labor, Nationalism, and Politics in Argentina*. New Brunswick, N.J.: Rutgers University Press.

Bank of London and South America (1979). "Argentina: Economic Policy Since April 1976," *Bank of London and South America Review* 13, pp. 277–284.

Barnett, Anthony (1982). "War over the Falklands," *New Left Review*, Special Issue 134 (July-August).

Belloni, Alberto (1962). *Peronismo y socialismo nacional*. Buenos Aires: Coyoacán.

———— (1960). *Del anarquismo al peronismo*. Buenos Aires: Peña Lillo.

Beyhaut, Gustavo, et al. (1965). "Los inmigrantes en el sistema ocupacional argentino," in Di Tella, Torcuato, et al., *Argentina, sociedad de masas*. Buenos Aires: Editorial Universitaria de Buenos Aires.

Blackman, Morris J., and Hellman, Ronald G., eds. (1977). *Terms of Conflict: Ideology in Latin American Politics*. Philadelphia: ISHI Press.

Blanksten, I. George (1953). *Perón's Argentina*. Chicago: University of Chicago Press.

Botana, Natalio (1977). *El orden conservador*. Buenos Aires: Sudamericana.

Botzman, Mirta; Lifschitz, Eduardo; and Renzi, Maria Rosa (1979). "Autoritarismo, 'libre cambio,' y crisis en el proceso actual," *Economía de América Latina* (CIDE, Mexico), No. 2 (March).

Braun, Oscar (1970). *Desarrollo del capital monopolista en Argentina*. Buenos Aires: Editorial Tiempo Contemporáneo.

Braun, Oscar, and Joy, Leonard (1968). "A Model of Economic Stagnation: A Case Study of the Argentine Economy," *Economic Journal* 78, No. 312 (December), p. 29.

Broner, Julio, and Larriqueta, Daniel E. (1969). *La revolución industrial Argentina*. Buenos Aires: Sudamericana.

Bruce, James (1953). *Those Perplexing Argentines*. New York: Longman.

Bunge, Alejandro (1940). *Una nueva Argentina*. Buenos Aires: Kraft.

Burgin, Miron (1946). *Economic Aspects of Argentine Federalism, 1820–1852*. Cambridge, Mass.: Harvard University Press.

Cafiero, Antonio (1961). *5 años despues . . . De la economía social-justicialista al régimen liberal-capitalista*. Buenos Aires, n.p.

Calvert, Peter (1982). *The Falklands Crisis: The Rights and the Wrongs*. New York: St. Martin's Press.

Canitrot, Adolfo (1981). "Teoría y práctica del liberalismo. Política antiinflacionaria y apertura económica en la Argentina (1976–1981)," *Estudios CEDES* (Buenos Aires) 3, No. 10.

———— (1979). "La disciplina como objetivo de la política económica. Un ensayo sobre el programa económico del gobierno argentino desde 1976," *Estudios CEDES* 2, No. 6.

———— (1975). "La experiencia populista de redistribución de ingresos," *Desarrollo Económico* (Buenos Aires), No. 59.

Canton, Darío (1970). *La política de los militares argentinos 1900–1970*. Buenos Aires: Siglo XXI.

———— (1969). *Materiales para el estudio de la sociología política en la Argentina*. 2 vols. Buenos Aires: Editorial del Instituto Di Tella.

———— (1968). *El parlamento argentino en épocas de cambio: 1890, 1916, y 1946*. Buenos Aires: Editorial del Instituto Di Tella.

Cardenas, Gonzalo, et al. (1969). *El Peronismo*. Buenos Aires: Carlos Perez.

Cardoso, Fernando H., and Faletto, Enzo (1969). *Dependencia y desarrollo en América Latina*. Mexico: Siglo XXI.

Cardoso, O. R.; Kirschbaum, R.; and van der Kooy, E. (1983). *Malvinas: La trama secreta*. Buenos Aires: Sudamericana/Planeta.

Cavarozzi, Marcelo (1983). *Autoritarismo y democracia (1955–1983)*. Buenos Aires: Centro Editor de América Latina.

_____ (1982). "Argentina at the Crossroads: Pathways and Obstacles to Democratization in the Present Political Conjuncture," *Working Papers*, No. 115. Washington, D.C.: Wilson Center.

Cheresky, Isidoro (1983). "Pouvoir et légitimité dans les regimes autoritaires," *Document de Travail* No. 2 (July). Paris: GRELAT.

Ciria, Alberto (1983). *Política y cultura popular: La Argentina peronista 1946–1955*. Buenos Aires: Ediciones de la Flor.

_____ (1964). *Partidos y poder en la Argentina moderna (1930–46)*. Buenos Aires: Jorge Alvarez.

Cochran, Thomas C., and Reina, Ruben E. (1962, 1971). *Capitalism in Argentine Culture*. Philadelphia: University of Pennsylvania Press.

Collier, David, ed. (1979). *The New Authoritarianism in Latin America*. Princeton, N.J.: Princeton University Press.

Comisión nacional sobre la desaparición de personas (1984). *Nunca más*. Buenos Aires: EUDEBA.

Constantini, Humberto (1983). *The Gods, the Little Guys, and the Police*. New York: Harper and Row.

Corradi, Juan E. (1979). "The Avatars of Socio-Political Discourse in Latin America," *Social Science Information* 18, No. 1 (February).

Cortés Conde, Roberto, and Gallo, Ezequiel (1967). *La formación de la Argentina moderna*. Buenos Aires: Paidos.

Cox, Robert (1981). "Timerman Shows that 'Authoritarian Generals' are Keepers, Captives of a 'Totalitarian Beast,'" *New York Times*, June 9, Op. Ed. page.

Cúneo, Dardo (1967). *Comportamiento y crisis de la clase empresaria*. 2d edition. Buenos Aires: Pleamar.

_____ (1965). *El desencuentro argentino 1930–1955*. Buenos Aires: Pleamar.

Cúneo, Niccolò (1940). *Storia dell'emigrazione italiana in Argentina, 1810–1870*. Milano: Garzanti.

Daniels, Ed (1970). "From Mercantilism to Imperialism: The Argentine Case," *North American Congress on Latin America, Newsletter* (New York and Berkeley) 4, Nos. 5 and 6.

De Ipola, Emilio (1982). *Ideología y discurso populista*. Mexico: Folios.

Delgado, Julián (1968). "Industria: El desafío a la Argentina," *Primera Plana* (Buenos Aires), No. 297 (September 3).

Delich, Francisco J. (1970). *Crisis y protesta social. Córdoba, mayo de 1969*. Buenos Aires: Ediciones Signos.

De Riz, Liliana (1981). *Retorno y derrumbe: El último gobierno peronista*. Mexico: Folios.

Diamandouros, P. Nikoforos (1984). "Transition to, and Consolidation of, Democratic Politics in Greece, 1974–83: A Tentative Assessment," *West European Politics* 7, No. 2 (April 1984), pp. 50–71.

Díaz Alejandro, F. Carlos (1970). *Essays on the Economic History of the Argentine Republic*. New Haven, Conn., and London: Yale University Press.

Diéguez, Héctor (1969). "Argentina y Australia: Algunos aspectos de su desarrollo económico comparado," *Desarrollo Económico* (Buenos Aires) 8, No. 332 (January-March).

Di Tella, Guido, and Zymelman, D. (1967). *Las etapas del desarrollo económico argentino*. Buenos Aires: Editorial Universitaria de Buenos Aires.

Di Tella, Torcuato (1964). *El sistema político argentino y la clase obrera*. Buenos Aires: Editorial Universitaria de Buenos Aires.

Di Tella, Torcuato, and Halperín, Tulio (1969). *Los fragmentos del poder*. Buenos Aires: Jorge Alvarez.

Dixon, Norman (1976). *On the Psychology of Military Incompetence*. London: Jonathan Cape.

Dorfman, Adolfo (1970). *Historia de la industria argentina*. Buenos Aires: Solar/ Hachette.

Doyon, Louise M. (1975). "El crecimiento sindical bajo el peronismo," *Desarrollo Económico* 15, No. 57 (April-June).

Eshag, E., and Thorp, R. (1965). "Economic and Social Consequences of Orthodox Economic Policies in Argentina in the Post-War Years," *Bulletin of the Oxford University Institute of Economics and Statistics* 27, No. 1 (February).

Fayt, Carlos S. (1971). *El político armado. Dinámica del proceso político argentino 1960-1971*. Buenos Aires: Ediciones Pannedille.

_____ (1967). *La naturaleza del peronismo*. Buenos Aires: Viracocha.

Ferns, H. S. (1969). *Argentina*. London: Ernest Benn Ltd.

Ferrer, Aldo (1980). "La economía argentina 1976-1979," *Economía de América Latina* (CIDE, Mexico), No. 5, 2d semester.

_____ (1979). "El retorno del liberalismo: Reflexiones sobre la política económica vigente en la Argentina," *Desarrollo Económico* (Buenos Aires) 18, No. 72 (January-March).

_____ (1967). *The Argentine Economy*. Berkeley and Los Angeles: University of California Press.

Ferrer, Aldo, et al. (1969). *Los planes de estabilización en la Argentina*. Buenos Aires: Paidos.

Fichas de Investigación Económica y Social (Buenos Aires), Nos. 1-9 (April 1964-May 1966).

Fillol, T. R. (1961). *Social Factors in Economic Development: The Argentine Case*. Cambridge, Mass.: MIT Press.

Fontana, Andrés (1983). "Fuerzas armadas, partidos políticos y transición a la democracia en Argentina 1981-1983." Mimeo., Kellog Institute for International Studies, University of Notre Dame, Indiana.

Frank, Andre Gunder (1969). *Latin America: Underdevelopment or Revolution*. New York: Monthly Review Press.

Frank, Rt. Hon. Lord, Chairman (1983). *Falkland Islands Review*. London: Her Majesty's Stationery Office.

Freels, John William, Jr. (1968). *Industrial Trade Associations in Argentine Politics*. Ph.D. dissertation, University of California, Riverside. Spanish edition, Buenos Aires: Editorial Universitaria de Buenos Aires, 1970.

Frondizi, Silvio (1956). *La realidad argentina*. 2 vols. Buenos Aires: Praxis.

Fuchs, Jaime (1965). *Argentina, su desarrollo capitalista*. Buenos Aires: Cartago.

Galbraith, John Kenneth (1981). "Up from Monetarism and Other Wishful Thinking," *New York Review of Books* 28, No. 13 (August 13).

Galletti, Alfredo (1961). *La política y los partidos*. Mexico: Fondo de Cultura Economica.

Gambini, Hugo (1969). *El 17 de Octubre de 1945*. Buenos Aires: Editorial Brújula.

García Lupo, Rogelio (1972). *Contra la ocupación extranjera*. Buenos Aires: Editorial Centro.

_____ (1962). *La rebelión de los generales*. Buenos Aires: Proceso.

Germani, Gino (1965). *Política y sociedad en una época de transición*. Buenos Aires: Paidos.

_____ (1955). *Estructura social de la Argentina*. Buenos Aires: Raigal.

Giberti, Horacio (1964). *El desarrollo agrario argentino*. Buenos Aires: Editorial Universitaria de Buenos Aires.

_____ (1961). *Historia económica de la ganadería argentina*. 2d ed. Buenos Aires: Solar/Hachette.

Gillespie, Richard (1982). *Soldiers of Perón: Argentina's Montoneros*. New York: Oxford University Press.

Goldthorpe, John (1978). "The Current Inflation: Towards a Sociological Account," in F. Hirsch and J. Goldthorpe, eds., *The Political Economy of Inflation*. London: Martin Robertson.

González Trejo, Horacio (1969). *Argentina: Tiempo de violencia*. Buenos Aires: Carlos Perez.

Haig, Alexander M. (1983). *Caveat: The Reminiscences of General Haig, U.S. Secretary of State from January 1981 to June 1982*. London: Weidenfeld and Nicholson.

Halperín Donghi, Tulio (1964). *Argentina en el callejón*. Montevideo: Editorial Arca.

Halperín Donghi, Tulio, ed. (1980). *Proyecto y construcción de una nación*. Caracas: Editorial Ayacucho.

Hastings, Max, and Jenkins, Simon (1982). *The Battle for the Falklands*. New York: W. W. Norton.

Hodges, Donald C. (1976). *Argentina, 1943–1976: The National Revolution and Resistance*. Albuquerque: University of New Mexico Press.

Hutchinson, Thomas J. (1865). *Buenos Ayres and Argentine Gleanings*. London.

Ibarguren, Carlos (1955). *La historia que he vivido*. Buenos Aires: Peuser.

Iestwaart, Heleen F. P. (1980). "The Discourse of Summary Justice and the Discourse of Popular Justice: An Analysis of Legal Rhetoric in Argentina," in Richard L. Abel, ed., *The Politics of Informal Justice*. New York: Academic Press.

Imaz, José Luis de (1970). *Los que mandan* (Those Who Rule). Albany: State University of New York Press.

_____ (1962). *La clase alta de Buenos Aires*. Buenos Aires: Editorial Universitaria de Buenos Aires.

International Monetary Fund. *International Financial Statistics* (Washington, D.C.). Monthly since January 1948.

Irazusta, Julio (1963). *Influencia económica británica en el Río de la Plata*. Buenos Aires: Editorial Universitaria de Buenos Aires.

Jefferson, Mark (1926). *Peopling the Argentine Pampa*, American Geographical Society Research Series No. 16. New York: Commonwealth Press.

Jitrik, Noé (1968). *El 80 y su mundo*. Buenos Aires: Jorge Alvarez.

Johnson, Kenneth F. (1976). "Guerrilla Politics in Argentina," *Conflict Studies*, No. 63 (October).

Jorge, Eduardo (1971). *Industria y concentración económica (desde principios de siglo hasta el peronismo)*. Buenos Aires: Siglo XXI.

Josephs, Ray (1944). *Argentine Diary: The Inside Story of the Coming of Fascism*. New York: Random House.

Kelly, Sir David (1962). *El poder detrás del trono*. Buenos Aires: Coyoacán.

_____ (1952). *The Ruling Few*. London: Hollis and Carter.

Kenworthy, Eldon (1967). "Argentina: The Politics of Late Industrialization," *Foreign Affairs* 45, No. 3 (April).

Kirkpatrick, Jeane (1979). "Dictatorships and Double Standards," *Commentary* (November).

_____ (1971). *Leader and Vanguard in Mass Society. A Study of Peronist Argentina.* Cambridge, Mass., and London: MIT Press.

Kogan, N. (1956). "Authoritarianism and Repression," *Journal of Abnormal Social Psychology* 52, pp. 34–37.

Laclau, Ernesto (1977). *Politics and Ideology in Marxist Theory.* London: New Left Books.

_____ (1970). "The Argentinian Contest," *New Left Review*, No. 62 (July-August).

_____ (1969). "Modos de producción, sistemas económicos y población excedente," *Revista Latinoamericana de Sociología* 5, No. 2 (July).

Latin American Perspectives (1974). Vol. 1, No. 3, Special Issue on Argentina (Fall).

Leiserson, Alcira (1966). *Notes on the Process of Industrialization in Argentina, Chile, and Peru.* Politics of Modernization Series, No. 3, Institute of International Studies. Berkeley: University of California.

Levene, Ricardo (1937). *A History of Argentina.* Chapel Hill: University of North Carolina Press.

Lux-Wurm, Pierre (1965). *Le peronisme.* Paris: Bibliotheque Constitutionnelle et de Science Politique.

McGann, T. F. (1966). *Argentina: The Divided Land.* Princeton, N.J.: D. Van Nostrand Co.

Magnet, Alejandro (1953). *Nuestros vecinos justicialistas.* Santiago, Chile: Editorial del Pacífico.

Martínez, A. B., and Lewandowski, M. (1911). *The Argentine in the Twentieth Century.* London: T. F. Unwin.

Martínez Estrada, Ezequiel (1942). *Radiografía de la Pampa.* Buenos Aires: Losada.

Martínez de Hoz, José Alfredo (1978a). "In an End-of-the-year Message to the Nation, the Minister of Economy of Argentina, Mr. Martínez de Hoz, Reviewed the Progress of the Argentine Economy in 1977 and Outlined Prospects for 1978," *Boletín Semanal del Ministerio de Economía*, anexo No. 218 (January 30), pp. 1–8.

_____ (1978b). "Address by Mr. José Alfredo Martínez de Hoz, Governor for Argentina and Minister of Economy, at the 3rd Plenary Session," *XIX Annual Meeting of the Board of Governors, Inter-American Development Bank*, Vancouver (April 18).

_____ (1977). "An Address by Dr. José Alfredo Martínez de Hoz, Jr., Minister of Economy, Argentina, Before the Open Plenary Session at the International Industrial Conference Jointly Sponsored by the Conference Board and Stanford Research Institute," San Francisco (September 12–15).

_____ (1976). "Programa de recuperación, saneamiento y expansión de la economía argentina," *Boletín Semanal del Ministerio de Economía*, No. 126 (April 19), pp. 1–15.

Martorell, Guillermo (1969). *Las inversiones extranjeras en la Argentina.* Buenos Aires: Editorial Galerna.

Mazo, Gabriel del (1955). *El radicalismo. Notas sobre su historia y doctrina, 1922–52.* Buenos Aires: Raigal.

Merkx, Gilbert W. (1968). *Political and Economic Change in Argentina from 1870 to 1966.* Ph.D. dissertation, Yale University, New Haven, Conn.

Mignone, Emilio Fermin (1981). "Desapariciones forzadas: Elemento básico de una política," *Punto Final* (Mexico), No. 194, supplement (June).

Moore, Barrington, Jr. (1966). *Social Origins of Dictatorship and Democracy*. Boston: Beacon Press.

————— (1965). *Political Power and Social Theory*. New York: Harper Torchbooks.

Mulhall, E. T., and Mulhall, M. (1863). *Handbook of the River Plate*. Buenos Aires: Editors of the Standard.

Murmis, Miguel, and Portantiero, Juan Carlos (1971). *Estudios sobre los orígenes del peronismo: 1*. Buenos Aires: Siglo XXI.

Navarro, Marysa (1982). "Evita's Charismatic Leadership," in Michael L. Conniff, ed., *Latin American Populism in Comparative Perspective*. Albuquerque: University of New Mexico Press.

————— (1968). *Los nacionalistas*. Buenos Aires: Jorge Alvarez.

Neumann, Franz (1966). *Behemoth: The Structure and Practice of National Socialism 1933–1944*. New York: Harper Torchbooks.

North, Liisa (1966). *Civil-Military Relations in Argentina, Chile, and Peru*. Politics of Modernization Series, No. 2, Institute of International Studies. Berkeley: University of California.

Nun, José (1969). *Latin America: The Hegemonic Crisis and the Military Coup*. Politics of Modernization Series, No. 7, Institute of International Studies. Berkeley: University of California.

Oddone, Jacinto (1967). *La burguesía terrateniente argentina*. Buenos Aires: Ediciones Libera (First edition 1930).

————— (1934). *Gremialismo proletario argentino*. Buenos Aires: La Vanguardia.

O'Donnell, Guillermo (1982). *1966–1973. El estado burocrático autoritario. Triunfos, derrotas y crisis*. Buenos Aires: Editorial de Belgrano.

————— (1977). "Estado y alianzas en la Argentina 1956–1976," *Desarrollo Económico* 16, No. 64.

————— (1973). *Modernization and Bureaucratic Authoritarianism: Studies in South American Politics*. Berkeley: University of California Press.

Orgambide, Pedro (1968). *Yo, Argentino*. Buenos Aires: Jorge Alvarez.

Organization of American States, Inter-American Commission on Human Rights (1980). *Report on the Situation of Human Rights in Argentina* (OEA/Ser. L/V/II.49, doc. 19, corr. 1). Washington, D.C.

Orona, Juan V. (1966a). *La Revolución del 6 de Septiembre*. Buenos Aires: Imprenta López.

————— (1966b). *La logia militar que derrocó a Castillo*. Buenos Aires: Imprenta López.

————— (1965). *La logia militar que enfrentó a Hipólito Yrigoyen*. Buenos Aires: Imprenta López.

Ortiz, Ricardo M. (1955). *Historia económica de la Argentina*. 2d ed. 2 vols. Buenos Aires: Plus Ultra.

Page, Joseph A. (1983). *Perón: A Biography*. New York: Random House.

Palacio, Ernesto (1960). *Historia de la Argentina 1515–1957*. 3d ed. 2 vols. Buenos Aires: A. Peña Lillo.

Panettieri, Jose (1969). *Síntesis histórica del desarrollo industrial argentino*. Córdoba: Macchi.

————— (1967). *Los trabajadores*. Buenos Aires: Jorge Alvarez.

Panorama de la economía argentina. Buenos Aires: 1957–1966.

Perelman, Angel (1961). *Cómo hicimos el 17 de octubre*. Buenos Aires: Coyoacán.

Pérez Amuchástegui, A. J. (1965). *Mentalidades argentinas 1860–1930*. Buenos Aires: Editorial Universitaria de Buenos Aires.
Perón, Eva (1955). *Historia del peronismo*. Buenos Aires: Ediciones Mundo Peronista.
———— (1953). *La razón de mi vida*. Buenos Aires: Peuser.
Perón, Juan Domingo (1968). *La hora de los pueblos*. Buenos Aires: Norte.
———— (1963). *Tres revoluciones militares*. Buenos Aires: Escorpion.
———— (1957). *La fuerza es el derecho de las bestias. La realidad de un año de tiranía*. Caracas: Garrido.
———— (1952a). *Política y Estrategia, por Descartes*. Buenos Aires, n.p.
———— (1952b). *Los mensajes de Perón*. Buenos Aires: Editorial Mundo Peronista.
———— (1952c). *Conducción política*. Buenos Aires: Subsecretaría de Informaciones.
———— (1948a). *Perón Expounds His Doctrine*. Buenos Aires, n.p.
———— (1948b). *The Argentine International Policy*. Buenos Aires, n.p.
———— (1948c). *Political and Social Situation Prior to the Revolution of 1943*. Buenos Aires, n.p.
———— (1948d). *Social Reform*. Buenos Aires, n.p.
———— (n.d.). *Del poder al exilio*. Buenos Aires: Norte.
Peronist Doctrine. Official Publication. Buenos Aires, n.p.
Peter, José (1968). *Crónicas proletarias*. Buenos Aires: Esfera.
Potash, Robert A. (1980). *The Army and Politics in Argentina, 1945–1962. Peron to Frondizi*. Vol. 2. Stanford, Calif.: Stanford University Press.
———— (1969). *The Army and Politics in Argentina, 1928–1945. Yrigoyen to Perón*. Vol. 1. Stanford, Calif.: Stanford University Press.
Puiggrós, Rodolfo (1969). *El Peronismo y sus causas*. Buenos Aires: Jorge Alvarez.
———— (1968). *La democracia fraudulenta*. Buenos Aires: Jorge Alvarez.
———— (1967). *Las izquierdas y el problema nacional*. Buenos Aires: Jorge Alvarez.
———— (1965a). *Pueblo y oligarquía*. Buenos Aires: Jorge Alvarez.
———— (1965b). *Historia crítica de los partidos políticos argentinos*. Buenos Aires: Argumentos.
———— (1952). *El proletariado en la revolución nacional*. Buenos Aires: Trafac.
Ramos, Jorge Abelardo (1965). *Revolución y contrarrevolución en la Argentina*. 2 vols. Buenos Aires: Plus Ultra.
Rennie, Ysabel (1945). *The Argentine Republic*. New York: Macmillan.
Rocca, Paolo (1980). "Aspetti della politica economica argentina dal 1976 ad oggi." Tesi di Laurea, Facolta di Scienze Politiche, Universita degli Studi di Milano. Matr. No. 157113.
Rock, David (1975). *Politics in Argentina 1890–1930: The Rise and Fall of Radicalism*. Cambridge: Cambridge University Press.
Rock, David, ed. (1975). *Argentina in the Twentieth Century*. Pittsburgh: University of Pittsburgh Press.
Romero, José Luis (1963). *A History of Argentine Political Thought*. Stanford, Calif.: Stanford University Press.
Romero, Luis Alberto, et al. (1968). *El Radicalismo*. Buenos Aires: Carlos Perez.
Rouquié, Alain, ed. (1982). *Argentina, hoy*. Mexico: Siglo XXI.
———— (1978). *Pouvoir militaire et société politique en Republique Argentine*. Paris: Presses de la Fondation Nationale des Sciences Politiques.
Rowe, James (1966). "Argentina's Durable Peronists: A 20th Anniversary Note," *American Universities Field Staff, Reports Service* 12, No. 2.
Rubinstein, Juan Carlos (1968). *Desarrollo y discontinuidad política en Argentina*. Buenos Aires: Siglo XXI.

Sarmiento, Domingo Faustino (1961). *Life in the Argentine Republic in the Days of the Tyrants.* New York: Collier Books.

Sarobe, José María (1957). *Memorias sobre la revolución del 6 de septiembre de 1930.* Buenos Aires: Ediciones Gure.

Sautu, Ruth (1968). "Poder económico y burguesía industrial en la Argentina, 1930–1954," *Revista Latinoamericana de Sociología* 4, No. 3 (November).

Scalabrini Ortiz, Raúl (1965). *Política británica en el Río de la Plata.* Buenos Aires: Plus Ultra.

————— (1964). *Historia de los ferrocarriles argentinos.* Buenos Aires: Plus Ultra.

Schmitt, Carl (1976). *The Concept of the Political.* New Brunswick, N.J.: Rutgers University Press.

Schmitter, Philippe (1980). "Speculations About the Possible Demise of Authoritarian Regimes and Its Possible Consequences," *Working Papers*, No. 60. Washington, D.C.: Wilson Center.

Scobie, James R. (1964a). *Argentina: A City and a Nation.* New York: Oxford University Press.

————— (1964b). *Revolution on the Pampas: A Social History of Argentine Wheat, 1860–1910.* Austin: University of Texas Press.

Sebreli, Juan José (1966). *Eva Perón: ¿Aventurera o militante?* Buenos Aires: Siglo Veinte.

————— (1965). *Buenos Aires: Vida cotidiana y alienación.* Buenos Aires: Siglo Veinte.

Sidicaro, Ricardo (1982). "Estado intervencionista, grandes propietarios rurales y producción agropecuaria en Argentina 1946–1976," *Nova Americana*, No. 5. Torino: Einaudi.

Silverman, Bertram (1969). "Labor Ideology and Economic Development in the Peronist Epoch," *Studies in Comparative International Development* 4, No. 11.

Silvert, Kalman H. (1963). "The Costs of Anti-Nationalism: Argentina," in Kalman H. Silvert, ed., *Expectant Peoples.* New York: Vintage Books.

Smith, Peter (1974). *Argentina and the Failure of Democracy.* Madison: University of Wisconsin Press.

————— (1969). *Politics and Beef in Argentina.* New York: Columbia University Press.

Snow, Peter G. (1979). *Political Forces in Argentina.* New York: Praeger.

Solberg, Carl (1970). *Immigration and Nationalism. Argentina and Chile, 1890–1914.* Austin: University of Texas Press.

Stein, Stanley J., and Stein, Barbara H. (1970). *The Colonial Heritage of Latin America.* New York: Oxford University Press.

Strickon, Arnold (1962). "Class and Kinship in Argentina," *Ethology*, No. 4 (October).

————— (1960). *Grandsons of the Gauchos.* New York: Columbia University Press.

Taylor, Carl C. (1948). *Rural Life in Argentina.* Baton Rouge: Louisiana State University Press.

Timerman, Jacobo (1981). *Prisoner Without a Name, Cell Without a Number.* New York: Alfred A. Knopf.

Torre, Juan Carlos (1984). *Sindicatos y trabajadores bajo el peronismo.* Buenos Aires: Centro Editor de América Latina.

————— (1980). "La cuestión del poder sindical y el orden político en la Argentina," *Criterio* 53, No. 1843 (September).

Touraine, Alain (1976). *Les sociétés dépendantes.* Paris: Editions J. Duculot.

United Nations, ECLA (1971). *Estudio económico de América Latina 1970.* E/CN.12/868/Rev.1. New York.

———— (1969). *Economic Development and Income Distribution in Argentina.* E/CN.12/802. New York.

———— (1964a). *Social Development of Latin America in the Post-War Period.* E/CN.12/660. New York.

———— (1964b). *The Economic Development of Latin America in the Post-War Period.* E/CN.12/659/Rev.1. New York.

———— (1959). *Análisis y proyecciones del desarrollo económico. El desarrollo económico de la Argentina.* E/CN.12/429/Rev.1. Mexico.

U.S. Chamber of Commerce in Buenos Aires. *Comments on Argentine Trade.* Monthly.

Valenzuela, Luisa (1983). *The Lizard's Tail.* New York: Farrar, Straus, Giroux.

Varela-Cid, Eduardo, ed. (1981). *Juicio de residencia a Martínez de Hoz.* Buenos Aires: El Cid Editor.

Viñas, David (1964). *Literatura argentina y realidad política.* Buenos Aires: Jorge Alvarez.

Walsh, R. J. (1964). *Operación masacre.* Buenos Aires: Continental Service.

Walter, E. V. (1969). *Terror and Resistance: A Study of Political Violence.* New York: Oxford University Press.

Weil, Felix José (1944). *Argentine Riddle.* New York: John Day Co.

Whitaker, Arthur P. (1965). *Argentina.* Englewood Cliffs, N.J.: Prentice-Hall.

———— (1954). *The United States and Argentina.* Cambridge, Mass.: Harvard University Press.

World Bank (1978). *Economic Memorandum on Argentina.* Report No. 2208-AR.

Other Titles of Interest from Westview Press

†*Latin American Politics and Development*, Second Edition, Fully Revised and Updated, Howard J. Wiarda and Harvey F. Kline

†*Latin America, Its Problems and Its Promise: A Multidisciplinary Introduction*, edited by Jan Knippers Black

†*Latin America: Capitalist and Socialist Perspectives of Development and Underdevelopment*, edited by Ronald H. Chilcote and Joel C. Edelstein

†*Politics and Public Policy in Latin America*, Steven W. Hughes and Kenneth J. Mijeski

†*Dynamics of Latin American Foreign Policies: Challenges for the 1980s*, edited by Jennie K. Lincoln and Elizabeth G. Ferris

†*Latin American Nations in World Politics*, edited by Heraldo Muñoz and Joseph S. Tulchin

†*Dependency and Marxism: Toward a Resolution of the Debate*, edited by Robert H. Chilcote

The Anglo-Argentine Connection, 1900–1939, Robert Gravil

Sovereignty in Dispute: The Falklands/Malvinas, 1493–1982, Fritz L. Hoffmann and Olga Mingo Hoffmann

†*The End and the Beginning: The Nicaraguan Revolution*, Second Edition, Revised and Updated, John A. Booth

†*Revolution in El Salvador: Origins and Evolution*, Second Edition, Revised and Updated, Tommie Sue Montgomery

PROFILES/NATIONS OF CONTEMPORARY LATIN AMERICA:

†*Mexico: Paradoxes of Stability and Change*, Daniel Levy and Gabriel Székely

†*Nicaragua: The Land of Sandino*, Second Edition, Revised and Updated, Thomas W. Walker

Colombia: Portrait of Unity and Diversity, Harvey F. Kline

†*Cuba: Dilemmas of a Revolution*, Juan M. del Aguila

Honduras: Caudillo Politics and Military Rulers, James A. Morris

Guatemala: A Nation in Turmoil, Peter Calvert

†Available in hardcover and paperback.

About the Book and Author

The Fitful Republic: Economy, Society, and Politics in Argentina

Juan E. Corradi

This book explains the varied political roles played by agrarian and industrial groups in the modernization of Argentina. It seeks to account for the attainment of a high level of social complexity that has not, however, been matched by steady economic growth or political stability. What have been the determinants of economic growth in Argentina? In what sense does its capitalist development differ from that of other advanced societies? Under what conditions has that development taken place? The answers to these questions, states Professor Corradi, are woven into a picture of a society that follows a path flanked by authoritarianism and political disorder.

Dr. Juan E. Corradi, a native of Argentina, was educated there and in the United States. Currently an associate professor of sociology at New York University, he has also taught at the University of Massachusetts, the University of California (San Diego and Santa Cruz), and Memorial University, Newfoundland. He is coauthor of *Ideology and Social Change in Latin America* (with June Nash and Hobart Spalding, 1977) and author of *Textures: Critical Essays on the Politics of Discourse* (forthcoming).

Index